Nerds, Goths,
Geeks, and Freaks

Children's Literature Association Series

Nerds, Goths, Geeks, and Freaks

Outsiders in Chicanx and Latinx Young Adult Literature

Edited by Trevor Boffone and Cristina Herrera

Foreword by Guadalupe García McCall

University Press of Mississippi / Jackson

The University Press of Mississippi is the scholarly publishing agency of
the Mississippi Institutions of Higher Learning: Alcorn State University,
Delta State University, Jackson State University, Mississippi State University,
Mississippi University for Women, Mississippi Valley State University,
University of Mississippi, and University of Southern Mississippi.

www.upress.state.ms.us

The University Press of Mississippi is a member
of the Association of University Presses.

First printing 2020
∞

Library of Congress Cataloging-in-Publication Data available
LCCN 2020932717
Hardback ISBN 978-1-4968-2745-6
Trade paperback ISBN 978-1-4968-2746-3
Epub single ISBN 978-1-4968-2747-0
Epub institutional ISBN 978-1-4968-2748-7
PDF single ISBN 978-1-4968-2749-4
PDF institutional ISBN 978-1-4968-2750-0

British Library Cataloging-in-Publication Data available

This book is dedicated to nerds and weirdos, and all those outsider kids who grew up on the fringes.

Contents

Section 1. Artists and Punks

Section 2. Superheroes and Other Worldly Beings

Section 3. LatiNerds and Bookworms

Section 4. Non-Cholos in the Hood

     Swimming While Drowning 145
     Trevor Boffone

11   What Can We Learn from Cool Cats?: Chillante Pedagogy,
     Gary Soto, and the Chato Series 159
     Elena Avilés

12   The Coming-of-Age Experience in Chicanx Queer Novels
     What Night Brings and *Aristotle and Dante Discover
     the Secrets of the Universe*......................................175
     Carolina Alonso

     List of Contributors....................................191

     Index 197

Foreword

Guadalupe García McCall

I met Cristina Herrera when I was appointed inaugural artist-in-residence at the Arne Nixon Center at California State University in Fresno, California, in 2017. She was warm and sweet, and so excited to meet me. Waving her nerdy geek flag high up in the air, she gushed about my work. I fed on the love she and the rest of the committee members lavished on me and welcomed the opportunity to talk about what I love most, literature and the way it has fed my soul and steered the course of my life. From huerfanita, to would-be drop-out, to teacher, to author, to university professor—that's the life my love of words and books has afforded me, a life full of blessings.

Cristina was one of the first people to encourage me to apply for university positions. At that time, I truly believed I was on my way to retirement and a part time job at our local community college. But she insisted that I had more to offer, more to give the world. She reminded me of my mother, and all the dreams she had for me. It is because of my mother that I am sitting here, at this particular desk at George Fox University.

It is winter here, in Oregon, and last night I braved the mal aire. I stepped out and inhaled that cold, bitter, drizzly foggy air that my mother warned against and drove myself to the next town in the dark to attend a party given for English majors at George Fox University. Why? Because I love my job? Because I love my students? Yes and yes, but also because I am a nerd! Everyone going to the party was bringing a book in the spirit of sharing great literature. There was no way I was staying home.

Needless to say, I stayed until the end and left the party with a copy of *Wicked* and a geeky smile on my face.

This morning, I stood in the dark, misty dawning of a new day, holding a computer bag with everything I need to be a successful writing professor. The fog was thick in the air, and I took it into my lungs, the way my mother always said I shouldn't. According to her, we should always avoid inhaling the air at night. Fog is considered mal aire—air that has been sitting too close to the filth and squalor of humanity, air that has touched the sordid nature of man's evil dreams and nightmares, air that will poison your thoughts and clog your lungs with its impurities.

But I don't give in to the poison. I don't allow the evil to infiltrate my thoughts.

All I feel is my mother's presence in the mild morning mist, the hallowed haze that softens every light crowning every light post in the vicinity, and I am overwhelmed by the love she brings me—the calor she provides even as I stand in thirty-degree weather.

"Mira donde ando, Mamá," I tell her, because even I can't believe I am standing in a parking lot in the Pacific Northwest in this blessed space—as Assistant Professor of English.

I smile because I know she came to share this moment with me, and I have to acknowledge that she brought me here, to this place. She dreamt this for me, believed it, sacrificed for it—one would say, she lived for it.

My mother left her family too, her mother and sisters in Mexico. When I was six years old, she picked up our tiliches and crossed the border with my father with the hope that her children, me and my seven brother and sisters, would go to school in los Estados Unidos—learn to speak, read, write, and love "the English," and have a better life.

But her dreams for us started before that, before I was even born. My mother sacrificed for this dream all her life. She scrubbed and scraped pots and pans for the Señoras who lived in the rich houses in Piedras Negras, Coahuila, from the age of ten. She swept and mopped floors, cleaned toilets, and had to make do with two meager meals a day and two square pieces of toilet paper from miserly Doñas all her life so that my siblings and I could have a better life, a decent life, where silent nodding and suppliant smiling wasn't a job requirement.

Her dreams for me were expansive, enlightened—emboldened by all that she had suffered, all the pride she'd had to swallow as ama de llaves in those cruel rich neighborhoods. My mother gave me the space to read books night and day. She let me burn through them like my eyes were on fire, so that I might learn how to express myself, how to speak out and show the world that my voice mattered, that the dreams God had put in my heart were not worth any less than the dreams of any other human being.

"Te amo," I tell her, as my husband pulls the car out of the garage and waits for me to get in. I don't miss her anymore. She is in this space with me. Her dreams for me didn't die with her. I am surrounded by them. They are the morning mist, the hallowed haze, the soft light crowning every light post in this part of the world. They are in the air. Air that was meant to poison me but which I, like so many nerds and geeks and outsiders, choose to take in and transform into something beautiful.

"I know," I tell her, as I look at the moon hanging low in the sky to the left of me. "I know. It's beautiful here." Because I realize that I am talking to myself again, I hug my bag and laugh.

My husband is standing inside the garage, about to get in the car. "What?" he asks. "Nothing," I say. "I'm just laughing."

He doesn't ask why. He's used to it. I am a thinker, a writer, a nerd—and like any good nerd, I talk to myself all the time. But I don't always laugh. That's different. That's changed.

My mother made that possible. She is that little voice inside my head that says, *It's okay to love school. It's okay to love reading and writing. It's okay to follow your dreams!*

If I had any advice to give nerdy kids today it would be, "Don't let the mal aire of our current climate poison your thoughts. Dream! Soar! Let the world hear you roar!"

Acknowledgments

In March 2014, Cristina had the privilege of directing a symposium on Latinx literature through the American Literature Association, "The Latina/o Literary Landscape." It was Cristina's first time undertaking such a large job, but the success of the symposium was largely due to the wonderful colleagues she met that day, many of whom are now some of her dearest and closest friends. One of those new colleagues Cristina met was someone named Trevor Boffone. From there, we bonded over our mutual love of Latinx literature, tennis, and our work, leading us to share our research in progress because we valued and trusted each other's feedback. Soon after meeting, we knew we wanted to work together one day. We just had to wait for the perfect project. This book is that project.

We thank our contributors for lending their time and talents to this volume. We have learned so much from each of you. We are inspired by your scholarship and the expertise you bring to this volume.

To Guadalupe García McCall, thank you for lending your voice and talents to our book's foreword.

We would like to thank our anonymous reviewers who gave us pointed feedback that only enhanced this volume.

We thank the staff at the University Press of Mississippi, especially Katie Keene, for her encouragement and enthusiasm while guiding us through the publishing process.

Trevor: First of all, this project wouldn't exist without my fabulous co-editor, Cristina Herrera, who has made this one of the most enjoyable collaborations of my career. Thank you for being a fellow nerd! I would like to thank my colleagues at the University of Houston who supported this work from the beginning, especially Gabriela Baeza Ventura, Ruth M. López, Sarah Luna, Sylvia Mendoza, Rachel Afi Quinn, Kavita Singh, Jess Waggoner, and anyone else who has shared a coffee while working together on our respective projects. To Claire M. Massey for our transnational Skype writing sessions, for always believing in my work, and for "goin' on patrol" with me. To Guadalís Del Carmen, Nelson Diaz-Marcano, Brian Eugenio Herrera, Jorge Huerta, Josh Inocéncio, Marci R. McMahon, Jasminne Mendez, Lupe Mendez, and Abigail Vega who have each offered me something special over the years and have only made me a better scholar in return. To my family, thank you for offering unwavering support of my work. To Kayla, thank you for being a sounding board for all my ideas—good and bad—and for providing me with a lifetime of love and companionship.

Cristina: Thank you to my colleagues at Fresno State, whom I'm privileged to call friends, for cheering me on, supporting me, and offering wisdom: Maria Lopes, Annabella España-Nájera, Ramon Sanchez, Luis Fernando Macías, Jennifer Randles, Amber Fox Crowell, Andrew Jones, Rosa Toro, Larissa Mercado-López, and Laura Alamillo. To my colleagues outside of Fresno State who have sustained me in more ways than I can count: Gabriella Gutiérrez y Muhs, Patricia Pérez, Marisela Chávez, Eliza Rodríguez y Gibson, Lourdes Alberto Celis, Ella Díaz, and Marci R. McMahon. Thank you to my terrific co-editor, Trevor Boffone, whose friendship has earned him the nickname of "hermanito." Lastly, gracias a mi familia, especially my twin sister, my mom, and my older brothers, for their love. My other half, Elena: love you, T. To my beloved Kris, everything is for you and our fur babies, Carmelita and Cleo. I love you all. Los amo.

Nerds, Goths, Geeks, and Freaks

Introduction

Weirding Out Latinx America

In Guadalupe García McCall's debut young adult (YA) text, the Pura Belpré-winning verse novel *Under the Mesquite*, the teenage protagonist Lupita struggles to negotiate her talent and love of dramatic arts with her bicultural Chicana identity amidst accusations by high school classmates who taunt her with the following lines: "You talk like / you wanna be white . . . you think you're / Anglo now 'cause you're in Drama? / You think you're better than us?" (80–81).

In the classmates' accusations that Lupita must "wanna be white" because she enjoys studying drama, Lupita is rendered an outsider, not a "real Mexican." These hurtful accusations undoubtedly stem from mainstream myths of Chicanx/Latinx intellectual inferiority, sentiments that are unfortunately internalized by Lupita's classmates. Although Lupita is shamed for her interest in so-called "white" academic pursuits, she insists on her right to create, to act, to be Chicana on her own terms.

This insistence on constructing an identity that pushes against and challenges mainstream or cultural pressures to be "hip" or "on fleek" forms the central tenet of the essays in *Nerds, Goths, Geeks, and Freaks: Outsiders in Chicanx/Latinx Young Adult Literature*. While sociological research has documented the ways in which teenagers and young adults form "cliques" (Ortner, Kinney) based on arbitrary markers of "coolness," popular culture has seen a recent resurgence of decidedly "uncool" Latinxs that redefine the ways we think about identity, culture, and how to be a Latinx teenager. For example, the Colombian band Bomba Estereo's music video for their song "Soy Yo" features a geeky young Latina who basks in this nerd identity and who became an instant internet sensation, and the Twitter account @LatinxGeeks provides "a community for Latinxs who love all things geeky," according to their page.

Moreover, the popular 2018 film *Spider-Man: Into the Spider-Verse* featured Milo Morales, an Afro-Latino teen who is often described as an "intelligent nerd" and attends a competitive middle school in a more affluent part of New York City. This resurgence also comes at a time when Latinx YA writers have published a plethora of texts documenting "outsider" Latinx teens, seen in texts like Benjamin Alire Sáenz's *Artistotle and Dante Discover the Secrets of the Universe*, Isabel Quintero's *Gabi, A Girl in Pieces*, Matt de la Peña's *Mexican WhiteBoy*, Erika L. Sánchez's enormously popular debut novel, *I Am Not Your Perfect Mexican Daughter*, or Meg Medina's *Yaqui Delgado Wants to Kick Your Ass*, among many others. These are worlds in which Latinxs are the mainstream. In this way, the protagonists in these YA texts must navigate their communities as outsiders within an already marginalized community. Given the established canon of Latinx YA literature and the growing body of those works that explore "weirdos," "nerds," and other "taboo" identities, an edited volume that examines such identities is warranted.

Nerds, Goths, Geeks, and Freaks ¡Y Qué?: Reclaiming Outsiders

Existing Latinx literary scholarship primarily expresses a concern with literature for "adult" audiences, and while this work reflects Latinx literature's emergence as a major cultural and financial player in the larger literary scene, our collection addresses literature intended for youth readers, who make up one of the fastest-growing demographics in the United States. In very recent collections, such as *The Cambridge Companion to Latina/o American Literature*, for example, a number of well-known scholars trace important developments in the large canon of Latinx writing. Yet not a single chapter addresses the growing number of books targeting children and young adults by Latinx writers, some of whom write only for this demographic. As Frederick Luis Aldama pointedly adds in his collection of interviews with Latinx children's and YA writers, "The two-thousand-plus-page behemoth, *The Norton Anthology of Children's Literature* (2005), does not include one US Latino author" (Aldama 10). Just under 6 percent of children's and YA books published in 2017 were written by Latinxs, according to a study conducted by the University of Wisconsin's Cooperative Children's Book Center (*Publishing Statistics*).

Moreover, in a much-circulated 2012 *New York Times* article, "For Young Latinos, an Image Is Missing," Motoko Rich sheds light on the scant Latinx representation that exists in classrooms and public libraries across the country. As Rich shows, this lack of proper representation can have negative impacts on how young Latinxs view themselves.[1] Even so, the literature that children are exposed to does not adequately reflect the growing canon of Latinx children's and YA literature that is being produced by Arte Público Press, Cinco Puntos Press, Children's Book Press, and Lee & Low Books, among others. Despite these presses publishing the work, as literature scholar and editor of Arte Público Press Gabriela Baeza Ventura notes, "We have yet to see this literature at the forefront of awards, curricula, and bookstore displays" (244). In the same vein, this literature has yet to be given serious consideration in the academy.

The title of our edited volume, *Nerds, Goths, Geeks, and Freaks: Outsiders in Chicanx/Latinx Young Adult Literature* (hereafter referred to as *Nerds*), signals a much-needed approach to the study of Latinx young adult literature. This edited volume addresses themes of outsiders in Chicanx/Latinx children's and young adult literature, a topic that has not been explored in edited volumes thus far. In recent years, the field of Latinx children's and YA literature has exploded with new imprints specifically dedicated to the field, such as Piñata Books from Arte Público Press and mainstream publishers such as Simon & Schuster Books for Young Readers and Lee and Low Books, which have consciously made efforts to publish Latinx texts. Despite the achievements of award-winning authors, such as Guadalupe García McCall, Meg Medina, Margarita Engle, Matt De La Peña, and Benjamin Alire Sáenz, scholarship on Latinx literature has overwhelmingly ignored texts written for younger audiences. Esteemed journals on the study of children's literature have published few scholarly articles examining Chicanx/Latinx children's and YA texts. As the Latinx population in the United States approaches becoming the majority by 2043, the need for scholarship centered on Latinx children's and young adult writing has become more pressing. In addressing this theoretical gap, we also acknowledge the important fictional literary work done by African American YA writers, such as Angie Thomas and Renee Watson, whose texts also examine similar themes explored in our collection.

Our collection adds to recent scholarship such as *Voices of Resistance: Interdisciplinary Approaches to Chican@ Children's Literature* (2017), edited by Laura Alamillo, Larissa Mercado-López, and Cristina Herrera. While our book shares some commonality with this text, *Voices of Resistance* is primarily focused on the field of education and mainly discusses children's and middle-grade literature. Further, the essays in our collection share a thematic concern with "weirdness," "nerdiness," and what it means to be an "outsider" in Latinx and mainstream communities. We are also expanding on the recent work by co-editor Cristina Herrera in children's literature journal *The Lion and the Unicorn*, which has examined Chicana nerd identities in YA literature, characters she dubs "ChicaNerds." Following Herrera's lead, this collection furthers the discussion of nerd and "weirdo" identities to include texts not explored in her study. As our book contends, these multifaceted identities need to be examined to account for the ways in which Latinx children's and YA literature has broadened the textual representation to include outsiders, those who exist on the margins.

While related titles have been recently published, such as *Multicultural Literature for Latino Bilingual Children*, or *Immigration Narratives in Young Adult Literature: Crossing Borders*, these texts do not consider themes that we explore in our collection. Of further significance, it should be noted that in studies such as *Contemporary Dystopian Fiction for Young Adults: Brave New Teenagers* and *Reading Like a Girl: Narrative Intimacy in Contemporary American Young Adult Literature*, Latinx/Chicanx-authored texts are not discussed, demonstrating the timeliness and necessity of our collection. The prevalence of studies on YA literature, though an important feat, exposes what we consider to be a troubling fact: YA literature has indeed been explored and has established itself as a viable field of inquiry, but work on Latinx YA literature remains disturbingly under-studied.

In the same way, Latinx YA literature has been systematically excluded from scholarship on Latinx literature. The gold-standard edited collections *The Latino Studies Reader: Culture, Economy, and Society*; *Performing the US Latina/Latino Borderlands*; and *The New Latino Studies Reader: A Twenty-First-Century Perspective* include very little scholarship dedicated to unpacking the nuances of Latinx youth identities as seen through a cultural studies lens. As these landmark studies demonstrate, there has been and still remains a historical erasure of YA texts from discussions of Latinx literature at large.

Towards a Typology of Latinx Outsider Identities

In Gloria Anzaldúa's seminal work *Borderlands/La Frontera: The New Mestiza*, she theorizes the US-Mexico borderlands as both a literal space of occupation and confrontation and a metaphorical site of rupture, identity-crossing, and of course literal and figurative border-crossing. For Anzaldúa, this "open wound" of the borderlands (*Borderlands* 25), while undoubtedly invoking violence, colonization, and separation, nevertheless allows for her theoretical New Mestiza to create and build a borderless society that liberates her from the confines of borders that seek to confine and contain. This borderland is home to what Anzaldúa calls "los atravesados," or border crossers: "The squint-eyed, the perverse, the queer, the troublesome, the mongrel, the mulato, the half-breed, the half dead; in short, those who cross over, pass over, or go through the confines of the 'normal'" (*Borderlands* 25). As an in-between space, these "weird" border-dwellers thrive in a zone that contains "contradictions" and "ambiguity" (Anzaldúa, *Borderlands* 101). In that spirit, we expand Anzaldúa's theory to include those nerdy, goth, geeky, freaky, and outsider Latinx teens that she does not name: those "troublesome" misfits that are caught somewhere between their communities and the Anglo world. These outsiders reflect Anzaldúa's notion of El Mundo Zurdo (the left-handed world), a liminal space that presents opportunities for re-envisioning weird Latinxs as the future of a less oppressive world. From an in-between borderlands space, the individuals in question can embark on "the path of a two-way movement—a going deep into the self and an expanding out into the world, a simultaneous recreation of the self and a reconstruction of society" (Anzaldúa, "La Prieta" 208). From here, they can transform the societies around them, the same societies that have previously marked them as outsiders.

In the same way, our collection engages with José Esteban Muñoz's theory of disidentification, which explains how racial outsiders mediate the dominant culture by transforming it for their own benefit rather than adhering to the dominant culture's mandates for appropriate forms of Latinx identity. While Anzaldúa's borderlands theory and Muñoz's disidentification are useful frameworks for the purposes of our book, we also insist on identifying their shortcomings; after all, these scholars have taken for granted an "adult" perspective that does not necessarily speak to the realities of young Latinx weirdos who are excluded from the grownup worlds of their families and communities at large.

As outsiders, these Latinx youth must take back their own narrative, ultimately responding to Chicana theorist Emma Pérez's notion of the "Decolonial Imaginary." Pérez views Latinxs as subjects within an environment that constantly reminds them that they are objects and must be controlled; she inspires the Latinx community to "revise our history and reinscribe it with the new" (127). With this in mind, the Latinx outsiders in *Nerds* write themselves into the community and revise the traditional identity scripts to be more inclusive of outsider identities such as LatiNerds and queer Latinxs.

This collection of essays by scholars whose work focuses on twentieth- and twenty-first century Latinx literature continues a critical dialogue and broadens the field of Latinx cultural studies to be more inclusive of YA literature. As such, this volume is the first critical anthology addressing thematic concerns around outsiders and other "taboo" identities. Our collection insists that to understand Latinx youth identities, it is necessary to shed light on outsiders within an already marginalized ethnic group: nerds, goths, geeks, freaks, and others who might not fit within Latinx popular cultural paradigms such as the chola and cholo, identities that are ever-present in films, television, and the internet. In light of this, *Nerds* establishes a typology of youth Latinx outsider identities such as the aforementioned. Nevertheless, the characters who take on these identities do not wish to separate themselves from the mainstream Latinx community. Rather, they theorize their identities to forge new paths for Latinx youth to follow in ways that harmonize notions of being different and fitting in.

In *Nerds*, the analytical category of outsiderness intersects with discussions of race, ethnicity, gender, and sexuality. Other topics include Latinx theatre for young audiences, queerness in YA writing, representations of reading/writing/science/math/art in YA writing, bullying, and violence. The volume addresses the following questions. What does it mean to be an outsider within an already marginalized community? What constitutes "outsider" identities? In what ways are these "outsider" identities shaped by mainstream myths around Latinx young people, particularly with the common stereotype of the struggling, underachieving inner city Latinx teen? How do these young adults reclaim what it means to be an "outsider," "weirdo," "nerd," or "goth," and how can the reclamation of these marginalized identities expand much-needed conversations around authenticity and narrow understandings of what constitutes Latinx identity? How does Chicanx/Latinx children's and YA literature represent, challenge, question, or expand discussions surrounding identities that have been deemed outsiders or outliers? How have Chicanx/Latinx children's and YA writers contributed to these thematic and theoretical discussions?

This book is divided into four sections that interrogate varying outsider identities. While we have employed the identifier "Latinx" to demonstrate the shifting terminology in the field, our contributors make use of diverse terms, and as such, we have kept the terms they have chosen to also show the ways in which terminology continues to be a major focus of scholarly debate within our discipline. To facilitate a more inclusive discussion of outsiderness, some of the chapters address texts intended for middle-grade readers. Section one, "Artists and Punks," features chapters that examine artist protagonists who are deemed weird for their interests. In chapter one by Amanda Ellis, "Chicana Teens, Zines, and Poetry Scenes: *Gabi, a Girl in Pieces* by Isabel Quintero," Ellis investigates the YA novel and its use of zine culture to argue how the protagonist uses poetry and zines to make sense of her life as a young, fat, "weird" Chicana artist in the making. Lettycia Terrones analyzes the middle-grade novel *The First Rule of Punk* in her chapter, "Praxis of Refusal: Self-Fashioning Identity and Throwing Attitude in Pérez's *The First Rule of Punk*," which argues that the novel's protagonist finds affinity in the figure of Chicana punk rocker Teresa Covarrubias. As Terrones states, "Malú self-fashions an integrated identity by activating a punk rock ethos to refuse agents of assimilation."

Following Terrones is chapter three by Adrianna M. Santos, "Broken Open: Writing, Healing, and Affirmation in Isabel Quintero's *Gabi, a Girl in Pieces* and Erika L. Sanchez's *I Am Not Your Perfect Mexican Daughter*." In this chapter,

Santos argues that the central characters struggle with their "otherness" and their "Mexican-ness" and "use language as not only a means of self-expression but also as a way to both unravel and remake themselves." As artists and punks, these characters use creative means to adapt and thrive in a world that makes little room for them.

The chapters in section two, "Superheroes and Other Worldly Beings," examine texts that introduce concepts of the obscure, dark magic, and spirit worlds to speak of those teens whose other-worldly lives are under constant surveillance and attack. For example, in chapter four, "Bite Me: The Allure of Vampires and Dark Magic in Chicana Young Adult Literature," Christi Cook explores the ways in which the Anzaldúan paradigm of the New Mestiza, which embraces an in-betweenness and hybridity, does not fully speak to the experiences of teenage Chicanas; the writers' use of dark magic, according to Cook, emphasizes this painful teenage world.

Following Cook is chapter five by Domino Pérez, "Afuerxs and Cultural Practice in *Shadowshaper* and *Labyrinth Lost*," which looks at the world of fantasy and shadowshaping to examine how the young women protagonists in both texts, "through acts of refusal, are outside of the material, ritual, and cultural practices of their communities." Ella Diaz concludes section two with chapter six, "The Art of Afro-Latina Consciousness-Raising in *Shadowshaper*." In her chapter, Diaz examines the representation of street art and muralism in Daniel Older's novel, arguing that the protagonist Sierra uses muralism to insert herself and other Afro-Latinx peoples into an art world that has historically refused to see them.

The chapters in section three, "LatiNerds and Bookworms," discuss texts that explore nerd identities and characters who enjoy subjects that have traditionally been deemed "inappropriate" interests for Latinx youth. LatiNerds, or Latinx Nerds, represent "bookish" characters that challenge the ways in which mainstream culture has oversimplified Latinx youth as intellectually stunted, struggling, or not interested in books or reading. In chapter seven, "*The Smartest Girl in the World*: Normalizing Intellectualism through Representations of Smart Latinx Youth on Stage," Roxanne Schroeder-Arce explores how Miriam Gonzalez's play offers youth a look at young Latinx intellectuals who never question their smartness in relation to their ethnic and racial identity. By engaging with theories around Latinx youth identity development and culturally responsive pedagogy, this chapter shows how the play may affect Latinx youth who see themselves represented in a legitimate space. Cristina Herrera's chapter, "'These Latin girls mean business': Expanding the Boundaries of Latina Youth Identity in Meg Medina's YA Novel *Yaqui Delgado Wants to Kick Your Ass*," explores the ways Medina's novel expands what it means to be a young, urban Latina. As Herrera discusses, the novel questions the ways in which those Latinas who do not model themselves as cholas are victims of identity-policing, rendered not "really" Latina, and dismissed as weir-dos or outsiders within this narrow gender-racial identity script that defines the chola as the only "authentic" young, urban, Latina identity that exists. In chapter nine, "Tomás Rivera: The Original Latinx Outsider," Tim Wadham focuses on one of the most pervasive figures of Latinx literature: Tomás Rivera, author of the canonical *. . . y no se lo tragó la tierra/ . . . And the Earth Did Not Devour Him*. The chapter sheds light on Rivera's own journey becoming a reader and a writer through an overview of the play *Tomás and the Library Lady*, which demonstrates how a fellow outlier helped Rivera break from the constraints of the stereotypes forced on him and find a way to belong through the power of literature. Ultimately, the LatiNerds in this section find ways to embrace their identity through reading and their love of literature.

The chapters in section four, "Non-Cholos in the Hood," tackle one of the most pervasive stereotypes of Latinx urban identity. Also known as the home-boy, the cholo has been visible in films such as *Colors*, *American Me*, and *Cheech and Chong*, to name only a few. Although there are variations, popular culture has depicted the homeboy/cholo as a young male in baggy pants and flannel who may or may not drive lowrider cars. With this in mind, these chapters open up new possibilities for how young Latinx children engage with identity politics in such a way as to forge new paths for Latinx childhoods in the bar-rio. For instance, in chapter ten, "Young, Gay, and Latino: 'Feeling Brown' in Emilio Rodriguez's *Swimming While Drowning*," Trevor Boffone examines gay Latino teen coming-out and coming-of-age narratives and the issues affect-ing this often-forgotten demographic, specifically the perils of LGBT youth homelessness. Through an analysis of Emilio Rodriguez's play *Swimming While Drowning*, Boffone engages with José Esteban Muñoz's notion of "Feeling Brown" to present the ways in which queer Latino outsider identities manifest, ultimately pushing against stereotypes of both urban and queer youth. In her chapter on Gary Soto's Chato Series, Elena Avilés argues that Soto rewrites the iconic figure of the "cool cat" to reconsider urban male Chicano masculinity. In Chapter 12, "The Coming-of-Age Experience in Chicanx Queer Novels *What Night Brings* and *Aristotle and Dante Discover the Secrets of the Universe*," Carolina Alonso establishes a dialogue between canonical coming-of-age queer YA novels by renowned authors Carla Trujillo and Benjamin Alire Sáenz to demonstrate how both writers destabilize the genre by centering queer youth identities. The novels' protagonists break from traditional gender binaries and stereotypes, thus becoming outsiders who endure violence to varying degrees. As such, Alonso's chapter presents the difficulties that can manifest when Latinx urban youth question traditional identity scripts. Ultimately, these chapters present characters that push against the chola/cholo archetype to forge a new typography of Latinx urban youth identity.

Note

1. https://www.nytimes.com/2012/12/05/education/young-latino-students-dont-see-themselves -in-books.html.

Works Cited

Alamillo, Laura, Larissa M. Mercado-Lopez, and Cristina Herrera, eds. *Voices of Resistance: Interdisciplinary Approaches to Chican@ Children's Literature*. Rowman and Littlefield, 2017.

Aldama, Frederick Luis. "Introduction: The Heart and Art of Latino/a Young People's Fiction." *Latino/a Children's and Young Adult Writers on the Art of Storytelling*, edited by Frederick Luis Aldama, University of Pittsburgh Press, 2018, pp. 3–25.

Anzaldúa, Gloria. *Borderlands/La Frontera: The New Mestiza*. Aunt Lute, 1987.

Anzaldúa, Gloria. "La Prieta." *This Bridge Called My Back: Writings by Radical Women of Color*, edited by Cherríe Moraga and Gloria Anzaldúa, Third Woman Press, 1983, pp. 220–23.

Baeza Ventura, Gabriela. "Latino Literature for Children and the Lack of Diversity." *(Re)mapping the Latina/o Literary Landscape: New Works and New Directions*, edited by Cristina Herrera and Larissa M. Mercado-Lopez, Palgrave Macmillan, 2016, pp. 241–54.

Basu, Balaka, Katherine R. Broad, and Carrie Hintz, eds. *Contemporary Dystopian Fiction for Young Adults: Brave New Teenagers*. Routledge, 2014.

Brown, Joanne. *Immigration Narratives in Young Adult Literature: Crossing Borders*. The Scarecrow Press, 2011.

Clark, Ellen Riojas, Belinda Bustos Flores, Howard L. Smith, and Daniel Alejandro Gonzalez, eds. *Multicultural Literature for Latino Bilingual Children: Their Words, Their Worlds*. Rowman and Littlefield, 2015.

Cooperative Children's Book Center (CCBC). *Publishing Statistics on Children's Books about People of Color and First/Native Nations and by People of Color and First/Native Nations Authors and Illustrators*, 2018. https://ccbc.education.wisc.edu/books/pcstats.asp.

Day, Sara K. *Reading like a Girl: Narrative Intimacy in Contemporary American Young Adult Literature*. University Press of Mississippi, 2013.

Herrera, Cristina. "Soy Brown y Nerdy: The ChicaNerd in Chicana Young Adult (YA) Literature." *The Lion and the Unicorn: A Critical Journal of Children's Literature*, vol. 41, no. 3, 2017, pp. 307–26.

Kinney, David A. "From Nerds to Normals: The Recovery of Identity among Adolescents from Middle School to High School." *Sociology of Education*, vol. 66, no. 1, 1993, pp. 21–40.

McCall, Guadalupe García. *Under the Mesquite*. Lee and Low, 2011.

Pérez, Emma. *The Decolonial Imaginary: Writing Chicanas Into History*. Indiana University Press, 1999.

Ortner, Sherry B. "'Burned Like a Tattoo': High School Social Categories and 'American Culture.'" *Ethnography*, vol. 3, no. 2, 2002, pp. 115–48.

Rich, Motoko. "For Young Latino Readers, an Image Is Missing." *New York Times*. https://www .nytimes.com/2012/12/05/education/young-latino-students-dont-see-themselves-in-books.html

Section 1

Artists and Punks

1

Chicana Teens, Zines, and Poetry Scenes: *Gabi, A Girl in Pieces* by Isabel Quintero

Amanda Ellis

Isabel Quintero's 2014 young adult novel *Gabi, A Girl in Pieces* imagines a teenager's transformative senior year of high school. Quintero's title and cover image announce much about the form and content of the novel, given that *Gabi* is composed of various kinds of fictional "pieces" of writing that narrate pivotal events in the main protagonist's life. Gabi Hernandez, like most adolescent characters in YA fiction, is all but consumed by life's transitions. Gabi's self-conceptions, her ideas about sexuality, her father's substance abuse, and her constant wrestling with body shame drive Quintero's narrative. Through Gabi, Quintero gives readers a depiction of a witty teenager's life by way of a narrative that culminates with Gabi's unique rebellious evolution and triumphant agency as a geeky Chicana teenager who experiments with activist art, creative writing, and performance poetry. Quintero's plot also maintains fidelity to the title because through the course of the novel Gabi risks psychologically being brought to "pieces" by tumultuous personal circumstances. Quintero's narrative highlights the multifarious forces shaping Chicana teenage life, and more significantly the importance of creative writing and revision. The novel affirms that creative personal writing proves crucial for Gabi as she presses through trials and navigates the nebulous and liminal experience of Chicana adolescence.

Though Gabi experiences exclusion, she does not try to fit in. Instead, she learns to pen her way out of shame, homophobia, lurking sexual violence, and grief by embracing who she is through her writing. In fact, Quintero pushes back against those who write off fat girls by inviting readers to engage Gabi's character through the fraught processes of identity formation made legible through the pages of Gabi's diary. Close reading the formal and material features of Quintero's book to analyze Gabi's burgeoning relationship to creative writing, performance poetry, and independent print media-making, I argue that Quintero exposes the transformative power of artistic expression and alternative publishing to offer a powerful representation of a geeky Chicana. Gabi's story has the power to "effect socially and politically transformative change" (Alamillo et al. xi). Exploring Gabi's relationship to the printed word, I trace the formation and evolution of a geeky teenage Chicana feminist political rhetoric that Gabi ultimately leverages as a survival strategy deployed squarely within the throes of adolescence. Moreover, I contend that Quintero revises the fictional diary form to build on a larger cultural investment in harnessing creative power as a form of political power. This power transforms the contemporary con(texts) that fail to value both Chicanas and their creative labors. The novel reveals that the creation of political art, the practice of writing, and the power of performance poetry serve as vital creative outlets for Chicana outsiders, be they nerds, goths, geeks, or freaks.[1] *Gabi* elaborates the ways expressive writing and performative outlets can serve as the tools by which Chicana geeks fashion forms of agency and create pathways for individual and communal transformation.

What Is a Chicana Poet Geek?

What a geek is, is arguable, but in *Gabi* a Chicana poet geek is someone who does not belong, who writes her own poetry, and who refuses to play by the rules. Mainstream conceptualizations of geeks may recall socially aloof white men in the science/tech industry, but Quintero imagines a Chicana who abandons fantastical notions of belonging and embraces a desire to write across forms, genres, and mediums. Gabi self-describes as lamentably not "Morena. Bonita. Preciosa. Flaca. Flaquita" but instead as "Güerra [sic]. Casper. Ghost. Freckle Face. Ugly. Whitey. White girl. Gringa" (Quintero 35). Phenotypically defying stereotypical understandings of what counts as Mexican, Gabi is physically unable to adhere to racial constructs linking Mexican identity to brown skin, and therefore she experiences racial disjuncture.[2] Though she offers a staunch critique of gender, Gabi fails both at being brown and at openly interrogating her own privilege as a "Güerra."[3] White privilege notwithstanding, Gabi asks, "Well, what is a Mexican supposed to look like? Am I supposed to be brown and short? Carry a leaf blower on my back? Speak with a thick accent?" (Quintero 36). Inscribing her humor and sardonic wit, Gabi admits she is "a girl who thinks that being good at housework and having an intact hymen are totally overrated" (Quintero 275). Pushing back against ethno-national patriarchal ideologies inflected by misogyny and preoccupied with much more than race and gender, Gabi shows herself to be an irreducibly complex intersectional singular subjectivity. She is a writing enthusiast who experiments in her diary, zine, and performance poetry, who readers can imagine will continue to create communities in which to hone her love of the printed form and cultivate an expertise in creative writing.

Gabi, a Girl in Pieces opens with a diary entry penned the summer before Gabi's senior year. Quintero introduces her main protagonist by fictively deploying the conventions of formal realism. The diary entry, which subtly invites readers to understand Gabi and her private thoughts as sincere and genuine, also plots Gabi on a continuum Gabi reveals in her opening entry where she fits both within a transnational, multi-generational, maternal family structure and within a Chicana cultural and societal context that is inflected by rejection and shame, and is mediated by cultural and religious codes of conduct. Gabi's first entry notes, "My mother named me Gabriela after my grandmother who—coincidentally—didn't want to meet me when I was born because my mother was not married and was therefore living in sin" (Quintero 7). Keenly aware of the national, generational, moral, and ethical differences between herself and the other older women in her family, Gabi asserts herself from the onset of the novel as a Chicana outsider. She is an outsider in relation to the most intimate of arrangements, namely the dynamics of her own home and extended family. In the privacy of her diary Gabi breaks ranks and rejects the ideologies upheld and sustained by the older women in her family. She writes, "This is America and the twenty-first century, not Mexico one hundred years ago," and in doing so, her first diary entry not only works to inaugurate Quintero's novel as one about contemporary American life, but also becomes the place where Gabi composes the earliest seedbed of her ever-evolving Chicana poetic rebellion (7).

Quintero's Piecemeal Narrative

The novel's structure, unique form, and use of visual images are as singular as Gabi. Fittingly, the cover image of the novel brings into visual focus a collaged female cyclops. Like Quintero's narrative and main protagonist, the material text itself artistically centers and visually gestures to the notion of personhood as a racialized and gendered embodiment of unfinished, fluid (and at times monstrously surreal) processes that challenge Gabi to shift from harsh self-loathing and self-criticism to brave self-construction. The novel's cover image is presented to readers twice, and the second time is on the cover of the zine Gabi authors. A significant pictorial source of Gabi's deepest self-projections, the collage is composed of revealingly asymmetrical images of dismembered body parts on torn papers. Each piece creates a central (albeit distorted) body. The paper fragments form an image of a young brown teen through collage (see Figure 1). The ensemble, presumably depicting layers of Gabi (her clothing, body, and bones and flesh), prominently displays her pierced heart. Materially, Quintero's novel brings Janice Radway's understanding of "selfhood as collage" into view (Radway 194). Radway describes acts of girlhood self-construction as animated "by the desire to project a self that might move about in the world" and among particular kinds of people in specific, intensely desired ways. As such, they are mixes of creation and constraint. They are products of inchoate, genuinely prospective desires, of a willed determination to make something of what has been offered by a contradictory, contested cultural environment that cannot, for all its trying, either predict or determine the future"[4] (195). And yet Quintero reveals that Gabi the Güerra has body-image struggles, and therefore the collage functions as a projection of her desire to be thin and brown.

Interestingly, the collage depicts her heart outside her body, as if on her sleeve. Larger than her entire upper torso, the heart signals that Gabi's story, told through diary entries, will be one of magnified candid openness, sensitivity, and vulnerability. Indeed, Gabi's heart is figuratively pierced by the pressures of diet culture, racism, and misogyny, morality policing by her family members, and her own personal depression after her father overdoses on meth. An empty rib cage displaces her midsection, revealing her desire to be (dangerously) thin, and a humerus bone stands in for one of fleshed limbs. The illustration visually manifests her body-image distortion, common among teenagers, and it hyperbolically figures Gabi's body as equal parts teenager and surreal monster. It also shows Gabi's bones and organs as layers on display, demanding that her very person be seen as a fragile and complex anatomy under construction and scrutiny, capable of defying static fixity and norms and expectations.

Her identity in effect marks her as always already misunderstood. The cover figure shows a body "trapped" in an orange coquettish crop top and mini skirt and adorned with jewelry and makeup, inviting readers to question Gabi's agency and identity expression since the novel reveals that "the way [Gabi sees] it, a dress is restricting. It's a trap" (23). An unopened bag of chips, a half-eaten cookie, and a stack of books frame Gabi's collaged body. The composition evokes the power of various competing cultural and societal expectations, by drawing the reader's gaze to the profound impact various pressures impose on the bodies of young women of color. It also announces that while Gabi does not evolve out of a vacuum, what she does consume (or decidedly refuses to)

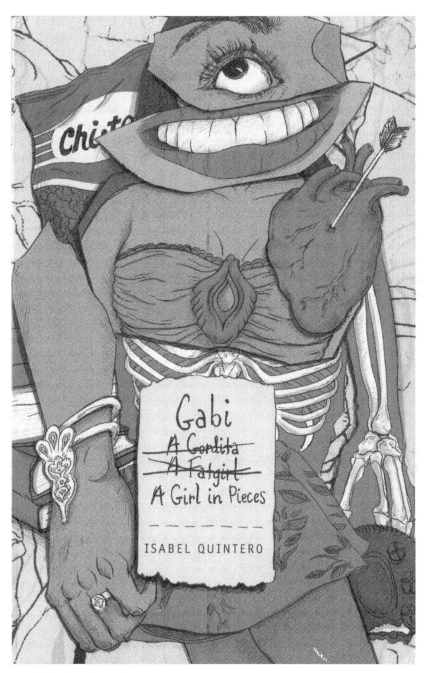

Cover of *Gabi, a Girl in Pieces*. © Zeke Peña

threatens to consume her, resonating with what Janice Radway refers to as "insubordinate creativity,"[5] or the kinds of creative constructive inscription and publication practices young people undertake on their own (Radway199). The materiality of the novel constructs Gabi as palimpsestic—under revision and self-construction. As the central architect of her life and the author of her diary, Gabi maintains an evolving societal awareness, and actively pieces together who she is and who she wishes to become.

This novel is not your standard diary fiction. While it is a fictional first-person novel that purports to be a teenager's diary, its unique form mirrors aspects of the novel's cover image's collage technique also. Far from a simple series of chronologically dated fictional diary entries, the novel is also comprised of Gabi's poetry, drafts of Gabi's unsent letters, and a copy of Gabi's first illustrated zine titled: "The Female Body" (Quintero 194). Hence, one of Quintero's strategies for revealing Gabi's agency is to interrupt the novel's diary mode by writing, "Here's my zine" and by including a copy of Gabi's zine squarely within the novel, further underscoring the subliminal and overt effect of the diary mode's non-traditional narration.[6]

The inclusion of the zine as a representational strategy further effects the novel's stream of time. H. Porter Abbot, in *Diary Fiction: Writing as Action*, notes that "the interrupted composition of the diary brings us back to a new beginning in the present. Each entry, as it begins, returns us to that point of temporary withdrawal, outside of the action, necessary for the putting down of the words on paper" (25). The inclusion of Gabi's zine heightens the diary mode's interruptions of narrative temporality. Through Gabi's diary and, more prominently, her zine, readers grasp Gabi's burgeoning identity as a developing writer. Quintero alters the standard diary-novel form and exposes readers to a powerful media form. Gabi's zine is solely dedicated to exploring the subjects of female body diversity and health, topics at the forefront of many teenagers' minds. *Gabi* speaks to the pliability of Chicana teenage personhood through its imaginative rendering of Gabi as a rebellious teen, by pressing on the traditional boundaries of the standard diary-novel form, and by departing from contemporary depictions of Chicana teenage personhood. It declares that Chicana teenage poets exist and they can write their way through and out of all kinds of conscripting con(texts), including those shaped by their own unique personal struggles. It asserts and materially models the fact that Chicanas engage with multiple discourses to produce a variety of rhetorics, writing across genres and forms, and even by creating original forms of participatory media.

Further fomenting the idea that writing itself and the concept of critical revision is central to Quintero's figuration of Gabi's evolution, craft, and agency are the book's titles. Inscribed directly atop the book cover's image and title page are a series of three titles. Two of the three titles are crossed out as if editorially rejected, signaling that even the book's title itself (like our understanding of youth in general, the genre of the YA diary novel, and Quintero's central Chicana protagonist Gabi) is "under revision." While under erasure, the crossed-out titles function as a means of bilingually translating the troubling pressures associated with fat shaming, the policing of girls who fail to conform to normative body and beauty standards, the pressure of compulsory body conformity, and the unrealistic standards of beauty that teenagers contend with across cultures. The titles center Gabi's pervasive struggle with weight stigma, body shame and acceptance, and her intuitive awareness of revision and rewriting as central to the act of writing itself, as well as to the very processes of identity formation taking place in her life, processes that are undeniable hallmarks of adolescence as figured through the genre of the YA novel.

Reimagining Border(land)s of Chicana Young Adulthood

As in many other fictional Chicana mother-daughter relationships imagined throughout contemporary Chicana literature, Gabi does not reject her mother or the older women in her family altogether, but she does "reject and contest cultural patriarchal, and heteronormative gender roles that would have [her] follow in [her] mother's footsteps" (Herrera, 10–11). Thus, Quintero's young diarist is intent on interpreting, deconstructing, narrating, upending, and reshaping the borders of what Chicana girlhood and adolescence means, and she achieves this by focusing on the power of personal writing. Through Quintero's use of the diary strategy, one understands Gabi's character as actively undertaking the process of reflexively contemplating and indexing her own growth and development, or turmoil and loss, through writing. One can presume that each of the entries Gabi pens are intended only for Gabi's own view. Quintero stages an illusory voyeuristic access to a private landscape through this mode of narration that is meant to be read as a sincere glimpse into the most private of *borderlands*; the ones comprising Gabi's uncensored raw feelings, secret thoughts, and her inner consciousness recorded by Gabi's own pen. The documentation of Gabi's "secret" thoughts via Quintero's fictional diary strategy coupled with the sense of access to her interiority and most intimate emotions take precedence over any other landscape. Put another way, the physical and metaphoric borderlands that occupy much theoretical and literary space for Chicanas since the 1990s boom of Chicana feminist writing and Gloria Anzaldúa's watershed 1987 *Borderlands/ La Frontera:*

The New Mestiza here are not figured through geographic spaces, or the physical south Texas geography that resulted from the territorialization of the US-Mexico border, "Where the first world grates against the third and bleeds" (Anzaldúa 25). Rather, they are imagined through the shifting contours of Gabi's evolving thoughts and emotive landscapes and through the pages of Gabi's writing. Quintero's novel offers readers an opportunity to engage and affirm the complex borderlands within the mind-space and written works of a nonconformist teenage Chicana poet geek and zinester.

Gabi's borderlands are different. Gabi's identity as a poet geek departs from dominant fictive filmic and literary imaginings of Chicana/o youth, as well as from Anglo mainstream representations of YA girl protagonists. As Kameron Hurley notes in *The Geek Feminist Revolution,* "Inside geek circles, what geekiness is, and how it's defined, is becoming . . . a hotly contested issue. [Recent] mainstream coverage . . . has focused primarily on predominately white, male geeks suffering a keen sense of nostalgia for the days when they were the assumed default audience," which belies the fact that women have always been geeks (13). Gabi is not like Margaret from Judy Blume's 1970 YA novel[7] *Are You There God? It's Me, Margaret,* nor does she resemble Katniss Everdeen from Suzanne Collins's 2008 dystopic trilogy *The Hunger Games.* She is a Chicana writer, a voracious reader, and a sharp thinker who becomes a poet and zinester inspired by Sandra Cisneros and other poets and writers. For these reasons, Gabi's character departs from many depictions of young Chicanas. More specifically, she is unlike Chicanas in YA novels who not only face the traditional challenges associated with teenage life, but also perform the arduous labor associated with the US farm worker's experience. Take for instance Pam Muñoz Ryan's character Esperanza, a girl who must negotiate west coast teenage life as an agrarian laborer in her 2000 young adult novel *Esperanza Rising,* or Maria Helena Viramontes' character Estrella in the classic 1996 novel *Under the Feet of Jesus.* Gabi's character also departs from the readily available fictively imagined figure of the gang member or gang-affiliated misfit such as in Yxta Maya Murray's 1997 *Locas,* which imagines Chicana girl gang life, or even the 2012 gang memoir *Always Running: La Vida Loca: Gang Days in L.A.* by Luis J. Rodriguez.

One of a growing cadre of writers that includes Matt de la Peña, Malin Alegria, Benjamin Alire Sáenz, Erika Sánchez, Ashley Hope Pérez, and Mario Alberto Zambrano, Quintero broadens the scope of characters within Chicana/o and or Latinx youth in YA fiction.[8] *Gabi* does not focus on the figure of the urban gang member, or the child agrarian laborer; instead she offers us the often hilarious and sarcastic personal writing and self-examination of a Chicana teenage poet geek desperately trying to figure out who she is and make peace with the fact that she will more than likely be forever widely misunderstood. Gabi's outsider status only further animates her willingness to push beyond the limitations of her age, body size, race, class, and gender and more importantly to do whatever it takes to continue to hone her skills as a writer.

 ## Producing Performance Poetry from Pain

At the start of her senior year, Gabi "had to change [her] schedule around to fit [her] poetry class," an act that proves incalculably life-changing (Quintero 27). In this class Gabi meets her English teacher Ms. Abernard, builds a poetry-workshop community, and meets her secret crush Martin Espada. Ms. Abernard introduces Gabi to a variety of poetic forms. As Larissa Mercado-López notes, "Chicana feminist youth literature can have serious implications for young Chicana readers living in the in-between spaces of childhood and adulthood" (Mercado-López 5) Gabi learns that "Poetry helps heal wounds / Makes them tangible" in this class (141).

Immersed in the study of poetry, Gabi is challenged to author, revise, publish, and bring her own poetry to life by performing it. Through this class Gabi builds a portfolio of haiku, prose poems, list poems, and spoken word pieces. Thus, while her senior brings the tragic overdose of her father, the teenage pregnancy of her closest friend, the rape of one of her schoolmates, and the homophobic rejection of her friend Sebastian by his family, her senior year introduces her to the literary worlds of Edgar Allen Poe, Sylvia Plath, Michelle Serros, Allen Ginsberg, Sandra Cisneros, Pablo Neruda, Aldous Huxley, e.e. cummings, John Steinbeck, Maya Angelou, Alexander Pope, Tracie Morris, William Shakespeare, and Robert Burns. Engrossed by a palliative written world, she experiments with poetic writing and confesses, "I really like poetry. It's therapeutic. It's like I can write something on paper and part of it (not all of it, obviously) disappears. . . . I didn't realize how powerful it could be" (83–84). Hence, Ms. Abernard helps Gabi go beyond being a consumer of poetry and become a poet. Most importantly, Gabi learns to harness poetry's therapeutic potential to dress her own emotional wounds. Beyond merely refining her craft as a burgeoning creative writer, Gabi actively sharpens the tools for her own cathartic healing, political mobilization, and community building.

Led by Ms. Abernard's guidance and her new penchant for poetry, Gabi accepts an invitation to make her own private writing public.[9] Gabi goes against her family's wishes and performs her spoken word poetry at the Grind Effect poetry cafe. She reveals, "My hands started shaking as soon as I stepped up to the mic, but then something happened about two stanzas in. I got so lost in the poem—and in getting all the emotions out that came with it—that I forgot where I was" (137). Her poem about her father's addiction, titled "In Light of the Fear of My Father's Death I Write This Down," is an unflinching cathartic elegy to her father that solidifies Gabi's decision to pursue her dreams despite her pain and the gendered policing taking place within her family. Gabi laments her Tia Bertha's unbearable lack of support for her poetry and her constant moralizing, noting, "I already had to listen to her go on about poetry reading and how horrible it is that I'm going. She says that a nice young woman does not expose her thoughts like that to the public. That writing is something only men should do, like going to college" (131). In the space of three sentences, Quintero links Gabi's expressive poetic agency with her willingness to resist the misogynistic expectations constraining, restricting, and limiting her pursuits. While Chicana pain does not have to be made available for public consumption and performative display to be validated, for Gabi performing her poetry is an empowering act of defiance and a bold assertion of her budding expressive freedom. Rather than echo her Tia Bertha, Gabi's teacher urges her to go to college and even suggests that she "study English and take creative writing classes but then get a Masters in Fine Arts—an MFA—in poetry" (84).

Indeed, poetry helps Gabi heal, but zines turn out to provide Gabi with a purpose beyond her own personal healing; they offer her a political platform.

Chicana Zinesters: Feminist Agency, Recalcitrant Writing

Writing helps an undeniably geeky Chicana acclimate to being in her own skin. It helps her to deal with pain and loss. However, the incisive critiques that were privately housed in her diary begin to slip into her poetry and spill into her zine titled "The Female Body."[10] This seven-page verbal-visual text included as an inset in Quintero's novel is made up of seven diagrams. Each of the seven illustrated pages concern themselves with one aspect of the body: the shape of a biologically female body, breasts, vagina, hair, hands, legs, and mouth. The zine openly critiques oppressive misconceptions and ideologies of health, well-being, morality, sexuality, and the Chicana body. As Allison Piepmeier notes, "Zines are a living medium with both historical and contemporary relevance for the lives of girls and women and for feminism's third wave. Historically they are a space where many third wave ideas and iconography developed, and as a contemporary phenomenon they allow for different kinds of community and different modes of activism" (17). Gabi's zine read here as evidence of her burgeoning Chicana feminist identity works to question ideas about the female body and the degree to which it can be understood as unitary or stable.

The zine creates the ideological space to unpack contradictory feelings about embodiment and about the contradictory messages surrounding teenage personhood. For instance, "Diagram Two" notes, "These are the breasts. As they develop they will hurt. You will be teased because your breasts are too small. You will be teased because your breasts are too large. You will be teased because you have breasts. . . . You may realize that you are more than your breasts. You may not" ("The Female Body," see Figure 2). The few moments when Gabi expresses body positivity in her diary are scarce when compared to her expressions of self-loathing about her body weight. Her zine, however, indexes that Gabi is actively deconstructing the very ideologies that lead women to devalue aspects of their own body and, though she admits "this is the thing: I'm fat. I don't want to be fat for many reasons," Quintero offers no romantic notions about gendered identity and body image (170). Gabi has not entirely made peace with her physical body, her unrealistic self-conceptions and prevailing gendered body standards, but one can believe that by becoming a zinester, perhaps one day she will. As Adela C. Licona notes in *Zines in Third Space: Radical Cooperation and Borderlands Rhetoric*, "Zinesters often work to disrupt the order imposed by the normativising gaze and the perceived materialized order it imposes by rendering visible the previously invisible, indecent, invalid, and unacceptable" (Licona 71). Similarly, "Diagram Three," the third page of Gabi's zine that includes a partial sketch of a uterus and is dedicated to the topic of vaginas, notes, "You will be taught that this part of your body is more private and more dirty than any other part of your body. But you will never be given an explanation why. And if you ask you might get into trouble" (see Figure 3, "The Female Body"). Gabi's zine promotes "a new literacy that allows the body to be read and represented differently and that identifies misrepresentations and distortions that have been normalized" (Licona 88). It reveals Gabi's "desire to connect, communicate, inform, and act" (Licona 3).

Despite feeling physically flawed and loathing her own body, Gabi fashions a space in which she becomes the authority on the female body. Her zine production is remarkable precisely because these "publications . . . forgo the gatekeepers of the traditional publishing marketplace—editors, publishers, and others who determine who's in and who's out," and therefore Gabi's choice to make her own zine speaks volumes about her own agency (Piepmeier 13). Her zine epitomizes her ability to write and create art forms that think through embodiment without the need for anyone's permission. In *Are You There God? It's Me, Margaret,* the title character privately critiques her school health science film on female reproductive health titled *What Every Girl Should Know,* for the opaque way it depicts menstruation. Blume's character laments in her own diary that the film, "just said how wonderful nature was" (Blume 97). Four

"The Female Body" from *Gabi, a Girl in Pieces*. © Zeke Peña

"The Female Body" from *Gabi, a Girl in Pieces*. © Zeke Peña

decades later, in contrast to Blume's Margaret, Quintero's Gabi (wittingly or unwittingly) takes her critiques about her own unique embodied experience and produces activist art and social commentary, which deconstruct prevailing ideologies surrounding gendered embodiment. Gabi the zinester then can be understood as a brazen Chicana feminist activist writer. Gabi's personal struggles with her body image and her identity as a geeky Chicana misfit do not inhibit her from creating participatory media forms. Licona notes, "Through acts of contortion, distortion, aggression, confession, desire, and reconciliation, bodies and be-ings are being re-membered and re-configured in zines" (70). Quintero novel frames Gabi's struggle with her own embodiment as the impetus that drives Gabi to create con(texts) where she can revise and produce knowledge about her body and experience. Therefore, Gabi's zine can be understood as a space where she will continue to discursively fashion and reconstruct her own identity.

Gabi's commitment to being an ally to other young women goes beyond the pages of her zine. When her high school nemesis Georgina finds out she is pregnant after having been raped, Gabi takes Georgina to a clinic when she decides to terminate her pregnancy. Through Gabi, Quintero pushes against depictions of young women as passive, weak, divisive, competitive, and catty, or as only achieving voice through the pages of their diary. Rather than shame Georgina, Gabi affirms and supports her by reminding Georgina precisely what one imagines Gabi has likely had to say to herself many times. She tells Georgina, "You are not alone. I know we don't get along . . . but . . . Don't feel alone. There has to be a solution out there. We just haven't thought of it yet'" (178).

Chicana (Body) Struggles for Safe Space

Quintero's novel is composed of equal parts levity and woe communicated through its images and verbal text. Through the diary mode and the inclusion of Gabi's zine, Quintero's novel achieves biting sarcasm, humor, and boldness. Gabi's diary serves as a safe house for her deepest desires and her worst fears, but Gabi's agency goes beyond her ability to pen the pages of her diary. Gabi deliberately constructs safe spaces for those around her. Though she self-describes as merely a misunderstood teenage poet, she is also an advocate to the most vulnerable people around her. Through her unabashed rebelliousness she creates paradigm shifts in her home and community. For instance, when Gabi's best friend Cindy finds out she is pregnant, Gabi finds a way to show her love and support during her pregnancy and the birth of her son. Also, when Gabi's friend Sebastian is thrown out of his own home for admitting he is gay, Gabi creates a safe space for him in her own home. Gabi also helps her bible-beating and prude tia Bertha by calling out her hypocrisy and by resisting her judgmental statements, thereby freeing her tia to be open and honest about her own desires and longing for a guilt-free love life. She even helps her nemesis Georgina. Most importantly, Gabi finds a way to help herself through her own writing, and one can easily imagine a future for Quintero's character as a writer. Though Quintero's novel is admittedly triumphalist because it depicts a Chicana teenage poet geek who chooses to chase her dreams, not all of Gabi's struggles are totally resolved. Upon opening a series of college acceptance and rejection letters, Gabi notes, "Me. The Mexican fat girl. Accepted to Berkeley!" (186). In this way, Quintero closes her novel with a Chicana who is equipped to build a coalitional community through her poetry and her zines, and who will continue her ongoing struggle to accept and love herself, her body, and her geeky wit for who and what it is.

Notes

1. Although geek and nerd are often interchangeably used, because Gabi self-identifies as an "English geek" and her brother Beto refers to her as such, I decisively refer to Gabi as a poet geek (261). Gabi struggles in math but affirms the fact that she excels in English.

2. Theorizing black geeks in "Post-Integration Blues: Black Geeks and Afro-Diasporic Humanism," Alexander G. Weheliye contends that "racial identities have shifted and multiplied, despite the continued existence of white supremacy and structural racism, the awkward and self-conscious, yet verbally skilled geek persona serves as an ideal vehicle for amplifying the vexed politics and aesthetics" of the contemporary era (226).

3. Gabi's gender critique is far more pronounced than her discussion of race, but her understandings of the formation of race are evolving. Commenting on progressive notions of gender in children's and YA literature, Philip Serrato notes that texts always leave something to be desired, and can be read as part of "an ongoing, evolutionary process of authors relentlessly seeking out efficacious strategies for translating the insights of feminism, gender studies, and queer theory into personally and socially transformative books for children" (150).

4. Radway asserts, "We make ourselves with materials and in conditions that are *not* of our own making. Thus, those materials and conditions inevitably exert their own kind of force and constraint on our acts of fabrication. . . . We make ourselves out of the very stories, songs, objects, performances, and characters that people our daily lives and point us and our imaginations toward an only dimly discerned future" (194).

5. Radway notes, "There are many forms, practices, and modes that one could point to in girl culture today to illustrate this kind of insubordinate creativity. I think of the many collages girls construct to adorn their rooms, their notebooks, and their diaries" (199).

6. It warrants noting that the complex formal dimensions of this novel dovetail with other Chicana works that experiment with form and give voice to borderland's experiences. Take for instance Guadalupe Garcia McCall's 2011 *Under the Mesquite*, written in verse, or Gloria Anzaldúa's 1987 *Borderlands*.

7. Though identifying with Judy Blume's character, Gabi notes her irreducible difference from her; she writes, "I feel like Margaret in Judy Blume's *Are You There God, It's Me Margaret?* Except instead of waiting for my period, I am waiting for my first time to see a boy naked. I wonder if that is normal? Probably not good in any case. Argh!!! *FML*. Seriously" (234). Thus, one can conclude that Gabi cannot locate representations that speak directly to her experience in YA fiction, and because of her frustration, she feels compelled to seek out or construct con(texts) where her experience and her ideas can freely take shape, such as the spoken word café.

8. See Cristina Herrera's article "Soy Brown y Nerdy: The ChicaNerd in Chicana Young Adult (YA) Literature" for a critical understanding of how Ashley Hope Pérez and Isabel Quintero subvert the mainstream nerd stereotype by fictively imagining the "ChicaNerd."

9. Suzanne Bost's, *Encarnación: Illness and Body Politics in Chicana Feminist Literature*, considers pain in the creative works and in the personal, shifting identity politics of Moraga, Castillo, and Anzaldúa. Bost notes, "Pain and illness remind us about the needs of bodies. . . . Foregrounding pain . . . undermines the myth of self-reliance and demands more expansive ways of understanding individual agency" (5). Hence, Gabi's decision to grapple with the pain of losing her father through poetry centers her crucial need to deal with emotional pain even as it foments her personal evolution as a Chicana poet geek.

10. Allison Piepmeir asserts that zines "cover every imaginable subject matter, from food politics to thrift shopping to motherhood. They are an example of participatory media—media created by consumers rather than by corporate cultural industries" (Piepmeier 2).

Works Cited

Abbot, H. Porter. *Diary Fiction: Writing as Action*. Cornell University Press, 1984.

Alamillo, Laura, Larissa M. Mercado-López, and Cristina Herrera, editors. *Voices of Resistance: Interdisciplinary Approaches to Chican@ Children's Literature*. Rowman & Littlefield, 2018.

Anzaldúa, Gloria. *Borderlands/ La Frontera: The New Mestiza*. San Francisco: Aunt Lute. 1987.

Blume, Judy. *Are You There God? It's Me, Margaret*. Simon & Schuster, 1970.

Bost. Suzanne. *Encarnación: Illness and Body Politics in Chicana Feminist Literature*. Fordham University Press, 2010.

Herrera, Cristina. *Contemporary Chicana Literature: Rewriting the Maternal Script*. Cambria Press, 2014.

Herrera, Cristina. "Soy Brown y Nerdy: The ChicaNerd in Chicana Young Adult (YA) Literature." *The Lion and the Unicorn*, vol. 41, 2017, pp. 307–26.

Hurley Kameron. *The Geek Feminist Revolution*. A Tom Doherty Associates Book, 2016.

Licona, Adela C. *Zines in Third Space: Radical Cooperation and Borderlands Rhetoric*. SUNY Press, 2012.

Mercado-López, Larissa M. "Entre Tejana y Chicana: Tracing Proto-Chicana Identity and Consciousness in Tejana Young Adult Fiction and Poetry." *Voices of Resistance: Interdisciplinary Approaches to Chican@ Children's Literature*, edited by Laura Alamillo, Larissa M. Mercado-López, and Cristina Herrera, Lanham, Rowman & Littlefield, 2018, pp. 3–16.

Piepmeier, Alison. *Girl Zines: Making Media, Doing Feminism*. New York University Press, 2009.

Quintero, Isabel. *Gabi, A Girl in Pieces*. Cinco Puntos Press, 2014.

Radway, Janice. "Girls, Reading, and Narrative Gleaning: Crafting Repertoires for Self-Fashioning within Everyday Life." *Narrative Impact: Social and Cognitive Foundations*, edited by Melanie C. Green, Jefferey J. Strange, and Timothy C. Brock, Taylor and Francis, 2002, pp. 183–204.

Serrato, Phillip. "Promise and Peril: The Gendered Implications of Pat Mora's *Pablo's Tree* and Ana Castillo's *My Daughter, My Son, the Eagle, the Dove*." *Children's Literature*, vol. 38, 2010, pp. 133–52.

Weheliye, Alexander G. "Post-Integration Blues: Black Geeks and Afro Diasporic Humanism." *Blacks in Diaspora: Contemporary African American Literature: The Living Canon*, edited by Lovalerie King and Shirley Moody-Turner, Indiana University Press, 2013, pp. 213–34.

2

Praxis of Refusal: Self-Fashioning Identity and Throwing Attitude in Pérez's *The First Rule of Punk*

Lettycia Terrones

At the age of eighteen, Marianne Elliott-Said (aka Poly Styrene), a non-conformist brown girl punk rocker, wrote and belted out organic critiques of consumerist capitalist culture and the suffocating gender norms of her 1977 London surroundings. Through her band, X-Ray Spex, Poly Styrene leveraged punk performance to engage directly in a radical praxis that sought, as Jayna Brown writes, "liberation from the effects of racial and sexual violence" (463). This radical praxis is evident in her song "Identity," which calls out the epistemic violence inherent in race-making projects that would seek to erase and misrepresent girls of color by normalizing their lack and non-presence in mainstream society and media narratives. The power of Poly Styrene's rebellion is not lost on Malú, the protagonist of Celia C. Pérez's middle-grade novel *The First Rule of Punk* (2017). Like her predecessor and hero, Poly Styrene, Malú also uses creative expression in punk to contend with the complex threads of her racial identity comprised by her Mexican and white heritage. Pérez's novel interrogates what this process of unraveling and reweaving a bicultural heritage looks like for mixed girls. Through Malú's first-person narrative, Poly Styrene's question, "When you look in the mirror / Do you see yourself," becomes the exploration of a young girl's integration and self-fashioning of an identity squarely located within an activist punk-rock ethos that refuses assimilation. By tracing Malú's resilient acts of refusal to assimilate into social norms and the meaning-making practices she activates in self-fashioning her identity, my essay locates Malú's rebellion within a rich and defiant feminist brown-girl punk genealogy. I analyze Malú's instinctual connection to Teresa Covarrubias, singer of East Los Angeles's legendary punk band the Brat, to situate her amongst this radical genealogy. Malú's *corazonada*, or the culturally informed gut-feeling she gets when first connected to Covarrubias, I argue, demonstrates Malú's aesthetic kinship to other brown punk feminists, who, like Covarrubias, also resist conformity and practice a politics of refusal. I examine these politics of refusal through the lens of Stefano Harney and Fred Moten's work in *The Undercommons: Fugitive Planning & Black Study,* in which they theorize practices of refusal as being those creative potentialities enacted independent of defining and commanding power structures. In describing the black radical tradition's deep legacies of radical refusal, Harney and Moten offer racialized minoritatian and deviant people vibrant optimism and resistant strategies found in creative, life sustaining non-conformity. My reading of Malú's zine-making art practice will show how she leverages this creative act as a strategy for interrogating and self-fashioning her identity. Moreover, I argue how Malú's zines themselves enact a performative site that not only allows Malú a praxis space for exploring her identity and ethics but further connects her to a larger collective of brown feminist punks.

Indeed, Harney and Moten's framework offers a vantage point from which to interrogate Pérez's *The First Rule of Punk* as itself being a creative work that holds up a mirror to all the weirdo outsiders, all the underrepresented Chicanx and Latinx youth, the deviant punks who are also refused through misrepresentations, erasures, and omissions by the various mainstream institutional systems they navigate. Through Malú's process of identity meaning-making, Pérez's narrative models the vibrancy of Chicanx and Latinx youth who have, and always will, create spaces wide enough to carry all their truths. In this way, Pérez's creative work likewise resists dominant narratives that continue to limit access to #OwnVoices authors, illustrators, and literary critics to the dominant United States children's literature publishing market. The larger project of my analysis of *The First Rule of Punk* is to connect it to a lineage of Chicanx cultural productions that resists domination of conformity through creative resistant acts. This rasquache[1] sensibility reminds us of José Esteban Muñoz's analysis in *Disidentifications: Queers of Color and the Performance of Politics*, which calls out the "particular hegemonic mandate" and imposed positionality of minoritorian subjects to perform their "alterity as a consumable local spectacle" for social elites (182). Naming this form of oppression, the "burden of liveness," Muñoz illustrates how minoritarian black, brown, and queer artists directly subvert oppressive norms through creative acts. This direct negotiation, if not unabashed defiance, alters dominant ideologies and narratives, breaking open spaces for Latinx non-conformists to create and self-fashion their own representations and knowledges.

Malú's Punk Rock Corazonada

María Luisa (Malú) O'Neill-Morales is a second-generation biracial daughter of a Chicana woman and white father who together maintain a harmonious co-parenting relationship despite being divorced. The novel opens with Malú's unhappy protest against her move from Gainesville, Florida, to Chicago, where her mother, Magaly, will start a two-year visiting professorship. On her last night in Gainesville, Malú and her father, Michael, an old punk rocker, dance the night away to the Smith's classic ballad "Please Please Please Let Me Get What I Want." Michael gives Malú a set of worry dolls to help ease her mind about the move, but it is Malú's trusty zine supplies that will help chase the homesick blues away as she contends with starting seventh-grade in a new town, making friends, and dealing with her mom fussing over her non-señorita fashion style.

Malú and Magaly's relationship is fraught with contention over fashion choices. This space of tension becomes a crucible for Malú's acts of self-fashioning, where she explores and negotiates her racialized identity. Marci R. McMahon's scholarship on Chicana feminist artist Patssi Valdez theorizes on the performativity of self-fashioning as a process which "highlights the intersections of dress with bodily performance and the possibility of these sites in the negotiation of gendered and racialized ideologies" (132). I connect McMahon's formulation of self-fashioning, where creative acts, through the medium of clothes, makeup, and style, perform "political negotiation and critique" against normative ideologies (132). Malú's self-fashioning is not so much motivated by posing a direct opposition to Magaly's desire for her to act and dress like a *señorita*. Rather, Malú is interested in the boldness and non-conformist attitude of punk fashion as a site for exploring and expressing her differences, and her instinctual rejection of social norms. Malú's self-fashioning offers her an organic, changing, and unfixed site for processing her identity and ethics. Often vulnerable in this site of exploration, punk fashion offers Malú a sense of protection.

The protective function of punk fashion is evident in Malú's style choices. On the first day of her new school, José Guadalupe Posada Middle School, she dons her best punk rock armor: green jeans, Blondie t-shirt, *trenzas*, silver-sequined Chuck Taylor high-tops in homage to her hero, the original Dorothy from the *Wizard of Oz*. She layers the "heavy eye makeup, dark lipstick" so classic to Chicana punk rock feminine aesthetics (McMahon 141). Malú resists being boxed in. She doesn't want to assimilate and is courageous enough to risk the ridicule of her peers, as they too must negotiate the socializing institution of school. By foregrounding Malú's self-fashioning, I call attention to the intuitive gravitation toward this Chicana punk aesthetic. Up to this point,

Malú's primary reference point to punk is her dad, whose influence informs her love of 1970s punk bands like Blondie, the Ramones, and X-Ray Spex. Despite looking up to Poly Styrene of X-Ray Spex, Malú does not yet connect her own biracial heritage to that of Poly Styrene's Somali and white British biracial roots. However, Malú's unawareness of the deep genealogy of black and brown women's contributions to punk does not last long.[3]

Malú's instinctual desire to make meaning of her mixed cultural identity through a punk self-fashioning materializes when having just wrapped up the first practice session of her newly formed punk band, the Co-Co's, she hears the voice of Teresa Covarrubias for the first time.

Enthralled, she asks, "Who is she?" To which her mentor and fellow punk rocker Mrs. Hidalgo knowingly replies, "That's Teresa Covarrubias. . . . The Brat was a Los Angeles band in the early eighties, . . . And they're Chicanos, Mexican Americans. *Like us*" (C. C. Pérez 162, emphasis added). Prior to this moment, Malú's identification as a punk rocker is squarely situated within traditional punk narratives of non-conformity but is not so much attuned to the intersections of race and feminism in punk. Mrs. Hidalgo's "like us" indexes a kinship that shakes up Malú's prior assumption that she was "the only brown punk in the whole world" (C. C. Pérez 105). Indeed, the phrase "like us" illuminates in Malú a *corazonada*, or deep cultural knowing that gestures towards what it means to be Chicanx in the United States. Malú's *corazonada* gestures toward a larger effect of the Chicanx experience, that making meaning of one's identity is born from a deep-in-the-bones experience of cultural liminality—a liminality often described as the existential knowing that you are neither from here nor there.

In this powerful moment, Mrs. Hidalgo confirms for Malú the beautiful liminality, the quintessential *nepantla* quality, of Chicanx ontology. Gloria Anzaldúa's seminal theoretical work describes this unique Chicanx state of consciousness where through liminality, a new decolonial consciousness can emerge. Anzaldúa writes, "Negotiating with borders results in mestizaje, the new hybrid, the new mestiza, a new category of identity. Mestizas live in between different worlds, in nepantla" (71). Living and creating in this liminality opens up a potentiality for curing, what critic Laura E. Pérez calls "the cultural *susto*: that is, the 'frightening' of spirit from one's body-mind in the colonial and neocolonial ordeals" (21).[4] This moment of cultural transference from Mrs. Hidalgo to Malú expands her prior knowledge and understanding of the punk narrative. Mrs. Hidalgo teaches Malú about Chicana feminist punk contributions and includes Malú as a participant in this group. Mrs. Hidaldo's mentoring introduces Malú to the survival strategies of brown feminist punks who themselves deploy self-fashioning to negotiate the pain and healing of cultural fragmentation experienced in *nepantla.* Malú too belongs to this lineage of Chicana artists who make their own rules, which she will go on to learn is indeed the first rule of punk (C. C. Pérez 310).

Pérez's reference to Teresa Covarrubias is strategic. Covarrubias indeed makes her own rules. This self-fashioning, resistant aesthetic is clearly evident in the widely viewed YouTube video of Covarrubias, whose performance with her band the Brat captures her magnetism and undeniable impact on the Chicanx punk scene. The Brat's classic punk rock song "High School" hits you fast and tight in this bootleg video recording shot in 1979 at Plaza de la Raza cultural center located in the Mexican American working-class neighborhood of Lincoln Heights, East Los Angeles. Covarrubias commands our attention like a brown siren. The camera focuses on her face as she sings. At first ignoring its low-angle shot, Covarrubias, powerful and in full control, draws the lens up to meet her straight-ahead gaze. She wrecks all our ships! Then, dismissing the camera's gaze, she looks back to check if her band of four Chicano punks are still afloat. Her hair cropped short, no make-up, Covarrubias, grabs the standup mic and tears it up full stop, juxtaposing a high-femme cry, shaking up the visual effect of her baby blue housedress. She belts out her resistance: "Catholic high school's just a game / Driving kids like me insane" (1–2).

Scholarship documenting Covarrubias's impact on Chicana feminisms and her undeniable influence on the nascent Los Angeles punk rock scene of the late 1970s and early 1980s points to the power of her vocal command to provoke what cultural critic Licia Fiol-Matta calls "the thinking voice." Fiol-Matta theorizes the "thinking voice" as being the phenomenon of voice at once transcending performance and its sociomaterial apparatuses while still yet emerging from it, such that the singer's voice calls out to and draws in the listener, "impelling her public toward an exercise of thought through the sense of hearing and the act of listening. This is, in Heideggerian terms, the 'gift' of the thinking voice" (172–73; 227). Likewise, Covarrubias calls to us, and to Malú; her voice a multivalent siren with messages proclaiming a Chicana feminist resistant politic. Covarrubias's voice, like her performance, rejects the male heteronormative gaze and institutionally enforced patriarchy. In her song, "High School," Covarrubias draws lines against the "short grey skirts" mandated by school uniforms. She contrasts her defiance, opposing the conscripted gender norms of "looking cute" by declaring, "I'm looking worst" (3–4). McMahon examines fashion and performance as aesthetic political strategies deployed by the Chicana avant-garde, noting how artists of Covarrubias's milieu defied gender/race/class norms that were heavily inscribed in school, as well as in the punk rock scene. Michelle Habell-Pallán further describes how Chicana singers like Covarrubias and Alicia Armendariz Velasquez (a.k.a. Alice Bag) leveraged their songwriting and lead-singer presence to "critique gender norms with song titles like 'Misogyny,'" despite persistent sexism in the punk scene (160). Indeed, Covarrubias's lyrics telling us she "idn't learn a goddamn thing / Didn't buy that fuckin' ring" concretize her refusal to conform to the socializing norms delimiting the prospects for good Catholic (Mexican) girls (8–9).

However, it is Covarrubias's refusal to seek recognition, signaled by her words, "I won't prance won't make romance / Wish I could? But I can't," which draws Chicana feminist interlocutors to engage Covarrubias's thinking voice (10–11). Harney and Moten theorize this praxis of refusal, noting how creative potentialities are used to reject powers of domination, describing it as the radical move to "be part of another project" (152). This politics of refusing recognition is precisely what effects Chicana feminists' responses to Covarrubias. The feminist collectivity of this response is marked by Chicanas' diverse responses to Covarrubias's brown, feminist siren song. The effect of Covarrubias's thinking voice is evident in the academic and organic theorizing that attempts to describe the *it-ness* of her voice.[5]

Covarrubias articulates a Chicana feminist punk aesthetic. "Punk to me was about all these oddballs and people who didn't really have any other place to express themselves and being given a forum where no one was judging you on how good you were, who you know, or what clique you were in. . . . Whoever wanted a go at it, punk was there and you could express yourself in that movement" (quoted in Alvarado 159). It is no wonder then that Malú finds affinity with Covarrubias. Malú's *corazonada* resonates with Covarrubias's refusal to assimilate. In Covarrubias's voice, Malú recognizes her own impulse to reject norms that seek to delimit who she should be. She turns to punk as a creative space for interrogation of her complex bicultural heritage. In punk, Malú self-fashions an integrated identity by activating a punk rock ethos to refuse agents of assimilation. Specifically, Malú uses creative punk expression found in making zines, fashion, and forming a band as mediums to negotiate the complex threads of her racial identity. With Mrs. Hidalgo's mentoring in punk, Malú begins to weave the mixed brown-girl feminist genealogies comprising her Mexican and white heritage.

Malú's Performative Zine

Malú's zines throughout *The First Rule of Punk* illustrate her process of self-fashioning an identity that integrates her biracial heritage and punk aesthetics. Zines as a medium for self-fashioning projects further situates Malú within a lineage of brown girl punks. I draw upon two examples to illustrate the creative and political function of zine-making that connects Malú to brown feminist punk genealogies. Jim Mendiola's 1996 film *Pretty Vacant* chronicles a summer in the life of La Molly, a young Chicana feminist punk rocker from San Antonio, who uses the creative outlet of her zine, *Ex-Voto*, and her all-girl punk band, Aztlán-a-Go-Go, to write herself into the world. Habell-Pallán's critical history on the cultural work of Chicana feminist punk rockers posits *Pretty Vacant* as exploration of unfolding Chicana mestiza consciousness, writing, "Molly's art production serves as an index of the 1980s explosion of Chicana writing and art. A useful way to interpret the film, then, is to read the figure of Molly as an allegory for the development of a Chicana feminist epistemology" (174). For Molly, *Ex-Voto* performs as a site for the development of her mestiza consciousness, evident here in her description of its contents.

Ex-Voto, right? I published it 'cause no one was addressing my interests or my needs. Simple as that. For those of you who've missed my first issues, I'll catch you up: Number one had articles on Emma Tenayuca, a profile. The only band the matters [The Clash], a history. Pictures of my girlfriend Lourdes's band, Los Niños Héroes Girlfriends. An interview with Terry Cisneros (Henry's daughter; I went to high school with her) all about Ivy League grad schools—how to get in, what they're like. And, an illustrated history of *retablos*, from 18th century Mexico to postmodern Tijuana kitsch. (La Molly, *Pretty Vacant*)

Ex-Voto touches the pulse of Chicana feminist imperatives that seek to teach about Chicana histories and contributions often excluded from normative sites of education. Molly compiles a snapshot of the deep legacy of Chicana-led radical class-struggle, signaled by her Emma Tenayuca profile. Through *Ex-Voto*, she performs the work of D.I.Y. college preparation and mentoring through resource sharing. She further presents Mexicana and Chicana artistic contributions seen through the women-centered aesthetic spiritual expressions of *retablos*. Molly's coverage of her girlfriend's femme punk band also unabashedly communicates a love and attention for Chicana queers. Specifically, Molly notes her activist impulse to create *Ex-Voto* in order to bring into the world what she does not see represented elsewhere, be it school or media narratives.

Indeed, zines have served as critical sites for writing oneself into the world and are an especially powerful medium for exploring minoritarian voices and racial intersections in punk. In an interview with Elizabeth Sinton, Osa Atoe describes the political intentionality of her influential zine *Shotgun Series*. "I wanted to provide images and writing that reinforces my own identity as a black, queer, punk musician and also that made D.I.Y. culture and anti-consumerist ideals accessible to other black people. . . . Instead of seeing my own identity as some sort of novelty, or error, I found comfort and empowerment, and pride through interviewing folks like Kali Boyce, Mick Collins, Rachel Aggs and many others" (quoted in Stinton 263). Atoe's description of political praxis through zine-making points to another important function of zines. By writing herself into the punk world, especially one that persists in maintaining a white-supremacist narrative of non-inclusion for people of color, Atoe calls attention to collective anti-capitalist practices of archive-making projects that directly challenge erasure. Atoe's construction of a counter-archive also brings to focus the critical importance of writing and imparting genealogies of radical black punk expression. By prioritizing "other black people," as her primary audience, Atoe enacts the type of "like us" performativity that Mrs. Hidalgo conjures in her cultural mentoring of Malú. Mrs. Hidalgo, Atoe, and La Molly articulate the role of black and brown feminist cultural mentoring in punk. However, it is through zine-making that the actualizing consequences of self-fashioning a brown feminist punk identity reify.

Three of Malú's zines in particular illustrate cultural mentoring and the subsequent development of her identity through a process of self-fashioning. Malú's "La Mano" zine results from a family-tree homework assignment for Spanish class. Although it makes sense that Magaly would be the best person to provide Malú with information about her family genealogy, she is reluctant to ask for help given her mother's criticisms. Malú thinks her mother sadly considers her to be a "weird, unladylike, sloppy-Spanish-speaking, half-Mexican kid" (C. C. Pérez 112). But Malú is eager to learn about the Mexican side of her family and is deeply affected when Magaly recounts her grandfather's work as a Bracero. Malú uses the symbol of *la mano* to synthesize connections between her often-alienated Mexican roots and her punk identity. In her zine, Malú lists facts about the Bracero Program, evidencing her research into the United States-Mexico guest-worker labor program of the Cold War. She also begins to formulate a political critique, noting in her zine the violence of racial and economic discrimination faced by Mexican Braceros. When Magaly shares that her *abuelo* picked strawberries as a Bracero, Malú connects his labor to a wider scope of capitalist consumption: "The thought of my abuelo's hands picking the strawberries I saw in the supermarket" boggles her mind (110). Through zine-making, Malú makes sense of her world by synthesizing the new information she has learned about her family history to create new knowledge by weaving herself into her Mexican heritage. "BRACEROS like my abuelo worked with their arms but also with shovel, hoe, baskets, backs, legs and their . . . HANDS MANOS (Abuelo's tools). I work with my hands too. Not in a hard way like Abuelo. But we both create (my tools) . . . scissors, paper, glue stick, and markers, tape, stack of old magazines" (C. C. Pérez 116–17). Through the creative process of making zines, Malú weaves herself into her tapestry of lived experiences and values that have collectively shaped her family. Malú's bracero-themed zine exemplifies what Chicana artist Carmen Lomas Garza describes as the resilient function of Chicano art, which works to heal the wounds of discrimination and racism faced by Mexican Americans—a history that is also part of Malú's cultural DNA (Garza 19). The zine performs an act of resilience by leveraging a creative process to construct strategies of cultural survival through maintaining collective memory. Malú calls on herself, and by extension her reader, to "REMEMBER" (C. C. Pérez 118). For it is in the act of remembering and honoring who and where we come from that enables us to integrate and construct our present lives. Malú exemplifies this process of cultural survival through collective memory by employing the symbol of the hand to signify transformation or self-fashioning of her cultural identity. She ends the zine by drawing a direct parallel between herself and her *abuelo*, noting how they both use their hands to cultivate and bring to life something new: *Abuelo* cultivates the land; she cultivates zines. In this way, Malú connects the materiality of her Mexican side to the aesthetics of her punk side.

Malú's family tapestry also includes her father, who, although geographically far away, is firmly present throughout Malú's journey. Despite their close relationship, Michael as a white man is unable to help Malú fully process her emotions when Selena calls her a coconut, i.e. a racial slur meaning brown on the outside, white on the inside. Selena, the popular girl at Posada Middle School, embodies all of the right "Mexican" elements that Malú does not. She dances *zapateado* in *ballet folklórico*, speaks fluent Spanish, and dresses like a *señorita*. Malú partly deals with the painful insult by reappropriating the pejorative term, naming her band the Co-Co's. However, she turns to her zine to engage the difficult psychoaffective work of processing how to reckon with an internalized inferiority complex, which as Malú puts it, "Makes me feel like there's something wrong with who I am" (C. C. Pérez 143). Pérez, here, addresses with tenderness the effects of racialized differentiations that happen within our culture, where demarcations of who is more "Mexican" often mimic the very stereotypes we fight against. Pérez's narrative intentionality, focalized through Malú's zine, "A Handbook for Coconuts," suggests an ethics of care by offering children of color an example of how to use creative avenues for doing the necessary work of decolonizing internalized racisms.

Malú opens her "Coconuts" zine with a clarification: "A 'COCONUT' is a mean name for someone who doesn't meet expectations" (C. C. Pérez 146). She then enumerates all the traits that disqualify her Mexicanness, including the fact that she is allergic to cilantro and her "weirdo" tastes in music and fashion (149). Considering the zine emulates a handbook genre, Malú alerts other possible coconuts to the type of questions they may frequently encounter, such as the proverbial, "What are you?" (150). With this question, Malú locates precisely how the insult functions. Being called a coconut is insulting because it reveals whiteness. The insult not only brings to the fore the hegemony of race-making and its necessary oppressive hierarchies, it also associates a white complicity in this race privileging system of difference. Thus, the coconut is both caught in this unjust racist system, but also benefits from it. Wielding the insult, the accuser asserts their non-complicity in this racist trap by claiming a cultural authenticity in contrast to the coconut's cultural deficiency.

The insult agitates Malú because it exposes her biracial vulnerability in not feeling Mexican enough. When Malú instructs her fellow coconuts to clip out their official membership card in her zine to show "at restaurants so that you don't have to embarrass yourself telling them to hold the cilantro," she communicates a justified frustration (151). This frustration, I argue, opens an analysis that critiques deficit narratives that so typically dominate and inform minority discourses. Research studies across disciplines, for instance, often assume minoritarian people to be deficient or lacking. Closing the so-called "achievement gap" exemplifies one of many rhetorical examples of deficit discourse. Arguably, the function of the coconut insult, however negative, may be seen as an act of resistance against normative discourses of deficit. Thus, Malú's pain is compounded not only because coconut suggests a cultural deficiency, but because the insult can only happen from within the culture. Malú uses her zine to process the hurt that results from the layered racialized hierarchies from both dominant and insider narratives. Malú's "Coconuts" zine in this way opens a safe space to interrogate and reckon with her biracial positionality. It is in this space that her zine, "Coconuts," serves its performative function to illustrate Malú's process of working out or negotiating her identity.

Whereas the "Coconuts" zine shows Malú grappling with identity negotiation, her final zine, "Quetzal's Guide to Dyeing Your Hair," presents the creative synthesis of her self-fashioning project. In "Quetzal's Guide," Malú activates her punk aesthetic to access aspects of the Mexican culture she is starting to integrate and make her own. With the help of Mrs. Hidalgo, the Co-Co's stage a D.I.Y. Alterna-Fiesta to coincide with the Posada Middle School 30th Anniversary Fall Fiesta talent show. Their event welcomes all the weirdo and misfit students "who got left out of the talent show because they didn't fit in" with Principal Rivera's idea of traditional, family-friendly, Mexican-type talent acts (296). Malú crops and dyes her hair vibrant green for the occasion. Her inspiration is the resplendent quetzal, whose symbolism takes on important dimensions that reflect Malú's self-fashioning project. Malú finds instant affinity with the resplendent quetzal (commonly associated with Quetzalcóatl the plumed serpent) when upon thumbing through an informational picture book about the bird, she notes how its green feathers spike up in a fuzzy mohawk, like "a little punk rock bird" (246).

However, it is the quetzal's signification to Mayan and Aztec culture that holds psychoaffective influence on Malú. An important detail from Miguel León-Portilla's comprehensive historiography of Aztec philosophy and culture describes how Nahuas, since the time of Teotihuacán, associate Venus with Quetzalcóatl.[6] This connection was especially important in Nahuatl astronomy and society, particularly in establishing chronologies and complex calendars. Noting the association between Venus and Quetzalcóatl, León-Portilla points out how Venus's reflection upon the Pacific Ocean is "not unlike a serpent with brilliant scales and plumes" (51). Venus, as a feminine symbol, imprints upon the ocean, resulting in the visual effect of blue and green plumage. Clara Román-Odio's scholarship on sacred iconographies deployed in Chicana feminist art, describes the particular use of the Quetzalcóatl symbol. Her analysis of Yreina Cervántez's lithograph tryptic, *Nepantla*, describes the iconography of the spiral of Quetzalcóatl as indexing nonlinear temporalities and the confluence of "multiple worldviews," that combine to spark decolonial praxis in aesthetic indigenous resistance to traditions in European art making. Cervántez, Román-Odio argues, activates the symbol of Quetzalcóatl to cross "beyond the painful, self-loathing effects of *nepantla*" (60). Malú's growing connection to this Chicana feminist lineage of resistant aesthetic cultural productions, I argue, resonates with her own deployment of the resplendent quetzal figure. The *corazonada* she feels toward the quetzal harmonizes with the *corazonada* she feels for Teresa Covarrubias, who symbolizes for Malú her own direct connection between punk and Chicana sensibilities.

In her zine, Malú writes, "Punk Rock Bird aka The Resplendent Quetzal," next to her drawing of a mohawked, sassy-looking, perched quetzal (C. C. Pérez 272). The quetzal proudly wears on its heart the symbol of anarchy, a capital letter A over a circle. Malú's fluency in anarchist theory and struggle aside, the symbol's iconography in punk marks the instinctual connection Malú makes by combining the resistant aesthetic of punk to the cultural signification of the quetzal. It is through this connection that Malú self-fashions her identity, transforming the pain of her *nepantla* into a restorative resilience. She demonstrates the psychoaffective work characteristic of self-fashioning projects required in decolonial praxis.[7] Thus, cutting and dyeing her hair, Malú physically and psychologically transforms in resistance to assimilationist pressures that seek her conformity to the norms established by her school and mother.

Furthermore, Malú situates herself within a collective of other punks, other nonconforming weirdos, by using the guidebook genre. Unlike her "Coconuts" zine, which illustrates Malú's internalized process of identity formation, "Quetzal's Guide" directly addresses an audience of her peers. The zine includes instructions for hair coloring using bright colors, recommendations for what to tell your parents to help them process the shock, facts about the resplendent quetzal, and closes with a fortune cookie note that reads, "Your hard work is about to pay off" (278). Malú encourages other teens like herself to use creative expression to support their own courageous acts of self-fashioning. Signaling towards the spirit of collective action, she broadcasts these words of affirmation to have faith in the positive consequences found through the tough work of fashioning and integrating one's identity.

Conclusion

Just as Malú engages modes of self-fashioning, so likewise Celia C. Pérez engages this self-affirming and creative praxis. Her narrative asks us to defamiliarize fixed rules of cultural authenticity that limit Latinx youth literature to static notations and definitions. Chicanx culture is always changing and dependent on the creative acts, political struggle, and organic resilience of our people. Eschewing nostalgia, Chicanx people draw broadly from living pedagogies and experiential knowledges rooted in our beautiful struggles to write living and life-affirming stories, which we tell, share, and use across temporalities and geographies. Furthermore, Pérez communicates her own kinship to the genealogy of Chicana feminist punk rockers by tethering Malú to the punk feminist Chicanx stories shared with her. Indeed, her participation in feminist punk and *nepantla* aesthetics runs deep. As the biographic note on the book jacket of *The First Rule of Punk* indicates, Pérez "has been making zines inspired by punk and her love of writing" for years. *The First Rule of Punk* carries exactly the attitude and voice that can only come from one who has directly experienced what it is like to live in the liminal spaces where you are neither from here nor there. Pérez' describes how her bicultural Cuban and Mexican heritage informs the politics of her narrative, recalling in an interview with the *Chicago Tribune* that it was not until college, when she read *Pocho* by José Antonio Villareal, that she recognized her own experiences reflected in the pages of literature for youth (Stevens para. 9–10). Thus, Pérez suggests the impulse behind writing her middle-grade novel is to challenge the discriminatory disparity of #OwnVoices in United States children's literature publishing. Moreover, by centering the experience of Malú as a young biracial *look up disidentification / queer found text /*

Chicanita, who comes to negotiate and understand her location within a larger brown feminist punk genealogy, Pérez challenges narratives that seek prescribe limits of authenticity in Latinx youth literature. Muñoz's scholarship on brown and queer cultural productions describes how minoritarian people perform what he calls disidentification, or creative acts of survival (including punk) that at once subvert and evade sociocultural and political hegemonic norms. Muñoz's formulations here offer an optic for understanding the cultural resilience and punk ethos of Pérez's disidentificatory narrative project. *The First Rule of Punk* shakes up our notions of cultural authenticity in Chicanx youth literature and makes its own rules.

Notes

1. In "'Domesticana': The Sensibility of Chicana Rasquache," Mesa-Bains theorizes a working-class subaltern Chicanx aesthetic positionality of cultural resistance and creative defiance against Anglo norms and structures. This "feminine rasquache," Mesa-Bains writes, "has grown not only out of both resistance to majority culture and affirmation of cultural values, but from women's restrictions with the culture" (161).

2. McMahon argues that Chicana artists—including Patssi Valdez, Alicia Armendariz Velasquéz, Diane Gamboa, and Teresa Covarrubias—in the (East) Los Angeles art scene and punk milieu of the late 1970s and early 1980s leveraged fashion to challenge the racialized heteropatriarchy inherent in prescribed gender roles for Latinas.

McMahon locates a distinct Chicana punk aesthetic that saw Chicanas using clothes, make-up, and style to enact "social commentary . . . [and] negotiate the normative discourses of gender and femininity" (142). Similarly, Ramírez discusses Chicana Pachuca fashion as a tool of political expression against normative white middle-class and nationalist norms.

3. See Stinton's "Writing Zines" for an outstanding genealogy of black and brown punk feminists. Ngô and Stinton edit a collection of essays on identity formation and radical politics, which references a broad genealogy of feminist punk queers of color.

4. Chicana feminist queer theory richly interprets Gloria Anzaldúa's classic theory of the nepantla state. That nepantla state contributes to what Anzaldúa calls mestiza consciousness, or a way of knowing or operating in liminality, where Chicanas' lived intersectionalities and ambivalences are navigated across spectrums of identities including genders, sexualities, ethnicities, races, and spiritualities.

5. In addition to Habell-Pallán's excellent critical history of Chicana feminist cultural productions in punk, which analyzes Teresa Covarrubias and Alice Bag's disruption of heteropatriarchal discourses within punk, see Alvarado's discussion of Covarrubias's contribution and legacy in Los Angeles punk history.

6. See Miguel León-Portilla, along with Alfredo López Austin, for comprehensive scholarship on Quetzalcóatl's significance and symbolism in Nahuatl cosmology and thought.

7. In *Black Skin, White Masks*, Frantz Fanon formulates his classic liberatory praxis of decolonization, which necessarily requires a transformative self-fashioning of the pscyhoaffective state of inferiority in order to destroy the domination of capitalist racialized oppression at the heart of white supremacist colonial and imperial projects.

Works Cited

Alvarado, Jimmy. "Backyard Brats and Eastside Punks: A History of East LA's Punk Scene." *Aztlán: A Journal of Chicano Studies*, vol. 37, no. 2, 2012, pp. 157–80.

Anzaldúa, Gloria, and AnaLouise Keating. *Light in the Dark: Rewriting Identity, Spirituality, Reality—Luz En Lo Oscuro*. Duke University Press, 2015.

Brown, Jayna. "'Brown Girl in the Ring': Poly Styrene, Annabella Lwin, and the Politics of Anger." *Journal of Popular Music Studies*, vol. 23, no. 4, 2011, pp. 455–78.

Covarrubias, Teresa. "High School." The Brat. *Attitudes*. Fatima Records, 1980.

Fiol-Matta, Licia. *The Great Woman Singer: Gender and Voice in Puerto Rican Music*. Duke University Press, 2017.

Garza, Carmen Lomas. *Pedacito De Mi Corazón*. Austin, Laguna Gloria Art Museum, 1991.

Habell-Pallán, Michelle. *Loca Motion: The Travels of Chicana and Latina Popular Culture*. New York University, 2005.

Harney, Stefano, and Fred Moten. *The Undercommons: Fugitive Planning & Black Study*. Minor Compositions, 2013.

McMahon, Marci R. *Domestic Negotiations: Gender, Nation, and Self-fashioning in US Mexicana and Chicana Literature and Art*. Rutgers University Press, 2013.

Mesa-Bains, Amalia. "'Domesticana': The Sensibility of Chicana Rasquache." *Aztlán: A Journal of Chicano Studies*, vol. 24, no. 2, 1999, pp. 157–67.

Ngô, Fiona I. B., and Elizabeth A. Stinson. "Introduction: Threads and Omissions." *Women & Performance: Journal of Feminist Theory*, vol. 22, no. 2–3, 2012, pp. 165–71.

Pérez, Celia C. *The First Rule of Punk*. Penguin Random House, 2017.

Pérez, Laura E. *Chicana Art: The Politics of Spiritual and Aesthetic Altarities*. Duke University Press, 2007.

Pretty Vacant. Directed by Jim Mendiola, Mero Mero Productions, 1996.

Ramírez, Catherine S. "Crimes of Fashion: The Pachuca and Chicana Style Politics." *Meridians*, vol.2, no. 2, 2002, pp. 1–35.

Román-Odio, Clara. *Sacred Iconographies in Chicana Cultural Productions*. Palgrave Macmillan, 2013.

Stevens, Heidi. "Chicago Librarian Captures Punk Aesthetic, Latino Culture in New Kids' Book." *Chicago Tribune*, 23 Aug. 2017. chicagotribune.com/lifestyles/stevens/ct-life-stevens-wednesday-first-rule-of-punk-0823-story.html.

Stinson, Elizabeth. "Means of Detection A Critical Archiving of Black Feminism and Punk Performance." *Women & Performance: A Journal of Feminist Theory*, vol. 22, no. 2–3, 2012, pp. 275–311.

Stinson, Elizabeth. "Writing Zines, Playing Music, and Being a Black Punk Feminist: An Interview with Osa Atoe." *Women & Performance: A Journal of Feminist Theory*, vol. 22, no. 2–3, 2012, pp. 261–74.

"The Brat at Plaza de la Raza." *YouTube*, uploaded by Petelotli, 30 June 2006, https://www.youtube.com/watch?v=wUfRIowIKMo.

X-Ray Spex. "Identity." *Germfree Adolescents*, EMI, 1978.

3

Broken Open: Writing, Healing, and Affirmation in Isabel Quintero's *Gabi, A Girl in Pieces* and Erika L. Sanchez's *I Am Not Your Perfect Mexican Daughter*

Adrianna M. Santos

The publishing world has recently enjoyed an explosion of Chicanx/Latinx Young Adult (YA) Literature.[1] Thus, the need for scholarly work on texts written for Chicanx/Latinx youth has become more urgent, particularly on those that contend with questions of identity (Alamillo, Mercado-López, and Herrera). There is much to learn from stories that feature young women, first-generation immigrants, and working class Chicanxs/Latinxs, whose voices have historically been underrepresented in the canon of YA literature. In this chapter I take as my primary objects of analysis Isabel Quintero's *Gabi, a Girl in Pieces* (2014) and Erika L. Sánchez's *I Am Not Your Perfect Mexican Daughter* (2017), two novels that have contributed to the recent wave of YA literature about Mexican American communities while building on the legacy of Chicana feminist theory.

I explore these texts through an intersectional lens, focusing on the liminality of the main characters, their "in-betweenness" as teenagers on the verge of high school graduation, girls transitioning to young women, and burgeoning poets finding their voices through writing. I engage Anzaldúan theory in a close reading of the novels, employing critical multicultural analysis. The everyday resistance to patriarchy and sexism within the texts privilege young women's points of view. They beg an examination of the social conditions under which young Mexican American women are operating and how access to authentic narratives about their lives can support the broader concerns of social justice. Their narratives explore the value of writing as an activity of self-making and empowerment. The numerous uses of language itself, especially poetry, become the foundation of self-representation that moves Mexican American girls as characters from margin to center. I argue that while the visibility of Mexican American girlhood is important in and of itself, there is a particular need to tell authentic stories of Chicanx/Latinx teenagers as *writers* because of the specific social conditions that silence their narratives. This is not a new concept in Chicanx/Latinx literature. Some of the most well-known examples of Chicana writers that write about writing include Gloria Anzaldúa, Cherríe Moraga, Michelle Serros, Josefina López, Pat Mora, and Sandra Cisneros, just to name a few. This legacy has continued in the next generation of Chicana YA fiction writers and is particularly salient in Quintero and Sánchez's contributions.

In both *Gabi* and *Daughter*, the female protagonists struggle with their "Mexican-ness" as a basis for exploring identity and use language as not only a means of self-expression but also as a way to both unravel and remake themselves, an idea directly descended from Anzaldúan thought that permeated the Chicana feminist consciousness in the 1980s and continues to reverberate in academic, artistic, and activist circles today. Gabi, who lives in the desert region of Quintero's childhood, writes her daily lived experience in fragmented, diary entries and poems, longing for the MFA that will prepare her for life as a writer, mourning the death of her father by drug overdose. She describes her dual identity: "Your allegiance is always questioned. My mom constantly worries that I will be too Americana" (34). Ultimately, she recognizes that her positionality requires the straddling of borders and writes, "There's no escaping my roots, and I guess it's better to embrace them than cut them" (85). On the other hand, Julia defies her family's and society's expectations for her in a more direct manner. An aspiring writer who struggles to cope with her sister's sudden accidental death, she resists every trope of the "perfect Mexican daughter" with her snarky attitude, everyday acts of rebellion, and dreams of going away to college. But she also struggles with depression and attempts suicide midway through her senior year of high school, representing the lived experiences of many young women in Chicanx/Latinx communities who are facing similar challenges. The situation is exacerbated after her sister Olga is suddenly killed in a car accident. Julia had always felt like an outsider, which adds to her distress. She writes, "I don't understand why everyone just complains about who I am. What am I supposed to do? Say I'm sorry? I'm sorry I can't be normal? I'm sorry I'm such a bad daughter? I'm sorry I hate the life that I have to live? There are times I feel completely alone, like no one in the world can possibly understand me" (117). This loneliness propels the narrative, capturing Julia's state of mind as she embarks on her coming of age journey. Her parents are traditional, with deeps roots in their Mexican heritage, and do not understand Julia's sin verguënza attitude and desire to leave the family to go away to college. Julia responds to this by expressing feelings of isolation and depression that escalate throughout the novel.

Gender and Multicultural Representation in YA Literature

It is crucial to study Chicana/Latina YA literature because young Mexican American women face specific struggles in their transitions from child to adult that are informed by multiple factors not limited to race and ethnicity, socioeconomic location, culture, and language (Gándara; Garcia, 2012). To examine the YA genre in a social justice context, I engage with critical multicultural content analysis. According to Kathy G. Short, this involves "locating power in social practices by understanding, uncovering, and transforming conditions of inequity embedded in society" (5). Furthermore, Botelho and Rudman identify critical multicultural analysis as "reading power within a complex web of social relations" with the potential to "disrupt binary thinking" that is similar to Anzaldúa's project in *Borderlands/La Frontera*. Each protagonist faces challenges related to race and class and gender. Stories that reflect the trauma of institutional oppression resonate in marginalized communities and the importance of continuing to explore heterogeneous representations of coming of age in YA literature is especially prescient in Quintero and Sánchez's texts, which reflect the realities that Mexican American teenage girls are facing.[4] The stakes are high and we know that representation matters.

The intersections between ethnic studies and children's literature are tenuous and there has been resistance to interdisciplinary work that marries the two fields, but the interest in them is growing (Capshaw; Thomas). Specialists in the field of children's literature itself emerged in the late eighteenth century, but scholarship about literature for children and young adults often operates separate from general literary studies (Airey and Stevens). It is interdisciplinary and intellectually rich but has been marginalized, partly because of hierarchical notions of children's issues as "women's work." Chicanx/Latinx studies has struggled to achieve prominence within academic departments and publishing houses, similar to the related fields of ethnic studies, women's and gender studies, and queer studies. But Marilisa Jiménez Garcia underlines how children's literature in the humanities and Latinx studies converge in ways that "function as a counter-canon to both U.S. and Latin American tropes and norms. Today's Latinx authors for youth challenge the kind of internal and external racism, sexism, and classism that has rendered Latinxs invisible in U.S. and Latin American literature and society" (117). As many contemporary scholars on Chicanx/Latinx YA and children's literature argue young Mexican American women need to see themselves represented in complex coming-of-age narratives. Quintero and Sánchez address subject matter that is often stigmatized in the conservative, Catholic, immigrant, Mexican American communities from which they come.

Moreover, Amy Cummins and Myra Infante-Sheridan delve deeply into the Chicana YA novel as a genre from a feminist perspective, advocating strongly for novels that show how "empowered protagonists navigate efficaciously the borderlands of multiple identities, cultures, and languages" in the classroom (36). The authors' main aim is to establish criteria for a Chicana *bildungsroman*, which includes "narrating the coming of age of a Chicana protagonist over an extended time, portraying her developing an understanding of a dual identity as a Mexican American, and connecting the protagonist's development with valuing of family, community, and collectivity" (19). Baxley and Boston also highlight the potential for "bildungsromans written by women of color [to] raise questions of equality, identity, and social assimilation in both American and Latina spaces" (74). This focus on genre is a useful approach to understanding identity development and representation in Chicanx/Latinx literature.

Narratives of Chicanx/Latinx childhood also have an important impact on the ways in which bilingual and bicultural experiences of childhood are depicted, theorized, and inform public policy. Many large cities are already minority-majority, with Latinx students whose needs are not being served through a model of teaching to the test, teaching only Anglo narratives of childhood, or focusing on a stereotypical representation of Latinxs that often gets repeated in publishing trends (Martínez-Roldán). Laura Alamillo and Rosie Arenas have acknowledged the lack of authentic Chicanx/Latinx characters in literature typically used in the classroom. They advocate for non-stereotypical textual and illustrative representations, arguing that culturally responsive pedagogy promotes equity. Chicanx literature, specifically, is rooted in the experiences of Mexican Americans and, additionally, is concerned with both the indigenous heritage and social justice issues of the Chicano Movement (Alamillo and Arenas 2012).

Similarly, YA literature for and about Chicanx communities is often concerned with intersectionality, focusing particularly on themes of immigration, hybridity, border crossing, language politics, poverty, education, sexuality, spirituality, and familism. These two texts show a commitment to making Chicana feminist coming-to-consciousness visible, another recent trend in the Chicanx/Latinx YA universe. Larissa Mercado-López notes the importance of reading Mexican American girl characters through the lens of Chicana feminisms, even in historical contexts that predate the terminology.

Literary code-switching is also a common technique of Chicanx authors. Anzaldúa writes, "Until I am free to write bilingually and to switch codes without having always to translate, while I still have to speak English or Spanish when I would rather speak Spanglish, and as long as I have to accommodate the English speakers rather than having them accommodate me, my tongue will be illegitimate" (45). In an interview, Erika Sánchez addresses bilingualism in her characterization of Julia. "I don't want to differentiate them because those words are just such a part of who she is. She can't separate English and Spanish. It's just part of her world" (Prado). In *I Am Not Your Perfect Mexican Daughter*, Julia not only code-switches but also acknowledges a burgeoning Chicana feminist consciousness in her understandings of the geopolitical border that divides the US and Mexico. "It's nothing but a giant wound, a big gash between the two countries. . . . How can anyone tell people where they can and can't go?" (280).[5] Julia's pilgrimage to Mexico after her suicide attempt shows the importance of reestablishing her connection to her roots, through relationships, culture, and of course, language. Furthermore, speaking of *Gabi, a Girl in Pieces*, Isabel Quintero remarks in an interview, "Sophomore year of college I took a Chicano lit class, where I read Michele Serros and realized that I could use all my languages—Spanish, English, Spanglish—in my writing and that my experiences and reality were worthy of poems" (Rhodes). Gabi references Michelle Serros and Sandra Cisneros as "superpoets" who inspired her to use both Spanish and English in her own poetry. Coming to terms with her dual identity and the intermingling of Spanish and English as a key part of it inform the character that she creates in Gabi. She writes in the novel, "Before we read their [Cisneros and Serros's] poetry, I didn't even know you could use two languages in one poem. I thought they either had to be in English or Spanish" (Quintero 67). Acknowledging this lineage of Chicana writers validates the characters' life experiences while at the same time holding space for the author to express gratitude for the pathbreakers that paved the way for Quintero herself.

Esperanza's Legacy

The House on Mango Street by Sandra Cisneros (1984) is arguably the most popular work by a Mexican American woman worldwide. The collection of vignettes features a young preteen protagonist who grapples with the everyday lived realities of racism, sexism, and violence in her working-class Chicago neighborhood. She and her friends discover what it means to cross the boundaries from girlhood to adulthood in sometimes funny, sometimes heartbreaking ways. Cisneros writes about body image, puberty, rape, marriage, pregnancy, domestic violence, the bonds of sisterhood, the power of friendship born of female relationships, and the sting of betrayal that can leave lasting scars. While Cisneros has confirmed that she did not specifically write *Mango* as a YA novel per se, it has found a place within the canon of American literature, being taught in middle schools, high schools, and colleges around the country, and has been translated and published in over thirty languages around the world. This novel stands as an important precursor that made Gabi and Julia possible. Esperanza longs to go away, get an education, and, importantly, come back to effect positive change in her community. The closing lines read, "One day I will pack my bags of books and paper. One day I will say goodbye to Mango. I am too strong for her to keep me here forever. One day I will go away. . . . They will not know I have gone away to come back. For the ones I left behind. For the ones who cannot out" (110). Cummins and Infante-Sheridan argue that "although *The House on Mango Street* remains ambiguous about what Esperanza does, the implication is that the text itself constitutes Esperanza's contribution by recording community stories" (34).[6] Highlighting the continuing impact of Cisneros's text on the next generation, postdoctoral research fellow Nichole Margarita García recently blogged, "At the age of 13, the first Chicana Ph.D I had ever met handed me *The House on Mango Street* by Sandra Cisneros. In the inside cover, she wrote: 'We offer this book to reflect on life's journey. We hope you enjoy it. May you continue to pursue and follow all your dreams so that you go away to come back for the ones who cannot out.' She changed my life trajectory" (García). The ongoing impact of Cisneros's novel is palpable. Quintero and Sánchez answer Cisneros's underlying "call to action" by writing and publishing literature for young people that directly speaks to Chicana experiences. Quintero muses, "I thought about the conversations I had had with other women my age and how they had gone through similar things and how we had felt alone, and how we weren't alone (Rhodes).

Sánchez expresses a similar sentiment. "I wanted to provide this story to young women of color because I think it's important for them to see themselves and to know that they're not alone. That their experiences are important and that they matter" (Prado). Chicana YA representation matters.

Because of the undeniable influence of *Mango*, other scholars have made connections between the coming-of-age story and contemporary representations of characters like Esperanza. Cristina Herrera writes, "By accepting Cisneros as a role model, Gabi looks for cultural, gender, class, and bodily affirmation embedded within the tradition of Chicana feminist poetry" (320). She notes Gabi's use of poetry as a method of identity formation and healing. Gabi explicitly connects with Cisneros' writing, invoking her poetry and taking inspiration from her focus on Mexican American girlhood and female empowerment. Her boyfriend Martin gets her a signed copy of *Loose Woman*, a Sandra Cisneros poetry collection, for her birthday. The inscription reads, "To la Gabi, on the loose" (144). Gabi wishes her mother would read it because "that's the kind of woman I want to be when I grow up. That's the kind of woman I wish my mom saw herself as" (149). She sees the strength in her mother articulated by her own love of poetry. They do not share this passion, but Gabi's recognition of her mother through her growing Chicana feminist consciousness is powerful, all the same.

In many ways, Julia too is an iteration of Esperanza. They both reside in Chicago in primarily working-class Mexican American neighborhoods. Julia, though, is a snarky twenty-first-century rebellion against the hopeful *Mango* protagonist, at least at first. While Sánchez does not explicitly refer to Cisneros, the references to writing, packing of a bag and leaving are reminiscent of Esperanza's famous last words. In the novel Sánchez writes, "Ever since I could pick up a pen, I've wanted to be a famous writer. I want to be so successful that people stop me on the street and ask, "Oh my God, are you Julia Reyes, the best writer who has ever graced this earth? All I know is that I'm going to pack my bags when I graduate and say, "peace out, mothafuckas" (2). She rejects a community-based model in the beginning, dreaming of breaking away from her family and neighborhood.

In many ways, both Gabi and Julia's transitional statuses as young women on the verge of adulthood recall the classic coming-of-age narrative that has continued to capture the imaginations of generation after generation. But Gabi and Julia's stories expand the depth of the themes that Cisneros raises for a contemporary audience by candidly depicting mental health issues, suicide, constrictive gender roles, the aftereffects of sexual assault, and more, bringing a twenty-first-century consciousness to Esperanza's legacy.

Writing as Self-Making

Affirming her multiple identities and linguistic expressions, Anzaldúa writes, "I will have my serpent's tongue—my woman's voice, my sexual voice, my poet's voice" (*Borderlands/La Frontera* 81). Gabi finds her voice though poetry about her own exploration of identity, sexuality, and social injustice. "I'm finding out that I really like poetry. It's therapeutic. It's like I can write something painful on paper and part of it (not all of it, obviously) disappears. It goes away somewhere and the sadness I feel dissolves a little bit. I've always like poetry, but I didn't realize how powerful it could be" (83–84). Her first spoken word performance emphasizes the centrality of writing to her life and sense of self, "I can't stop writing . . . A prophecy I wrote down. / Almost couldn't go through with it. / But it came out / hurried and hot / and by the end / my tongue was on fire" (141–42). Here is the first direct connection to Chicana feminist theory that appears in the novel. Anzaldúa writes to those with the "gift of the tongue" to "write with your tongues of fire" (*This Bridge* 173). Cristina Herrera reflects on this connection to Cisneros. She states, quoting one of Gabi's poems, "Voicing pain through poetry 'helps heal wounds / Makes them tangible' and is thus an act of burgeoning Chicana feminist agency" (321). Like Gabi, Julia also dreams of being a professional writer and longs for her own library with first-edition books, she spends much of her time at old bookstores taking in the smell and the knowledge. She derives her sense of self from her writing abilities and aspirations. She especially loves poetry and fantasizes about the books she will write one day and what their covers will look like (169–70). The tension between Julia and her mother is fraught with anger, mistrust, and unmet expectations and she is devastated when her mother destroys her journal, the contents of which include poems she has been working on for years. She feels like she has lost yet another part of herself, adding to the grief she feels about the loss of her sister. Julia's sardonic humor is telling about the kind of character that will be revealed throughout the novel. She is witty, sarcastic, angry, and hungry for something more than society has to offer her. "I just feel like it's unfair, that my whole life is unfair, like I was born into the wrong place and family. I never belong anywhere. My parents don't understand anything about me. And my sister is gone" (236). Julia seems to be experiencing something akin to the "Coatlicue state," which Anzaldúa describes as "an intensely negative channel . . . caged in a private hell; you feel angry, fearful, hopeless, and depressed, blaming yourself as inadequate" (332).[7] Julia continues, "I don't know why I've always been like this, why the smallest things make me ache inside. There's a poem I read once, titled 'The World Is Too Much with Us,' and I guess that is the best way to describe the feeling—the world is too much with me" (117). The poem she references, by English romanticist William Wordsworth, is a reflection on the speaker's frustration with the rise of consumer culture and the common man's lack of engagement with the beauty and wonder of the natural world.[8] Anzaldúa takes a different approach, writing, "Though you know change will happen when you stop resisting the dark side of your reality, still you resist. But despite the dread and spiritual emptying, the work you do in the world is not ready to release you" (*The Gloria Anzaldúa Reader* 325). Julia feels everything profoundly but is not yet ready to face the darkness within herself.

Examining Latina YA literature, Baxley and Boston note the connections between social pressure and suicidal behaviors specifically related to acculturation (69). Candid portrayals of depression and suicide are extremely important for Latinas, who attempt suicide at higher rates than their white and male counterparts. Through her expressions of anger and frustration, we slowly come to see Julia as depressed and eventually suicidal. Gabi also expresses heartbreak through poetry and uses her diary to write letters to her father that he will never read. In them, she works through anger, longing, shame, and love. One poem is about the death of her grandfather. It incorporates several Spanish phrases and describes a special song between them: "Because he sang that song to you / every time you said, / "Abuelito, cántame la canción. / And he knew what song you were talking about / because he knew you like nobody did" (71). The poem foreshadows some of the later feelings of grief Gabi will express over her father. A heroin addict who was often absent from her life, he remains a specter through the novel after his passing.

Despite his addiction, Gabi loves her father and is devastated when he dies. The effects on the rest of her family are palpable as well. Her mother is pregnant with her third child and her brother is showing signs of alcoholism. She thinks through the *familismo* within her culture that insists that "Good Mexican girls never turn away their parents, no matter how awful they've been" (88). Gabi questions the tenets of Catholicism, and the uncertainty of loving an addict. She wonders why his family is not enough for him and why he wants to kill himself. Expressing a fascination with the macabre, Gabi says she loves Sylvia Plath because she "is very dark and always talking about death and suicide" (59).

In *Gabi*, and *Daughter*, issues like mental health, suicide, and sex, are confronted head-on by amplifying the voices of young women who are coming of age and in many ways, coming apart. What helps put them back together, though, is the acknowledgement of writing as vehicle for self-making. Anzaldúa asserts that art is a tool of social transformation, what she calls *conocimiento*. She describes a process of regeneration and renewal called "the Coyolxauhqui imperative" as "an ongoing process of making and unmaking. There is never any resolution, just the process of healing" (*Anzaldúa Reader* 312).[9] Julia eventually finds that she must face the dark sides of herself to begin to heal. The narrative breaks from chronology in an important way regarding this rupture. Her attempted suicide is not described until the last few pages of the novel. By withholding a description of the event itself, the text emphasizes the importance of Julia's healing process in coming to terms with what happened. As she goes through therapy, she is forced to recount the experience again and again. The details of the incident are not relayed until Julia has acclimated to her medication, has worked through many feelings of shame in therapy, has sojourned to Mexico, has reconnected with her mother, and begins to forgive herself and her family. Following the final page of the narrative is a brief list of Mental Health Resources in which the author provides three suggestions for community programs that assist individuals who are thinking about attempting suicide. Finally, Julia comes to realize that she is changing and she accepts the uncertainty of the transformation as beautiful in itself. She writes, "She opened the vault, the box in which she kept herself—old filmstrips of her life, her truth. Broken feathers, crushed mirrors creating a false gleam. She takes it all apart, every moment, every lie, every deception" (331). Everything Julia sees as contained with herself must be examined to discover the truth of who she is, "Everything stops: snapshots of serenity, beauty, bliss surface. Things she must dig for in her mesh of uncertainty, in her darkness, though it still lies in the wetness of her mouth, the scent of her hair" (331). In her journey, she faces her fear of falling apart and instead resolves to keep moving and experiencing life to its fullest, "She digs and digs in that scarlet box on the day of her unraveling, the day she becomes undone. She thrives in her truth and travels the world like a nomad, stealing the beauty of the violet skies, fishing for pearls, pretty arabesques, paper swans, pressing them to her face, and keeping them in her palms. Forever" (331). This final reference to material objects that she touches and treasures are symbolic of the newfound hope with which she approaches the world, recalling that she read in a poem once about "terror being the beginning of beauty" (281).

Both novels end with the protagonists looking forward to college. As first-generation college students, Gabi and Julia will navigate the waters of higher education without the support that so-called "traditional" students will come equipped.[10] Establishing themselves as writers also entails understanding interpersonal relationships, and coming to terms with the structural inequities in which their communities have operated and that they will confront as they take the next step in their intellectual journeys. And though they reconcile by the end, Gabi must contend with her tía Bertha also admonishing her for writing poetry, saying "a nice young woman does not expose her thoughts like that to the public." And "writing is something that only men should do, like going to college" (131). Gabi muses at the end of the novel, "Seeing my beautifully crazy and colorful all-American family sit together at a slightly sticky table in one of the best hot wing restaurants in all the land, in a rundown shopping strip, made me feel like everything was as it should be, and that all the things I am worried about are gonna be all right" (284). Gabi affirms that she has every right to the same opportunities as all Americans, claiming her family and her identity as her own. She no longer worries what others will think of her and shows hope and optimism for the future, much of which is centered on her transition from high school to college, but at the same time basking in the glory of her working-class celebration at a local eatery.

but what if it isn't?

Julia's journey, as well, ends with her transition to higher education. Her parents do not understand her longing to go to college, but her mother eventually supports her decision. Julia learns that her mom endured sexual assault by a coyote when she crossed the border from Mexico, and this brings them closer together as Julia recognizes her mother's bravery and begins to see how their personalities are similar. In a final act of writing as healing, Julia visits her English teacher, Mr. Ingman, who advises her to write about her grief and sense of responsibility for her sister's death and her family. "That day, I sat in his classroom for nearly two hours, crying over my notebook, smearing the ink on the pages. . . . Though most of it came gushing out, it was the hardest thing I've ever written. At the end, I had eight handwritten pages, so sloppy, only I could ever read them. That's what became my college essay" (340). In a full circle return to her earlier expression of identity as a writer, she thinks, "Part of what I'm trying to accomplish—whether Amá really understands it or not—is to live for her, Apá and Olga. It's not that I'm living life for them exactly, but I have so many choices they've never had, and I feel like I can do so much with what I've been given. What a waste their journey would be if I just settled for a dull, mediocre life. Maybe one day they'll realize that" (339). This expression of agency is a powerful vocalization of self in relationship to one's family and community. A return to the earlier rejection of familia and another nod to Cisneros' (Esperanza's) legacy.

Conclusion

The protagonists in *Gabi, A Girl in Pieces* and *I Am Not Your Perfect Mexican Daughter*, break stigmas about mental health and body image issues that plague young women and are exacerbated for Chicanas due to social, cultural and economic factors. Gabi and Julia are complex, intelligent, dynamic, moody, creative, and resourceful. But, first and foremost, they are writers. Chicana feminist scholarship can help to illuminate the importance of claiming this identity as young, first generation Mexican American women. Writing is a source of identity formation and is healing for both of them. Gabi deals with the grief of losing her father and lashes out in anger towards a rapist and has to deal with the consequences, no matter how justified they may be in that she was avenging her friend. In the end she is supported in her educational pursuits by her family and friends. Julia has a "break down" after her sister's death in which her identity is shattered and then begins the process of rebuilding, putting herself back together on her own terms, with help from her community. This comes in the form of therapy, pilgrimage, family support, the prospect of going away to college. Gabi and Julia express themselves most fully through writing despite all these challenges. It is central to their characterizations. They are outsiders. They are bookworms who write poems. They dream of going to college. They are representative of countless other young Chicanas who can identify with their stories.

Representations of young Chicanas as brainy, creative, moody, witty, and rebellious are important to telling authentic stories about Mexican American teenagers. More scholarship needs to focus on them. Through this important representation young women who are intelligent, rebellious, flawed, and complicated, young audiences can critically witness and relate to their journeys. They can potentially apply these same tools of self-healing and critique to an understanding of themselves not only as empowered individuals but also as part of a community with agency and the ability to make a difference in their worlds, particularly through writing their own stories. The authors themselves are optimistic. Quintero says, "My writing is my activism. I had always talked about the power of writing and how it could change things, because it had changed my life" (Rhodes). Sánchez remarks, "I couldn't have imagined that my novel, about a brown girl who is snarky and is poor, could possibly win the National Book Award, or anything like it. The literary landscape is changing quite a bit, and I'm really happy about it." So are the young Chicanas who read their stories and find affirmation in them.

Notes

1. When speaking in general terms, I use the identifier Chicanx/Latinx in alignment with the subject of this volume. Chicanx refers to Americans of Mexican descent and grew from the politics of the Chicano Movement, while Latinx is a heterogenous umbrella term encompassing various groups of people of Latin American descent living in the US. This can include both citizens and immigrants. The use of "x" is a relatively new development in activist and scholarly communities and suggests solidarity with and inclusivity of LGBTQ and gender non-conforming identities. I sometimes distinguish between Chicanx and Latinx when necessary. While I refer to studies or theories that use alternative terms like Hispanic, Mexican American, Chicana/o, Latina/o, I maintain this preferred terminology but explain in further detail when a distinction is necessary. When describing women and girls, I use Chicana or Latina.

2. Hispanic children make up 22.7 percent of enrollment in all levels of education (Bauman). Since the number of school-aged Chicanx/Latinx youth continues to balloon, it is important that we uplift representation by authors from those communities by turning a critical eye on them. There is a growing need for and recognition of literature like this written for and about young people. In 2013 at the International Reading Association Conference in San Antonio, Texas, the first Social Justice Literature Award was given to *The House on Dirty-Third Street* by Jo S. Kittinger and illustrated by Thomas Gonzalez for Best Picture Book and *Summer on the Moon* by Adrian Fogelin for Best Non-Picture Book.

3. Women report more stress overall, which has life-threatening effects; health issues like heart disease, diabetes, and obesity are higher in communities of color; young Hispanic girls attempt suicide at much higher rates than their white counterparts. Conditions of poverty, social stresses of immigration, disproportionate sentencing and police brutality, and other kinds of institutional violence negatively affect Latinx communities in general (Hausmann-Stabile, Gulbas and Zayas 391). These important questions have implications for our society at large.

4. Reminiscent of Anzaldúa's famous line from *Borderlands/La Frontera*, "The U.S-Mexican border es una herida abierta where the Third World grates against the first and bleeds. And before a scab forms it hemorrhages again, the lifeblood of two worlds merging to form a third country—a border culture" (25).

5. The authors also seek to make connections between *HMS* and the contemporary Chicana YA novels *The Tequila Worm* (2005) and *Under the Mesquite* (2011) by focusing on the protagonists' development as artists in the context of the künstlerroman, a subgenre of the bildungsroman.

6. Anzaldúa, in her writings, recuperates Mesoamerican indigenous goddesses to describe contemporary lived experiences. Many scholars explore the significance of the mythological figures Anzaldúa invokes, particularly the female goddesses. I will not delve too deeply into these questions but rather focus on the processes stemming from these invocations that she theorizes in the context of mestiza consciousness and social transformation. I take a stance similar to Bost's reading of Chicana feminists' creative approaches to historiography: "Their vision of the past is not essentialist but motivated by contemporary political needs (and is thus indigenist, rather than European, revolving around goddesses, rather than gods)" (37–8).

7. Focusing on feminine power and everyday experiences that often involve both pain and healing in her personal journey of transformation, which she then theorizes and extends to include a collective consciousness.

8. https://www.poetryfoundation.org/poems/45564/the-world-is-too-much-with-us

9. Coyolxauhqui is a Mesoamerican goddess often associated with the moon. In Mexica mythology, she was killed and dismembered by her brother Huitzilopochtli after leading a revolt against her mother, Coatlicue. Anzaldúa recuperates this feminine figure in service to social justice and collective healing.

10. Latinas are enrolling in greater numbers than ever, but completion rates still lag. A White House report on Latinas in education reported in 2015 that only 19 percent of Latinas 29 or over had completed a BA.

Works Cited

Airey, Jennifer L., and Laura M. Stevens. "Young Adult Women's Literature." *Tulsa Studies in* *Women's Literature*, vol. 36, no. 2, 2017, pp. 287–94.
Anzaldúa, Gloria E. *Borderlands/La Frontera: The New Mestiza*. Aunt Lute Books, 2012.
Anzaldúa, Gloria E. "Now Let Us Shift . . . the Path of Conocimiento . . . Inner Work, Public Acts." *This Bridge We Call Home: Radical Visions for Transformation*, edited by Gloria E. Anzaldúa and AnaLouise Keating, Routledge, 2002, pp. 540–79.
Anzaldúa, Gloria E. "Let Us Be the Healing of the Wound: The Coyolxauhqui Imperative—la sombra y el sueño." *The Gloria Anzaldúa Reader*, edited by Analouise Keating, Duke University Press, 2009.

Bauman, Kurt. "School Enrollment Growth." *Census Blogs*. United States Census Bureau, 28 Sep. 2017. https://www.census.gov/newsroom/blogs/randomsamplings/2017/08/school _enrollmentof.html.

Baxley, Traci P., and Genyne Henry Boston. *(In)visible Presence: Feminist Counter-Narratives of Young Adult Literature by Women of Color*, Sense Publishers, 2014.

Bost, Suzanne. "Feeling Pre-Columbian: Chicana Feminists' Imaginative Historiography." *Encarnación: Illness & Body Politics in Chicana Feminist Literature*. Fordham University Press, 2009.

Botelho, Maria José, and Masha Kabakow Rudman. *Critical Multicultural Analysis of Children's Literature: Mirrors, Windows, and Doors*. Routledge, 2009.

Capshaw, Katharine. "Ethnic Studies and Children's Literature: A Conversation between Fields." *The Lion and the Unicorn*, vol. 38, no. 3, 2014, pp. 237–57.

Gándara, Patricia. "Fulfilling America's Future: Latinas in the U.S., 2015." The White House Initiative on Educational Excellence for Hispanics.

Garcia, Lorena. *Respect Yourself, Protect Yourself: Latina Girls and Sexual Identity*. New York University Press, 2012.

Garcia, Nichole Margarita. "The Risk of Displeasure: How to Write Without Permission." *Diverse Issues in Higher Education, A CMA Publication*, 18 Mar. 2018. http://diverseeducation.com /article/112403/. Accessed 1 Apr. 2018.

Hausmann-Stabile, Caroline, Lauren Gulbas, and H. Zayas. "Aspirations of Latina Adolescent Suicide Attempters." *Hispanic Journal of Behavioral Sciences*. vol. 35, no. 3, 2013, pp. 390–405.

Herrera, Cristina. "Soy Brown y Nerdy: The ChicaNerd in Chicana Young Adult (YA) Literature." *The Lion and the Unicorn*, vol. 41, no. 3, 2018, pp. 307–26.

Jiménez García, Marilisa. "Side-by-Side: At the Intersections of Latinx Studies and ChYALit." *The Lion and the Unicorn*. vol. 41, no. 1, January 2017. pp. 113–22.

López, Hernández Miriam. *Aztec Women and Goddesses*. Fundación Cultural Armella Spitalier, 2012.

Martínez-Roldán, Carmen M. "The Representation of Latinos and the Use of Spanish: A Critical Content Analysis of Skippyjon Jones." *Journal of Children's Literature*, vol. 39, no. 1, 2013, pp. 5–14.

Mercado-López, Larissa. "Entre Tejana y Chicana: Tracing Proto-Chicana Identity and Consciousness in Tejana Young Adult Fiction and Poetry." *Voices of Resistance: Interdisciplinary Approaches to Chican@ Children's Literature*, edited by Laura Alamillo, Larissa Mercado-Lopez, and Cristina Herrera, Rowman & Littlefield, 2018.

Prado, Emily. "*I Am Not Your Perfect Mexican Daughter* is the Coming-of-Age Novel Chicana Teens Deserve." *Remezcla*, Oct. 2017. http://remezcla.com/features/culture/erika-sanchez -debut-novel/.

Quintero, Isabel. *Gabi: A Girl in Pieces*. Cinco Puntos Press, 2014.

Quintero, Isabel. "Why I Write: Part I." *Isabel Quintero Blog*. WordPress, 2 Jun. 2014. https:// laisabelquintero.com/2014/06/02/why-i-write/.

Rhodes, Jackie. "'My Writing is My Activism': An Interview with Isabel Quintero." *Los Angeles Review of Books*, 1 Feb. 2017. https://lareviewofbooks.org/article/my-writing-is-my-activism -an-interview-with-isabel-quintero/#!

Sánchez, Erica L. "How a Chicana Finally Learned to Cook." *Huffpost*, 11 May 2012 https:// www.huffingtonpost.com/erika-l-sanchez/how-a-chicana-finally-lea_b_1506169.html. Accessed 15 Mar. 2018.

Sánchez, Erica L. *I Am Not Your Perfect Mexican Daughter*. Alfred A. Knopf, 2017.

Sánchez, Erica L. "I Wanted to Marry a Latino and Fell for a White Guy." *Jezebel*. 22 Jul. 2011. https://jezebel.com/5823561/i-wanted-to-marry-a-latino-and-fell-for-a-white-guy.

Schoenberg, Nara. "Chicagoan Erika Sanchez: From Daughter of Undocumented Immigrants to National Book Award Finalist." *Chicago Tribune*. 19 Oct. 2017. http://www.chicagotribune .com/lifestyles/books/ct-books-i-am-not-perfect-mexican-daughter-erika-sanchez-1022 -story.html. Accessed 15 Mar. 2018.

Short, Kathy G. "Critical Content Analysis as a Research Methodology." *Critical Content Analysis of Children's and Young Adult Literature: Reframing Perspective*, edited by Holly Johnson, Janelle Mathis, and Kathy G. Short. Routledge, 2017, pp. 1–15.

Thomas, Ebony Elizabeth. "Stories Still Matter: Rethinking the Role of Diverse Children's Literature Today." *Language Arts*, vol. 94, no. 2, 2016, pp. 112–19.

Section 2

Superheroes
and
Other Worldly
Beings

4

Bite Me: The Allure of Vampires and Dark Magic in Chicana Young Adult Literature

Christi Cook

Joining the ranks of the supernatural often provides a harbor of sorts for teenage characters in Young Adult (YA) fiction who face challenging life circumstances and experiences of being cast out of the mainstream. The fantasy worlds of vampirism and dark magic in Marta Acosta's *Happy Hour at Casa Dracula*[1] (2006) and Anna-Marie McLemore's *The Weight of Feathers* (2015) provide safety, escape, and sometimes ostracism for Milagro and Lace, the protagonists, who attain otherworldly power by entering these worlds. Fittingly, there is great risk involved in achieving this kind of power. Vampire narratives often include dangerous initiations into vampirism, and Milagro's tale in *Happy Hour at Casa Dracula* is no different.

Being a young vampire is a liminal existence—one may or may not survive the numerous foils of the vampire-hunting human world. Thus, early adulthood is posited as a life-or-death experience, which teen readers are likely to identify with. Similarly harrowing and emboldening is Lace Paloma's initiation into the world of *magia negra* in *The Weight of Feathers*. Like Milagro, Lace pursues a dangerous romantic interest who introduces her to a new space full of power but fraught with physical and societal danger. I examine the dangers of the characters' new worlds in light of the ubiquitous threat inherent to their prior daily lived experiences as young women of color who are doubly marginalized because of their ethnicity and their gender, and I investigate the authors' use of form and style in addressing their characters' hybridities. I explore the tension between a safe transitional space and a permanent home and how the supernatural affects their status as outsiders.

Vampires and the Supernatural in YA Literature

In *Happy Hour at Casa Dracula*, Milagro de los Santos, a thwarted writer, is struggling through a series of bad jobs and meaningless flings following her college graduation. At a book party celebrating the success of the new novel of her former beau, she meets an enchanting stranger, goes back to his hotel, and ends up in his room, where they kiss passionately, which results in a cut on both of their mouths and an exchange of blood. This is her initiation into the vampiric world; as is often the case with vampire initiations throughout vampire lore, it is painful and dangerous. Following this moment, which is ended by her ex bursting into the room while Milagro slinks away unnoticed, she becomes extremely ill and loses track of days. After she finds herself buying raw meat and sucking the blood out of it while being menacingly tracked down by strangers, she is rescued by someone who turns out to be a fellow vampire and is whisked off to his family retreat outside of town. The family members repeatedly and self-consciously deny that they are vampires. Additionally, during their medical examination of Milagro, they note that "it's been so long since an outsider has come into contact with the condition that we have no reliable scientific data," which serves further to emphasize Milagro's status as an outsider to the bourgeois vampire clan (Acosta 71).

The Casa Dracula inhabitants also refer to their idiosyncrasies as a condition in which "contact with our blood has consequences" (Acosta 61). This introduces the theme of blood as contagion that will be carried throughout the novel. Just as Bram Stoker "uses the figure of the vampire as thinly-veiled shorthand for many of the fears that haunted the Victorian fin de siècle," so can vampire novels since *Dracula* be read with the vampire serving as stand-in for whatever contemporary threat society is fixated on (Buzzwell). For example, as John S. Bak traces, *Dracula* was used in ad campaigns warning against HIV and AIDS throughout the 1980s and 1990s, and the renewed focus on the infectious nature of blood strikes a similarly menacing tone in this novel (xi–xv). When learning what might be wrong with her, Milagro expresses horror at the idea of becoming a monstrous vampire. The vampire she is talking to is tired of being stereotyped as a bloodsucking animal and replies, "I would think that a woman of color would understand prejudice" (50). Thus, the condition of being Chicana and the condition of being a vampire are overtly elided for the reader. As Teresa Goddu points out, the Gothic serves as a primary means of speaking the unspeakable in American literature" (quoted in González 49).

Ultimately vampire YA literature serves as an important bridge text in the larger conversation on race, ethnicity, gender, and hybridity because of its thematic focus on identity and power dynamics (Overstreet 15). Using vampirism as a metaphor for racial and ethnic discrimination allows the opportunity for death and the Gothic eventually to "become an act of love, facilitating social change" (González 50). Reminiscent of Margrit Shildrick's work on the monstrous and the other, this juxtaposition allows for "mutual becomings" that permit readers, alongside the characters, better to understand the other and themselves in a living, embodied manner (Shildrick 132).

Similar to the way Cherríe Moraga writes plays "utiliz[ing] ghosts, apparitions, shadows, madness, and murder in order to show the way cultural outsiders are treated by the patriarchal forces of Chicano nationalism," this and other Chicanx YA supernatural tales highlight the erasure of these bodies in the dominant vampire narrative and create a space for their compensation from that erasure (González 51).

Historically, a common interpretation of *Dracula* is that it is a prototypical text in the "invasion literature" genre that dates from the late 1800s to the early 1900s and is centered on the English anxiety of invasion by foreigners. In fact, "What distinguished Dracula from his vampire predecessors is that his attacks involved not only the possibility of death but the actual loss of one's identity, in particular one's racial identity" (Lyubansky). In much of its contemporary US manifestation, however, vampire mythos has involved vampires being upper-class and Anglo, so Milagro's inclusion is both an older vampire tradition along the lines of the ethnic outsider Dracula himself and a new innovation that bucks a current literary trend. Here, the vampire family seems to fear racial contamination with the introduction of Milagro into their tight-knit Anglo group, which exemplifies a white Anglo US version of invasion literature.

Hybridity, Homelessness, and the Chicanx Experience

Milagro, then, exists in several worlds at once, which is an obvious allegory for the Chicana condition. Milagro cannot return to her apartment because she is being hunted by an Anglo vampire hunting group, but for the majority of the novel she hasn't fully assimilated into vampirism, and she isn't a comfortable part of the vampire family that is hosting her. Thus, as an outcast with extraordinary gifts, she must attempt to find her path to a new way of being and a new hybrid identity that speaks to how Chicanx peoples must navigate the borderlands. Gaspar de Alba sums up this problem of Chicanx people finding their space in the world thus: "Chicano identity is, ultimately, a border identity; neither side wants you and you can't go home" (200).

The problem is, in Monika Kaup's words, that "neither place can adequately represent home any more, in the full symbolic sense of rootedness and belonging. For both places have been deprived of the anchoring quality of autonomous homes by the intervention of the outside economic and social forces of late capitalism" (180–81). As a Chicana, Milagro experiences poverty, discrimination, and lack of belonging before her vampiric encounter. Her Chicana experience is then writ large as she must flee to a new land: a wealthy Anglo vampire ranch that serves as her safety net during her acclimation to full vampirism. The Casa Dracula ranch is typical to the vampire genre in that vampirism is often associated with wealth, extravagance, and power, although vampires are often ethnic outsiders.

One solution for Chicana adolescents who are searching for home and for an authentic identity is to, as Gloria Anzaldúa recommends, embody *mestizaje* as the new cultural hybrid. In her New Mestiza model, Gloria Anzaldúa transforms the static "homeland" of her male forbears to an ever-changing "borderlands," which she describes as "physically present wherever two or more cultures edge each other, where people of different races occupy the same territory, where under, lower, middle and upper classes touch, where the space between two individuals shrinks with intimacy" rather than as exclusive to Chicano cultural heritage (19). Anzaldúa does not envision separatism for her people as a panacea in the manner her predecessors did; instead, she invokes complete inclusion as the Chicanx cultural ideal, which seems to be a less extreme and more humane approach than that of her forebears. She undercuts the Western tendency toward firm boundaries and calls instead for a "radical pluralism of Chicana identity" (Anzaldúa 79).

The borderlands are the feminist response to a patriarchal tendency to privilege one part of one's heritage over another and to prize land ownership above all else. However, this is not an easy ideal for an adolescent to attain. Children's literature author and scholar George Shannon states that "when two cultures cross, the nexus is most often a homeless land with its children feeling less than whole," since "cross-cultural children are caught between two mirrors—two ways of seeing—each presenting a different image of the self" (14). In *Casa Dracula*, Milagro falls into this homeless land, seeking "home" first in her ex, then a dear friend, and ultimately at Casa Dracula, where the vampire family has a long history of insularity, and consequently a high degree of suspicion regarding Milagro's motives. Her culturally influenced behaviors clash with their pretentious ways several times throughout the novel, and the matriarch remains judgmental of Milagro's manners, clothing, curvy body, and other ethnic "markings" for the majority of the tale. Since she is a consummate outsider, Milagro is miserable and homesick for a home and a harbor she cannot find until the end of the novel (282).

A sense of homelessness and of not belonging is often an intrinsic characteristic for those who feel torn among numerous identities. The intersectionality of the protagonists' marked hybrid status as young adult girls, Chicanas, and supernatural beings, two of which are obviously realistic marginalized depictions while one is a fantasy, creates an interesting space within which to explore hybridity. I argue that there is a limit to Anzaldúan hybridity, the go-to for many when discussing Chicana literature and hybridity, as the exemplar for the YA reader and character because of its overly idealistic portrayal of the New Mestiza, which doesn't work when applied to a teenaged coming-of-age that involves transitioning painfully and often amongst their borderlands identities in ways that do not reflect peaceful coexistence amongst hybrid influences. Chicana young adult literature's status as a marginalized, contradictory, hybrid art form can be understood with Anzaldúa's framework in mind—hybridity is a positive, empowering status, for the YA book as an artifact, the YA character in the book, and for the YA reader herself. The borderlands model invites formal experimentation and an all-encompassing acceptance of cultural "back-and-forths" that previously were neither tolerated nor even conceived of.

However, there is a limit to Anzaldúan hybridity as the exemplar for the YA reader and character. Although it is an appealing, all-encompassing ideal, I take issue with the overly idealistic portrayal of the New Mestiza as applied to a transitional, teenaged coming-of-age with its accompanying pain and confusion. I argue that the New Mestiza works best as a model for adults since most teenagers will have to transition painfully and often between their borderlands identities in ways that do not reflect peaceful coexistence amongst hybrid influences. I propose an alternate model for adolescent Chicana hybridity that takes into account the young adult experience. Similarly to Shannon's model, teens spiral back and forth through stages of difficulty in integrating different cultures before ultimately finding a hybridity that works for them.

Shannon's continuum includes (1) rejection by both of their conflicting cultures; (2) the acceptance of or by one culture while denying the other; (3) the attempt to be both conflicting cultures at once; and (4) the acknowledgement and acceptance of one's individual and evolving identity as a collage of cultures (14). Despite the idealistic dénouements of the novels, attention must be paid to the painful journeys as well. A realistic paradigm for exploration of young adult hybridity would look like a patchwork architectural structure: old and new identities are perpetually superimposed on one another in ways that are sometimes judged inadequate by outsiders. This judgment can be painful, and even though the building stands, it may never "belong" in its neighborhood.

Similarly to the sense of homelessness and lack of belonging that Milagro experiences, in *The Weight of Feathers,* the dual protagonists from rival itinerant performing families search for home and belonging despite their status as outsiders, both within their families and in the world at large, throughout this tale of magical realism. The novel features a Chicana named Lace Paloma who earns a living swimming with her cousins in a mermaid show and a Romani named Cluck Corbeau who fixes wings for his family members whose work entails "flying" in a tree-climbing show. The Palomas and the Corbeaus hate one another: the younger members of the families get into fistfights with each other while the older members spread racist warnings and prohibitions against the Other. For the purposes of this chapter, in which I interrogate gender and the Chicana experience, I will focus primarily on Lace's experiences and perspective.[2] Lace lacks a permanent home since she is part of a traveling show, but her search for home becomes even more desperate after her exile: her *abuela* kicks her out of the show for breaking the family's rules forbidding contact with the Corbeau family, and thus she is banished from her family, job, and home.

A prevalent theme in much Chicana young adult literature is navigation of the patriarchal home. In exploring this theme, it is helpful to begin with *Living Chicana Theory*, wherein Carla Trujillo reminisces about her own repressive childhood growing up constantly under her father's thumb. Trujillo, her sister, and her mother were at the beck and call of her father and brother, and this "house doctrine"[3] prevented her from discovering her real identity until she was able to spend several years in an apartment of her own. Monika Kaup also identifies the importance of deconstructing the home for Chicana theorists and artists. Examining Cisneros's *House on Mango Street*, Kaup asserts that, unlike Chicanos with their liberatory focus on the nation, Chicanas must begin with undoing the oppression of the home. Since Lace is a younger protagonist than Milagro, who is already living in her own apartment before fleeing to Casa Dracula, the reader watches Lace struggle to navigate challenges with gender roles that are entwined with the traditional values of her home.

In Lace's quest to alleviate the curse she believes the Corbeau family has lain on her that led to her being shunned by her family, she finds a temporary home living with and doing makeup work for the "enemy" Corbeaus. Lace gets to know the gentle Cluck Corbeau and empathizes with his outsider position in his family, and she and Cluck eventually fall in love with one another in this modernized Romeo and Juliet tale. However, for the first part of the novel, Lace is in constant turmoil worrying that she will be infected by the Corbeaus' touch or their feathers; she had been taught by her family to burn any black feathers she encountered and to eschew any further contact with the objects.

Part of the magic in this novel is that the Corbeaus grow feathers in their hair while Lace and her mermaid family members have scales on their bodies. As she lives alongside them, she thinks, "If her skin did not touch theirs, she would survive this" (McLemore 116). The fear of infection Lace experiences offers an obvious parallel to the fear Milagro and other characters in *Casa Dracula* associate with their blood contagion, and both center around fear of contamination by other races. Lace also hears "whispers from the other side of town," the warnings of her judgmental family members, every time she becomes emotionally or physically close to Cluck (145). She and Cluck find temporary harbor sometimes transcending and sometimes channeling their families' legacies of black magic: the magic embedded in the Corbeaus' feathers and the ability to make water and trees move the way one wants them to. They take turns encountering each other on one another's turf, having one love scene in the river Lace feels at home in and one love scene in Cluck's favorite cottonwood tree. Since Lace and her family earn their livelihood in the water, water is their second home. The same can be said for Cluck and his family regarding the trees. The symbolism contained in the equitable distribution of love scenes—each entering the other's safe space in order to experience full intimacy with the other—is a shining moment of the characters finally experiencing being *Heimlich*.[4] Even so, Lace spends the majority of the novel as an outsider who has been cast out of her family unit as she subsists amongst her lifelong enemies, whose ways are entirely foreign to her. The Corbeaus' side of the woods even smells different: "The scent of feathers pushed up from the trees," Lace is frightened that she'll be trapped "like a firefly in a jar" in the house they live in, and she is unable to understand the family when they speak French around her (McLemore 100, 122). She stays in Shannon's "homeless land . . . feeling less than whole."

Form and Style: "Outsider" Authors and Their Outsider Protagonists

The idea of not belonging to the niche that is expected of one is fitting for Marta Acosta, the author of *Happy Hour at Casa Dracula*, who refuses to write in the genre of magical realism since that is what editors and audiences expect of Latinx peoples. She tries, in her own words, to "change a preconception of what a Latina is supposed to be" ("Lost in Type"). Acosta chooses fantasy instead, but she subverts the vampire mythos in numerous ways, with the primary one being that vampirism, in her fictional world, is an infection one can eventually heal from. The protagonist of *Casa Dracula* says of her own zombie fiction writing, "I use the supernatural to represent the manifestation of various life forces, good, evil, the unconscious, the id, et cetera," and perhaps in this way she can be seen as a mouthpiece for the author, who uses both her unique voice and style and the metaphor of the vampire to address societal injustice (19). Acosta's tone in this novel is witty and breezy; chapter one is entitled "The Intolerable Lightness of Being Silly," which sets the stage well for Milagro's persona and voice.

Nonetheless, the protagonist makes several biting observations about racial and ethnic inequities. Every time she arrives at a party, she scans for people of color. When she spies a Latino waiter while doing one of these room scans, she sends him the silent message, "Right on, *mi hermano*. Power to the people" (6), and she reclaims one Anglo character's label of her as a "common Mexican girl," defying this character and saying, "You underestimate the determination of common Mexican girls" (256). Though this novel is a light and fun read, it is far from being devoid of political commentary on the unjust world faced by Chicanxs.

Anna-Marie McLemore, on the other hand, has a much heavier-handed, "weightier" style in her debut novel. She writes more self-consciously about discrimination and injustice. Each chapter begins with a bilingual axiom: sometimes Spanish-English and sometimes French-English. Thus, a moral greets the reader every few pages. Two exemplars are "*Volez de ses propres ailes* / Fly with your own wings," which communicates both literal advice to the Corbeaus to trust only their own equipment and metaphorical significance regarding staying true to one's self, and "*Los enemigos del hombre son los de su propia casa* / A man's enemies are those of his own house," which warns the protagonists and the readers to beware of potential dangers endemic to their own families and traditions. Bilingualism is one type of formal experimentation used by new Chicana authors in order to resist phallogocentrism and the privileging of Anglo languages and cultures.[5] McLemore experiments with bilingualism by setting Spanish and French against one another at the beginning of the novel, highlighting characters' isolation in not being able to understand the other language throughout, and then approaching, but not achieving, an Anzaldúan hybridity toward the end of the novel when the two cultures collide and begin an unsteady union. Throughout the novel, she code-switches, making some statements first in Spanish or French and then in English to emphasize an attempt at balance and parallelism with both worlds. The Spanish and French languages are granted predominance by being formulated in sentences that are full of wisdom and by being stated before their English equivalents. This setup, which is integral to the structure of the entire book, seems deliberate in its attempt to restore balance between warring cultures and to validate the primacy of the Spanish and French languages and

Lace's appreciation and growing understanding of her Mexican American roots even as she chooses to internalize and eventually to grow beyond them. Weight is a part of the title, and it is mentioned several times throughout the novel, primarily when referring to the weight of the Corbeaus's feathers, which signify the weight of judgment and discrimination Lace and Cluck experience. The Corbeaus's "feathers already had such weight," the reader is told on the second page of the novel. Although racial discrimination is most pronounced against Cluck, the Romani character whose "stain makes him darker, *le petit demon* in his own family," Lace is his constant champion, defending him from a fist fight at the hand of her cousins toward the beginning of the novel and one at the hands of Cluck's own brother toward the end (20). On top of the racial critique, McLemore adds capitalistic and patriarchal critiques: an adhesive factory sends down acidic rain that injures townspeople only to be covered up by ubiquitous Anglo men in blue suits who refuse to take any financial or environmental responsibility. It is revealed toward the end of the novel that the plant is responsible for the event that started the feud between the two families and that environmental toxicity is actually to blame, instead of "black magic," for several key disasters that unfold. When Lace understands that the greedy motives of an outside corporation are responsible for her family's longstanding bad feelings toward the Corbeaus, who are not guilty of all the evils she had been told about after all, she is able to leave the feud behind and set off for a new beginning with the refuge of her lover.

Conclusion

In the end, both Chicana protagonists find temporary harbor in the supernatural: the vampire home for Milagro, even though she herself has developed immunity to her vampiric infection, and love with a fellow participant and victim of *la magia negra* for Lace, as the two leave their quarreling families behind and embark for a yet-to-be-determined home of their own. Neither Milagro nor Lace is able to become integrated with her family of origin or with dominant culture, although Milagro, after vanquishing the violent vampire hunters, has the option of going back to her city and Lace and Cluck, in a cloud of red feathers created through a mother's love, sacrifice, and an act of magic, plan to attempt re-entry to the mainstream. The supernatural serves its purpose, though: it presents a readiness "to voice otherwise unspeak-able truths" (Clery 9). As Srdjan Smajić theorizes, supernaturalism, which constantly challenges the status quo, "is seen as performing an ideologico-political service inextricable from its aesthetics and frequently consonant with the suppressed voices of marginalized groups and discourses. In short, supernaturalism articulates what realism cannot or dare not" (3). With Milagro's immunity to vampirism and Lace's eschewing of her family, the container of much of *la magia negra,* it seems that the supernatural serves as a harbor during the protagonists' crises, but that it is partially laid aside as a quasi-rejoining of "the real world," and shedding of outsider status becomes possible. It is interesting that neither author holds the supernatural up as the ultimate goal or the ideal harbor; each communicates to the reader that the "real world," though deeply flawed, is where we must return.

Milagro and Lace journey through supernaturalism, which both authors use as a temporary refuge, a source of strength, and a magnifying glass emphasizing societal ills perpetrated against Chicanx peoples, women, and other outsiders, but both protagonists emerge on the other side of the supernatural. Their fictional hybrid identities are complicated, and readers are able more easily to understand the realities of their own nonfictional hybrid identities through the lens of the supernatural. The reader is left with confidence that both Chicanas have the strength to survive the real world after learning and growing from their struggles within the supernatural realm. Milagro's love interest says it best when describing how he fell in love with the plucky Chicana the first time he saw her: "You were trying to act demure, trying to fit in, but you had this attitude, and I could see it whenever you looked around the room." "What kind of attitude?" she asks. "Kind of a 'bite me! attitude," he responds (311). Both protagonists are on a journey to return to the real world of palpable injustices, but both Chicanas have their "bite me" attitudes to counter the inevitable injustices they will encounter.

Notes

1. The *Casa Dracula* series comprises four books; *Happy Hour at Casa Dracula* is the first in the series.

2. The narrative structure of the novel itself is focused equally on Lace and Cluck.

3. "House doctrine" is the patriarchal notion, found in the traditional Latin American practice of *machismo*, that a woman's place is in the home, cooking, cleaning, and serving the men of the household. This corresponds to the traditional roles of breadwinner husband and stay-at-home wife for Anglos in the US. Chicanas' focus on undoing the oppression of patriarchy at home is a trope from the Chicano Movement of the 1970s.

4. See Sigmund Freud's article "The Uncanny," for his theory of *heimlich* (canny, homelike) and *unheimlich* (uncanny)

5. Anzaldúa integrates numerous languages and styles in her book, which is innovative in a poststructural fashion (Kaup 208). Viramontes and Cisneros are other notable authors who implement these stylistic devices.

Works Cited

Acosta, Marta. *Happy Hour at Casa Dracula*. Pocket Books, 2006.

Anzaldúa, Gloria. *Borderlands/ La Frontera: The New Mestiza*. Aunt Lute Books, 1987.

Bak, John S. Ed. "Preface: Bad Blood; or, Victorian Vampires in the Postmodern Age of AIDS," Post/modern Dracula From Victorian Themes to Postmodern Praxis. Cambridge Scholars Publishing, 2007. www.bl.uk/romantics-and-victorians/articles/dracula.

Buzzwell, Greg. "Dracula: Vampires, Perversity, and Victorian Anxieties." Discovering Literature: Romantic and Victorian. 15 May 2014.

Clery, E. J. *The Rise of Supernatural Fiction, 1762–1800*. Cambridge University Press, 1999.

Gaspar de Alba, ed. *Velvet Barrios: Popular Culture and Chicana/o Sexualities*. Palgrave Macmillan, 2003.

González, Tanya. "The (Gothic) Gift of Death in Cherríe Moraga's The Hungry Woman: A Mexican Medea (2001)." Chicana/Latina Studies, vol. 7, 2007, pp. 44–77.

Kaup, Monika. *Rewriting North American Borders in Chicano and Chicana Narrative*. Peter Lang Publishing, 2001.

"Lost in Type: She-Hulk Author Marta Acosta Talks Miscommunication, Genre Confusion, and Sexism." *Misprinted Pages,* www.misprintedpages.com/2013/03/28/interview-she-hulk-marta-acosta.

Lyubansky, Mikhail. "Are the Fangs Real? Vampires as Racial Metaphor in the Anita Blake and Twilight Novels." *Psychology Today.* 10 April 2010.

McLemore, Anna-Marie. *The Weight of Feathers*. Thomas Dunne Books, 2015.

Overstreet, Deborah. *Not Your Mother's Vampire: Vampires in Young Adult Fiction*. Scarecrow Press, 2006.

Shannon, George. "Making a Home of One's Own: The Young in Cross-Cultural Fiction." *The English Journal*, vol. 77, no. 5, 1988, pp. 14–19.

Shildrick, Margrit. *Embodying the Monster: Encounters with the Vulnerable Self*. Sage Publications, 2002.

Smajić, Srdjan. "Supernatural Realism." *NOVEL: A Forum on Fiction*, vol. 42, no. 1, Spring, 2009, pp. 1–2.

Trujillo, Carla. *Living Chicana Theory*. Third Woman Press, 1998.

5

Afuerxs and Cultural Practice in *Shadowshaper* and *Labyrinth Lost*

Domino Pérez

In the young adult novels *Shadowshaper* (2015) by Daniel José Older and *Labyrinth Lost* (2016) by Zoraida Córdova, readers are presented with two courageous magic-wielding Latina protagonists, Sierra Santiago (Afro-Puerto Rican) and Alejandra Mortiz (Afro-Latina), respectively.[1] Female empowerment and folk practices play a central role in both of these Brooklyn-based books. Sierra and Alejandra (who prefers Alex) are the inheritors of exceptional magics rooted in cultural practices specific to their ethnoracial communities: shadowshaping, the ability to provide spirits with a physical form through drawing, music, murals, sculpture, or storytelling; the cantos used by brujas and brujos, those who harbor and practice a particular ability or abilities, including elemental control, healing, or defense, among others. Positioned on the margins of remarkable worlds, involuntarily and by choice, the outsiders or afuerxs take on evils that threaten their families and communities without having been properly trained about how to use their fantastic abilities. In these fantasy novels, folklore and cultural practice become sites of refusal for the protagonists, who reinforce social or affiliative relationships through the participation in and reframing of their respective cultural traditions. By doing so, these Latina characters and novels disrupt ideas about heroism and critique the obstacles (cultural or social) that limit these young outsiders' access to positions of power.

"Because You're Brown"

Harry Potter, the boy wizard with the lightning bolt scar, unruly hair, and green eyes, holds a beloved spot in the world of children's fantasy fiction, not to mention in the hearts and minds of readers around the world. The *Harry Potter* (1997–2007) series by J. K. Rowling features a host of wizards, witches, giants, and other magical creatures, but what it does not include is much in the way of racial or ethnic diversity, Cho Chang and the Patel sisters notwithstanding. Rowling does not identify Harry or the other two members of the "Golden Trio," Hermione Granger or Ron Weasley, as explicitly white in the novels. In the absence of racial or ethnic signifiers (which can come with their own sets of problems), the characters become white by default in the minds of readers, an assumption only reinforced by the casting of Anglo-British actors in the lead roles for the films.[2] Black British actress Noma Dumezweni brought unambiguous diversity to the franchise when she was cast as Hermione Granger in the theatre production of *The Cursed Child* (2016), a story set nineteen years after the events in *The Deathly Hallows* (2007), the seventh and final book. The decision to feature Dumezweni in the role sparked an uproar among Potter purists but Rowling gave the choice her unequivocal stamp of approval.[3] However, long before black Hermione, fans were racebending (the changing of race from one group to another), not to mention genderbending (disrupting or swapping gender) and "shipping" (imagined romantic pairings or groupings) well-known characters in the series. By aligning their own experiences with favorite characters, readers' efforts are an attempt to see themselves represented in the literature, or write themselves into the stories they love, though they should not have to.

Children's author Matt de la Peña, who is of Mexican and American descent, once asked, "Where's the African-American Harry Potter or the Mexican Katniss?" (Strickland). The answer lies, to some extent, in the way that "heteronormative heroism narrows the range of culturally viable narrative actions and plots" (Pugh and Wallace 261). When race, ethnicity, ability, or sexuality become additional factors, that range is narrowed even further, especially in popular YA literature, leaving limited space outside of the status quo. To be clear, De la Peña was not suggesting that there are no books featuring non-white protagonists. Rather his question was a means of expressing a need for "more commercial books [that] feature more characters of color." The appearance of such books, according to the author, "would change the game." As others have noted, such as Kate Capshaw, Cristina Herrera, Philip Nel, Ruth Quiroa, and Debbie Reese (Nambé Pueblo), among others, changing the game means transforming the white-dominated publishing industry.[4] The major publishing houses or "Big 5," from acquisitions editors to executives, are all looking for the next white, cis-male, heterosexual, commercially viable hero, preferably marketed across a series of books and optioned for a film franchise with tie-in merchandise.[5] It also means actively disrupting the assumption of whiteness in the manuscripts publishers acquire, produce, and promote. "The ubiquity of whiteness in popular media is so overwhelming that, in the absence of any racial signifiers," Lindy West observes, "the majority of white people and a significant number of non-white people automatically assume that characters are white." In light of these and other factors, de la Peña's inquiry speaks not only to the lack of commercially successful books featuring characters of color, but also to the ongoing lack of diversity in children's literature, an issue Nancy Larrick raised more than fifty years ago in "The All-White World of Children's Books" (1965).

The young adult novels *Shadowshaper* and *Labyrinth Lost*, because of the race and ethnicity of their authors and protagonists, are veritable outsiders in children's literature. Consider that in 2017, according to the Children's Cooperative Book Center, books by Latinx authors accounted for a mere 3.1 percent of the total published books ("Publishing Statistics"). While the amount represents a 1.5 percent increase overall from 2014 when de la Peña originally posed his question, the dearth of children's literature *by* Latinx authors is disproportionate to the Latinx population.[6] The protagonists of *Shadowshaper* and *Labyrinth Lost* are welcome disruptions to the pervasive whiteness of children's books, as well as to the narrative landscape of the YA fantasy genre more broadly. Depicted on the cover of Older's novel is a young black woman hovering above the city skyline, her chin raised slightly in defiance. As if taking the description of Sierra Santiago directly from the story, her "fro [stretches] magnificently around her in a fabulous, unbothered halo" (10). Her racialized features code her blackness but do not reveal her Latinidad, a detail that is confirmed early in the novel through language and family history. The image, striking and powerful, promises a very different kind of hero, or rather heroine, one that aligns directly with the Sierra as she is described and characterized throughout the novel.

Cultural practice takes prominence on the book jacket of *Labyrinth Lost*, where a woman, of an undetermined age, with her face painted in a manner reminiscent of *la catrina*, looks up at the title in gold overlaying a pair of cavernous dark eyes that appear to stare out from the flower and foliage in the background. The *calavera* design is associated with the *día de los muertos*, a Mexican cultural celebration, concentrated primarily in Oaxaca and the island of Janitzio, Michoacán, in which the dead are honored and remembered. In *Labyrinth Lost*, the image evokes a "death mask," the ceremonial face painting done on a bruja or brujo's Deathday so the "waking spirits feel at home" (Córdova 77). Signifiers of race and culture delineate the difference of these novels and their protagonists in a book-publishing industry with a history of whitewashing the covers of novels about characters who are clearly non-white.[7] As Annie Schutte notes, "When a YA book actually does have a protagonist of color, too often one of three things seems to happen: the cover is 'whitewashed' and shows a Caucasian model instead of a person of color; the cover depicts someone whose race seems purposefully ambiguous or difficult to discern; or the character is shown in silhouette." *Shadowshaper* and *Labyrinth Lost* do none of these; instead, they assert the race or cultural association of the protagonists within the novel and, in the process, refuse the expectation of heroic whiteness.

Outside Fantastical Worlds

Adding to their status as children's literature outsiders, both *Shadowshapers* and *Labyrinth Lost* are both fantasy novels. As Older himself points out, "The publishing industry, which is currently about 90% white, has focused inordinately on white protagonists, white communities, white stories, particularly when it comes to fantasy fiction" (368). Genre may not appear to be a significant factor in analyses of diversity, or lack thereof, but when we also consider Phillip Nel's statement about authorship in the realms of fantasy and speculative fiction, the category takes on additional significance: "Fantasy and science fiction are only two of the genres that publishers tacitly treat as mainly for White writers" (170). In other words, fantasy is outside of the purview of non-white writers. This idea is due to the ways that narratives inclusive of or by minoritarian writers are bound by certain expectations, creating what Christopher Meyers calls the "apartheid of literature." Meyers offers, for example, that "characters of color are limited to the townships of occasional historical books that concern themselves with the legacies of civil rights and slavery but are never given a pass card to traverse the lands of adventure, curiosity, imagination or personal growth." Black and brown children are rarely called on to lead great heroic adventures; instead, when included at all, they are relegated to sidekick or some other lower-tier status. The result is that children are denied a "sense of self-love that comes from recognizing oneself in a text" (Myers). Furthermore, they do not get the benefit "from the understanding that [their] life and lives of people like [them] are worthy of being told, thought about, discussed and even celebrated" because, as Myers explains to one boy, they are brown. For these and other reasons, the importance of Older and Cordova's works with their Latinx heroines in worlds filled with fantasy and magic cannot be overstated.

Shadowshaper and *Labyrinth Lost* further distinguish themselves in the fantasy genre: Older's novel falls into the intrusion variety, though it is also urban fantasy, while Córdova's is a portal variation with an attendant quest. Within each category, certain conventions exist that, in turn, create a set of expectations in the reader that the author may or may not provide. According to Farah Mendelsohn, "The trajectory of the intrusion fantasy is straightforward: the world is ruptured by the intrusion, which disrupts normality and has to be negotiated with or defeated, sent back when it came, or controlled" (115). Sierra learns about a supernatural force destroying the murals in her Bedford-Stuy neighborhood and the larger purpose behind these attacks. She finds out about the world of the shadowshapers and must discover her place in it to defeat the threats to her family and community. Regarding urban fantasy, Laura Miller describes it as "a cross of fairy tale, noir and classic coming-of-age narrative," a form that "is peculiarly suited to wrestling with the quandaries of early 21st-century womanhood, which is itself a hybrid of age-old preconceptions and fledgling, undreamed-of promise" (Miller). Apropos to these ideas, Sierra learns that gender is a factor in the withholding of cultural knowledge that infringes upon her potential as force within the world of shadowshaping. Conversely, Alex grows up in a family of brujas but wants to find a way to rid herself of magic. During what she thinks is a banishing spell gone awry, a portal opens to another world and her relatives, including her mother and sisters, are pulled into it. Subsequently, she must find a way to reopen the doorway to that unknown world to retrieve her loved ones. Whereas the "the portal fantasy is about entry, transition and exploration," the quest fantasy helps the protagonist meet a separate set of objectives (Mendlesohn 2). In attempting to send away her powers, Alex creates the conditions and circumstances for her journey. "Characteristically the quest fantasy protagonist goes from a mundane life" as Mendlesohn explains, "to direct contact with the fantastic through which she transitions, exploring the world until she or those around her are knowledgeable enough to negotiate with the world via the personal manipulation of the fantastic realm" (2). Alex's success depends upon her ability to summon and command her immense power.

    In addition to controlling powerful magics and understanding their places in heroic plots, Sierra and Alex are also teenagers, a stage of liminality between who they were as children and who they are becoming within or independent of their families. Laurence Yep reminds us that by "definition, adolescence is a period of feeling like an outsider. Teenagers are literally outsiders in their bodies because they are unable to stop or control the physical changes that are happening. They are also starting to develop their separate identities as individuals—which is a frightening, anxiety-generating enterprise" (53). Therefore, the introduction or manifestation of magic in the lives of these two protagonists becomes another aspect of their identities that are negotiated alongside the gender, social, and generational politics within their Latinx families. However, magic or fantasy serves an additional purpose. The fantastical elements of the narrative provide a means for these young women to critique or push back against cultural conventions, in part because "social political imagination takes into account the instability of identity, both individual and cultural, and the power structures in which we reside" (Botelho and Rudman 263). These power structures reveal the ways that knowledge of, access to, and participation in cultural practice define one's place in her respective community.

Cultural Practice and the Afuerx

Worldbuilding is the cornerstone of any successful work of fantasy. The mundane world must be as believable as its magical counterpart. Older acknowledges being inspired by Harry Potter, but that he "wanted a Harry Potter who would speak to my people and to other people that weren't white. . . . They needed a mythology that spoke to our mythology, a literature that speaks to our truth" (Diaz). Older does not give readers myth; instead he offers them a fantasy built on a fictional cultural practice that reveals larger truths in and outside the novel. Maria José Botelho and Masha Kabakow Rudman remind us, "Fantasy is not lack of truth. In order for it to work, it has to have a connection for the reader to a deep reality. We also have to remember that fantasy is not context-free and that class, gender, and race figure as largely in a work of fantasy as in any other genre" (214). Race and fictional cultural practices are central to the worlds found in *Shadowshaper* and *Labyrinth Lost*. The authors use folklore to create what Barre Toelken calls "narrative architecture," a method for "how plots are developed and how protagonists operate within them" (336). However, cultural practices also become sites of struggle and conflict that reveal deeper social realities, such as misogyny and threats to familial integrity. As afuerxs, Sierra and Alex occupy liminal spaces, both within and outside of culture or tradition because they refuse to accept either wholesale. These afuerxs are representative of a generational and temporal perspective that do not necessarily align with historical views of nationalism or conventional Latinx identity politics. Non-conforming in some way, they refuse the status quo, choosing instead to remake or reject culture and tradition from within.

For Sierra Santiago, shadowshaping is a cultural practice that members of her Puerto Rican family brought with them to New York from the island. They, along with other folk in their Brooklyn-based community, maintain the shadowshaping tradition, originally inclusive of men and women. The practice depends upon the cooperation of a figure known as Lucera, a figure of tremendous power around whom the spirits coalesce, and she then amplifies the energy of the spirits so the shadowshapers can channel that energy into material form. As a child, Sierra is unknowingly initiated into the world of shadowshapers by her grandmother, Mama Carmen, who secretly defies her own husband Lázaro Corona, who comes to believe that the cultural practice belongs exclusively to men. However, Mama Carmen dies before she can begin Sierra's shadowshaping training and the young woman grows up knowing nothing about the practice. In the wake of his wife's death, Lázaro refuses to educate Sierra, and his "old-school macho crap" influences his choice to teach only her brothers, who are either not interested in learning or as gifted as Sierra, as revealed later, about shadowshaping (Older 110). Lázaro's sexist attitudes create the conditions for the attack on the shadowshapers and places his granddaughter in immediate danger.

A small group of men, along with two younger apprentices, are all that remains of the shadowshapers, so the future of the practice is precarious and made even more so after Lázaro suffers a stroke. Although he recovers physically, he begins to ramble incoherently. However, during an uncharacteristic moment of lucidity, he alerts Sierra to the threat the shadowshapers face and expresses an urgency for Sierra to seek out a young Haitian artist and classmate named Robbie to help her finish the mural she is working on in the junk lot next to the tower. Sierra is caught in a double bind; she must protect a group of people she knows nothing about and seek out a classmate for reasons that are unclear, a process that puts her at risk. Folklore and fictional cultural practice in the novel become a reflection of cultural logics, namely gender, power, and control over knowledge circulation. That means male power is more important to Lázaro than generational gaps in knowledge. He even goes so far as to bring a white anthropologist, Jonathan Wick, into the shadowshaping fold instead of his own granddaughter. The author notes, "Many of us have to deal with the patriarchy of our forefathers and foremothers," and "All of those things are woven together into the world that Sierra's in" (Diaz). Lázaro's divisive decisions, which he later regrets, place the tradition, his family, and the entire community in peril from a malevolence that seeks to destroy a generation of shadowshapers.

The first intrusion of magic in Sierra's life occurs when she thinks she sees a memorial mural of Papa Acevedo, one of her grandfather's former domino buddies, crying while she is painting a dragon on the side of a tower that looms over the neighborhood, a sign of the gentrification taking place in her neighborhood. But the fantastical is encountered directly when Sierra is attacked by a corpuscule, a spirit made to animate a dead body, who demands to know the whereabouts of Lucera, who has been missing for over a year. The incident occurs at a party, when Sierra is telling Robbie about her grandfather's insistence that she seek out Robbie's help. The fellow artist begins to teach Sierra about the world of shadowshaping, disclosing, despite being sworn to secrecy, that he was trained "both in painting and . . . to work with the spirits" by Papa Acevedo before he died (Older 62). Robbie even tells her about the fight between Lázaro and Lucera, after which she disappeared. "Lucera, she was . . . is . . . a spirit. . . . But a really powerful one. They say she was the one first gathered the shadowshapers, that her power was in everything we do. But I guess no one realized just how crucial she was until she vanished, not long after your grandfather had his stroke" (64). Despite Lázaro's attempts to substantiate male power over and take control of shadowshaping, without Lucera the community of practitioners falls apart. "People just scattered. Some moved on to other traditions" (64). Robbie also tries to explain the fundamentals of the practice that involves the relationship between the spirits and the forms they can inhabit. Robbie reveals to Sierra that the two most important things in shadowshaping are "material and intentionality" (134). The deliberate purpose or mindfulness of the actions associated with the cultural practice, along with initiation rites and history, become a part of the culture at the center of the world Older builds. All of this information, including shadowshaping history, gives Sierra limited access to the tradition.

Dissatisfied with her position as an outsider to insider cultural knowledge, Sierra asks Robbie to attempt a shadowshaper initiation. She is infuriated by the fact that John Wick, who is behind the murders of the elders, "had shown up and gotten inducted into the family legacy that Sierra herself had been kept from her entire life" (131). His ability to gain access to the inner circle of the shadowshapers is made possible because Lázaro opens the door and invites him in. Robbie admits to not having the power necessary to do what Sierra asks, though he suspects that someone has already passed on his or her magic to Sierra, which is later confirmed. As she learns the extent of her abilities, the location of Lucera, and Wick's larger plan, she uses her position as an afuerx to break with tradition. Sierra enlists a diverse group of friends, allies, and select family to help her defeat Wick: her best friend Bennie, Izzy and Tee, a same sex couple, and Nydia Ochoa, a Puerto Rican graduate student in Anthropology at Columbia University, her brother Juan, a shadowshaper initiate whose form is music, and her godfather Neville Spencer. Breaking down the exclusivity of the practice, Sierra ensures the continuation of the cultural practice, at the same time infusing it with new life and new participants.

While Sierra grows up uninformed about the cultural practice of her community, Alex Mortiz is surrounded by hers. Magic is such a part of quotidian life in Sunset Park Brooklyn that the manifestation of magical ability or abilities is an expectation in her family. Still, ever since she was a little girl, Alex has had an uneasy relationship with her family's folk practices, the result of accidentally interrupting a ceremony for her dead Aunt Rosaria, whose exhumed body was dancing in the center of a circle of brujas and brujos. Images of her aunt and the stench of death have haunted Alex ever since. To add, at the age of ten, Alex accidentally kills her cat Miluna when it inexplicably attacks her on the same night her powers appear. Alex's father Patricio conceals all evidence of the incident, while also explaining that what happened was not Alex's fault because the cat was possessed by a demon. He makes his daughter promise not to tell anyone about what happened or that her abilities have manifested. All of these events, when coupled with her father's departure the next day, contribute to Alex's longing to rid her life of magic. She is an insider to the fantastical who longs for nothing more than to be an outsider. For five years, she hides her magic, even as her sister Lulu actively does cantos to facilitate the manifestation of her powers. However, when a bully attacks her best friend Rishi Persuad during gym class at school, Alex unleashes her power, making a snake emerge from the boy's mouth. Later at home, she unwittingly levitates everything in the kitchen. The materialization of these and other abilities indicate that she is an encantrix, the most powerful bruja in a generation.

Whereas shadowshaping is independent of race and ethnicity, as evinced by Wick's participation in the practice, in *Labyrinth Lost* bruja magic is intertwined with Latinx identity. Nowhere in the novel is this made clearer than in the repeated refrain, "Spells are for witches. *Brujas* do cantos" (Cordova 11). Alex pushes back against this idea; "Semantics," she tells her sister, adding, "All brujas are witches but not all witches are brujas." But the book makes distinctions between the two. More than a mere linguistic difference, they are identified as separate, though somewhat related, cultural practices. A bruja's power is derived from ritual, ancestry, and memory, factors that play a role in the continuation of the practice.

The Deathday celebration, which includes the familial blessings of both the living and dead, and the Mortiz *Book of Cantos* are central to bruja magic. They are the foundations on which Córdova builds her world. All action and conflict proceed from them. The first combines elements of other familiar celebrations: "Deathday: a bruja's coming-of-age ceremony. While some girls are having their bat mitzvahs, sweet sixteens, or quinceañeras, brujas get their Deathday. . . . Over the years, modern brujas like to have Deathdays line up with birthdays to have even bigger celebrations" (13). The comparing of the Deathday to other stage-marking rituals gives readers a sense of its cultural importance. With the Mortiz line of brujas and brujos extending back hundreds of generations, the continuation of the practice within the family is ensured because the ancestors can be called forth to give a new bruja a blessing that is essential to the initiation rites. Without it, a bruja who uses her abilities can burn her mind and body until there is nothing left. Of equal importance is the Mortiz *Book of Cantos*, an archive of generations of knowledge. Filled with personal wisdom, prayers, songs, tales, ceremonies, histories (related to ancestors, culture, and ritual), as well as encyclopedia-style entries, written in English and Spanish, it is the cornerstone of cultural practice within the Mortiz family. "It has every spell, prayer, and piece of information that our ancestors have collected from the beginning of our family line" (10). It tells a collective story about the magic central to their lives.

Alex wants nothing more than to break free of that story to choose a life of her own. Tey Diana Rebolledo and Eliana Rivero point out that "stories transmit moral values, tell us ideally how we should live, help distinguish correct behavior from incorrect, and identify those traits considered desirable by a group or society" (89). However, this is precisely the problem. Alex does not assign magic the same value as her mother and sisters, in part because she sees it as responsible for all the death and suffering that has touched her life. She thinks, "Magic killed my aunt Rosaria and Mama Juanita. My magic killed Miluna and set my father running. I could have hurt Rishi the other day. It destroys" (46). From Alex's point of view, magic forecloses all other possibilities before she even has time to understand what they are or who she is independent of it. The impending mantle of bruja troubles her in a way that it does not her sisters.

The quest to retrieve her family requires that Alex not only explore the full range of her powers, but that she master them, if she is to have any chance at saving her loved ones. It is an effort she does not undertake alone. Nova, a brujo revealed to have not had a Deathday, leads her on the journey to Los Lagos, a realm overseen by a powerful bruja known as the Destroyer, who, along with devouring life and magic, holds Alex's family captive. Rishi joins them, having followed Alex into the portal without her knowledge. As they travel together, Alex realizes that she is attracted to both Nova, at least until she discovers his betrayal, and Rishi. Her emergent bisexuality is far less complicated than her relationship to magic.

Alex's refusal to accept magic indiscriminately places her family in peril. It is also what allows her to defeat the Destroyer, with the help of her ancestors, rescue her family, and free her Aunt Rosaria, who is installed as the new protector of Los Lagos and will oversee its restoration. Through these efforts and more, Alex brings substantial change to an enslaved world, but does so by accepting the blessings of her family and her role as an encantrix. Back at home, the changes are on a smaller scale but no less important. Alex divulges her love for Rishi to her mother. She responds by inviting Rishi to Alejandra's second Deathday celebration and into their family of brujas. In the end, Alex recognizes and embraces her identity as an "encantrix, a bruja, a girl" (312).

Sierra and Alex are the chosen ones, the most powerful young women in their respective cultural traditions. They are a vision of heroism that we do not see nearly enough, but the question remains whether their stories resonate with audiences outside of the Latinx community. Both books have been well-received by a wide range of readers. For example, *Shadowshaper* has 3.8 (out of 4) rating on *Goodreads*, a website where readers can post book reviews. Similarly, *Labyrinth Lost* has a score of 3.7, with readers responding positively to the fictional cultural practices represented in the story. Both have been optioned for adaptation in other media: *Shadowshaper* in television and film, and *Labyrinth Lost* in film. Whether either will ever be made remains to be seen. In a time when Latinos are being narrated as criminals or a drain on economic resources almost daily, we need counter stories, particularly those highlighting Latinx heroism, now more than ever.

Waiting for Our Wakanda

For years, film studios insisted that movies with non-white leads fail to do well in the overseas markets. The reason was more of an excuse for their lack of effort to promote the films overseas, but it also meant that studios did not have to actively work to diversify the mainstream films it made and produced. And then *Black Panther* (2017) happened. With an African American director, majority black cast, a range of black characters, not to mention its focus on a fictional technologically advanced kingdom in Africa, the film gave audiences a superhero that defied previous representational limitations. Grossing more than seven million in the domestic market and one billion worldwide, the film was an unqualified blockbuster. Some attributed its success to its attachment to the Marvel universe and Disney machine, but, as Alissa Wilkinson rightly asserts, "Because the decision-makers at movie studios don't expect a 'black movie' to do well, they're less likely to allocate the kind of resources that can help a film become a hit." *Black Panther*'s remarkable performance at the box office should have dispelled the old pretext about films with black leads, yet it was not long before talk emerged about the film being a "one off" success. However, the film was successful in large part because people want to see themselves represented in the cultural forms they consume, a point supported by the fact that "in the U.S., 37% of the movie's overall audience was African-American, which is well

above the norm as the average movie audience is about 15% African-American"
(Huddleston Jr.). The film industry, like the publishing industry, functions along
a black and white axis in terms of diversity and representation. So despite the
fact that Latinos are the largest growing demographic in the nation, there were
more children's books published by and about Africans and African Americans
than Latinos.

Publishers have seen great success with Angie Thomas's *New York Times*
best-selling book *The Hate You Give* (2017) and Nicola Yoon's *Everything,
Everything* (2015), both YA contemporary novels focusing on black protagonists
that have been made into feature films starring Amandla Stenberg, who played
Rue in the *Hunger Games* (2012). Neither of these books has reached the fever
pitch of a Potter or Everdeen, but they do represent a significant intervention
in the types of stories being told for largescale audiences. Latinx readers of
YA are still waiting for our Wakanda moment in books and film. We have yet
to see a YA book with a Latinx lead catch fire or capture the imaginations on
a scale that de la Peña imagined. We deserve to see ourselves as heroes and
heroines in stories of our own making, ones that cast aside tired tropes to
reflect contemporary concerns and fantastical feats in this world and any others
we can envision. *Shadowshaper* and *Labyrinth Lost* show us what is possible
when outsiders and afuerxs move to the center of story, remaking narrative
and genre in process.

Notes

1. In the author's note, Cordova states, "Alex's ancestors come from Ecuador, Spain, Africa,
Mexico, and the Carribean" (318).

2. A term popularized by *Harry Potter* fandom to refer to the three main characters in the
series: Harry, Ron, and Hermione ("Trio")

3. In response to racist outrage about "black Hermione," Rowling famously tweeted,
"Canon: brown eyes, frizzy hair and very clever. White skin was never specified. Rowling loves
black Hermione."

4. Kate Capshaw's "Ethnic Studies and Children's Literature: A Conversation Between
Fields," Marilisa Jiménez García's "Side-by-Side: At the Intersection of Latinx Studies and
ChYALit," Oralia Garza de Cortés and Jennifer Battle's "The Politics of Publishing Latino
Children's Books," Phillip Nel's *Was the Cat in the Hat Black? The Hidden Racism of Children's
Literature, and the Need for Diverse Books*, Ruth Quiroa's "Promising Portals and Safe Passages,"
and Debbie Reese's website "American Indian Children's Literature" are but a few resources that
address this issue.

5. Hachette Book Group, HarperCollins, MacMillan, Penguin/Random House, and Simon
and Schuster make up the big five.

6. According to the United States Census Bureau, in 2016, Hispanics or Latinos made up 17
percent (55 million) of the total US population.

7. A frequently cited example of this practice is Justine Larbalestier's *Liar* (2009), a novel about a young black woman with short natural hair who was depicted on the cover of advanced copies as a white girl with what appear to be blonde highlights.

Works Cited

Botelho, Maria José, and Masha Kabakow Rudman. *Critical Multicultural Analysis of Children's Literature: Mirrors, Windows, and Doors.* Routledge, 2009.

Capshaw, Katharine. "Ethnic Studies and Children's Literature: A Conversation Between Fields." *The Lion and the Unicorn*, vol 38, no. 3, 2014, pp. 237–57.

Coats, Karen. "Author Talkbalk: Daniel José Older." *The Bloomsbury Introduction to Children's and Young Adult Literature.* Bloomsbury, 2018. 367–68.

Córdova, Zoraida. *Labyrinth Lost.* Sourcelife, 2016.

Diaz, Shelley. "Q&A, Urban Fantasy as Counter-Narrative: Daniel José Older on Shadowshaper." School Library Journal. 16 Jun. 2015. https://www.slj.com/2015/06/interviews/qa-urban -fantasy-counter-narrative-daniel-jose- older-on-shadowshaper/#_ Web.

Garza de Cortés, Oralia, and Jennifer Battle. "Publishing Latino Children's Books." *Diversity in Youth Literature: Opening Doors through Reading*, edited by Jamie Campbell Naidoo and Sarah Park Dahlen. American Library Association, 2013, pp. 63–66.

"Hispanic or Latino Origin" *U.S. Census Bureau, 2012–2016 American Community Survey 5-Year Estimates.* https://factfinder.census.gov/faces/tableservices/jsf/pages/ productview .xhtml?src=bkmk

Huddleston Jr., Tom. "An Especially Diverse Audience Lifted 'Black Panther' to Record Box Office Heights." *Fortune*, 21 Feb. 2018. Web.

Jiménez Garcia, Marilisa. "Side-by-Side: At the Intersection of Latinx Studies and ChYALit." *The Lion and the Unicorn.* 21.1 (2017): 113–22.

@jk_rowling. "Canon: brown eyes, frizzy hair and very clever. White skin was never specified. Rowling loves black Hermione." Twitter. 21 Dec. 2015 2:41 a.m. https://twitter.com/jk_rowling /status/678888094339366914?lang=en Web.

Larrick, Nancy. "The All-White World of Children's Books." *The Saturday Review.* 11 Sept. 1965.

Mendlesohn, Farah. *Rhetorics of Fantasy.* Wesleyan University Press, 2008.

Miller, Laura. "A Guide to Vampire Fiction with Real Bite." *Salon.* 23 June 2009. Online.

Myers, Christopher. "The Apartheid of Children's Literature." *New York Times.* 15 Mar. 2014. Web.

Nel, Phillip. *Was the Cat in the Hat Black? The Hidden Racism of Children's Literature, and the Need for Diverse Books.* Oxford University Press, 2017.

Older, Daniel José. *Shadowshaper.* Arthur A. Levine, 2015.

"Publishing Statistics on Children's Books about People of Color and First/Native Nations and by People of Color and First/Native Nations Authors and Illustrators." *Cooperative Children's Book Center*, 25 May 2017. https://ccbc.education.wisc.edu/ books/pcstats.asp.

Pugh, Tison, and David L. Wallace. "Heteronormative Heroism and Queering the School Story in J. K. Rowling's *Harry Potter* Series." *Children's Literature Association Quarterly*, vol. 31, no. 3, 2006, pp. 260–281.

Reese, Debbie. *American Indians in Children's Literature.* 26 Jun. 2018. https://americanindians inchildrensliterature.blogspot.com/ 15 Jun. 2018.

Schutte, Anne. "It Matters If You're Black or White: The Racism of YA Book Covers." *The Hub*, yalsa.org. 10 Dec. 2012.

Strickland, Ashley. "Where's the African-American Harry Potter or the Mexican Katniss?" *cnn. com* 2. Jul. 2014. Web. https://www.cnn.com/2014/04/09/living/young-adult-books -diversity-identity/index.html.

"Trio." *Harry Potter Wiki*. http://harrypotter.wikia.com/wiki/Trio. Accessed 15 Jun. 2018.

West, Lindy. "I See White People: *Hunger Games* and a Brief History of Cultural Whitewashing." *Jezebel.com*. 27 March 2012. Web.

Wilkinson, Alissa. "Black Panther Crushed Overseas Sales Projections. Can We Stop Saying 'Black Films Don't Travel'?" *Vox*, 20 Feb. 2018. Web.

Yep, Laurence. "The Outsider in Fiction and Fantasy." *The English Journal* vol. 94, no. 3, 2005, pp. 52–54.

6

The Art of Afro-Latina
Consciousness-Raising in *Shadowshaper*

Ella Diaz

The cover of Daniel José Older's *Shadowshaper* announces, "Paint a mural. Start a battle. Change the world." The three simple sentences are surrounded by the visual language of street art and a commanding portrait of a young Afro-Latina who stares directly at viewers with her head raised slightly, demanding respect as she returns their gaze. Her natural hair swirls around her in a rainbow of highlights and the novel's title protrudes from her T-shirt, making a visual wordplay on *Shadowshaper*. Below her, the Brooklyn skyline is stenciled in magenta, simulating a color-blocking technique used in aerosol murals called "pieces" in the late-twentieth century and that transformed New York City's subway trains, tenement walls, and billboards into "a gallery of the streets."[1] The cover foreshadows the forthcoming journey that readers will take with Sierra Santiago, a Puerto Rican teenager who discovers that she is part of an ancestral line of spiritual leaders through making art. From mural-making and chalk-drawing to hair and fashion, Sierra literally learns another way to see herself and the world—a tool that proves necessary for combatting forces of cultural appropriation and gentrification in her Bedford-Stuyvesant neighborhood of Brooklyn, New York.

The cover's image and message gesture to the historical role of art in consciousness-raising—a transformational process in one's thinking through exposure to the elided histories, cultures, and spiritual beliefs of disenfranchised peoples in the United States. While consciousness-raising is an intellectual project, it begins in the body and, often, amidst immediate or sustained circumstances of oppression. At every stage of Sierra's journey,

Older underscores the corporeal experience of consciousness-raising. From the opening scene in which Sierra makes a mural for the first time to the pain she endures in confronting the misuse of her heritage as well as the cultural borders of Afro-Latinidad, Sierra's artistic evolution lays bare the coloniality of power in the built environments of modern nation-states and the structural inequalities that they maintain for working class people of color (Quijano).

In fighting back against the appropriation of her heritage by the unscrupulous anthropologist Jonathan Wick, for example, Sierra confronts the intellectual tradition in the United States of studying colonized peoples by containing and then dividing their histories, cultures, and art within academic disciplines. As Wick seeks to possess Sierra's spiritual power, he destroys everyone in his path with such abilities, resonating in the social-spatial encroachment and destruction of Sierra's neighborhood. The neoliberal forces of urban redevelopment that seize the buildings and open spaces of working-class people of color and push them out of their home-places is *not* analogous to colonization; rather, it is its very extension, as the customization, personalization, and collective memories of a built environment are disrupted and lost to posterity once local businesses close, buildings are razed, and neighbors are forced to move away.[2]

Drawing on popular trends of zombies, magic, and superheroes in young adult fiction and films, *Shadowshaper* is not set in a galaxy far away or a post-apocalyptic world of ambiguous districts of poor people working in service to a Capitol. Instead, Older stays close to home in Brooklyn, localizing Sierra amidst another wave of gentrification. In doing so, he taps the rich art history of New York City and other urban centers of civil rights mobilizations in which artists of color merged their political principles with creative acts of consciousness-raising. Following the 1960s and 1970s civil rights era and amid the rise of hip hop, street art exploded in New York City's working-class and racial and ethnic neighborhoods in the late 1970s and 1980s. While more individually driven than civil-rights-era art, street art builds on the collectivist values of self-determination with which African Americans and Latinx artists challenged the stereotypes of US mainstream culture.

Sierra's spiritual legacy, then, is part of a distinctive art history in the US during the late twentieth century and part of the colonial histories that shape diasporic memory and cultural heritage. Living in a neighborhood in flux, Sierra represents the "alien consciousness" with which Gloria Anzaldúa describes the "New Mestiza" as a "confluence of two or more genetic streams, with chromosomes constantly 'crossing over,'" a mixture that provides "a mutable, more malleable species with a rich gene pool" (99). Alien consciousness is not fixed or biologically determined; instead, it is performative and, for Sierra, a conduit through which she bridges the historical gaps of her knowledge as she learns to discern the "shadows" of Afro-Latinidad, an identity and culture that fuses multiple spatiotemporal realities.

Building the New, Old World: the Historical Shadows of Afro-Latinidad

In an interview with the *Guardian*, Daniel José Older discusses the origins of *Shadowshaper* and the influence that young adult fiction like *The Hunger Games* trilogy had on his work, particularly its lack of racial-ethnic diversity. For Older, the absence of people of color in future worlds "based on *this* world" reflects a "phenomenal lack of imagination" on behalf of authors. Considering that a central plotline of most fantasy and science fiction pertains to an individual or collective resistance to a status quo, Older's assertion is evinced by "the histories of many communities of color in the United States, and of many colonized and diasporic peoples of the (aptly named) 'New World'" (Ramírez, "Cyborg Feminism" 396). "To be able to figure out all these quirky things about what you imagine the future will be like," Older adds, "and not somehow have any folks of colour [sic] doing anything heroic or worthwhile in it, what happened? . . . Where did we go?" (Ford).

Older's questions resonate in Catherine Ramírez's meditations on the continual whitewashing of the science-fiction genre that fails to "link theories of race, class, gender, and sexuality" or explore "the relationship of African Americans and other people of color to the discourses of modernity" ("Afrofuturism/Chicanafuturism" 187). Drawing on Afrofuturism and the work of Octavia Butler, Ramírez proposes Chicanafuturism to foreground the diasporic experience of Mexican Americans and other mixed-race peoples in their everyday use of technology as expressions of "the colonial and postcolonial histories of *indigenismo, mestizaje*, hegemony, and survival" (187).[3] Reading Butler's black and female protagonists as the New Mestiza that Gloria Anzaldúa proposes in *Borderlands/La Frontera* (1987), Ramírez positions the "theory of 'alien' consciousness" as the speculative basis "of and for 'New World,' feminist science fiction"—an idea that extends Donna Haraway's concept of "cyborg identity" to women of color as subjects that both exceed and illuminate the boundaries of identity, community, and historical location ("Cyborg Feminism" 375).[4]

In her use of "alien," for example, Anzaldúa redirects the exclusionary function of the term in hegemonic discourse.[5] The ability to both see and be seen as "alien" makes assimilation impossible but is also an oppositional tool for the New Mestiza, who "endeavors to undo the legacies of patriarchy, homophobia, and white supremacy in the United States by rejecting Enlightenment epistemology and ontology, as represented in great part by empiricism and the Cartesian subject" (Ramírez, "Afrofuturism/Chicanafuturism" 189). Sierra is one such "alien" as readers meet her atop scaffolding and while making art publicly. Armed with a paint brush and her conscious streams of thought, which move back and forth between the creative task at hand and dialogue with other characters, Sierra begins to see the world differently, pushing her experience of reality beyond linear notions of past, present, and future.

In the middle of making her first mural, Sierra is in dual conversations with herself and "Manny the Domino King." A close friend of her grandfather Lázaro, Manny invited Sierra to create a mural on a wall of the neighborhood's eyesore that borders the "Junklot," where he and "the other older guys play dominos" (2). The wall belongs to a "five-story concrete monstrosity" called the Tower that sits vacant "on a block otherwise full of brownstones" (2). Having built its outer structure, the developers abandoned it with "unpaned windows staring emptily out into the Brooklyn skies" (2). Questioned from below by Manny who notices her staring at another mural, Sierra dismisses his concern, but thinks to herself, "Blatant lie," and glances "down from the scaffolding to where Manny the Domino King stood with arms crossed over his chest. 'You sure?' he said. 'Yeah'" (1). Sierra's lie is that she had already stopped painting because she noticed the portrait of a recently passed community elder, Papa Acevedo, appeared to be crying. Backtracking in her mind to when she arrived at the Junklot to work on her enormous dragon mural, Sierra witnessed Papa Acevedo's mural fade at an unusual rate. Now she sees a "single tear" glistening from the corner of his painted eye.

As a closeted artist who fills "notebook after notebook with wild creatures and winged, battle-ready versions of her friends and neighbors," Sierra is anxious about creating her first public mural since, if "she messed up, all of Brooklyn would see it" (2–3). But Manny persisted in his request, convincing Sierra to do it by telling her that Lázaro would have wanted her to, if he was able to talk following his stroke (3). Between worrying about her public debut as an artist, her bewilderment over the changes to Papa Acevedo's mural, and her exchanges with Manny, Sierra continues to dab "dark green paint along the neck of the dragon [that] reared all the way up to the fifth floor of the Tower," which she "could tell . . . was gonna be fierce" (2). With most of the dragon's body an outline, Sierra shades "rows of scales and spines, and smiled at how the creature seemed to come to life a fraction more with each new detail" (2). Sierra's pleasure over the mural as it comes into being alludes to consciousness-raising as a performative act that fosters intellectual transformation. What is alive, what is real, and who decides are the subtext of the details with which

Older characterizes Sierra's natural artistic abilities over formal arts training. Drawing the dragon's form and instinctively filling it in, Sierra's creative process destabilizes Eurocentric notions of art and ontology, both of which detach the artist from the art object, codifying the borders between human and nonhuman in subject-object relationships. Not knowing what will come into being but taking pleasure in its incarnation, Sierra's consciousness blurs with the dragon, upending empirical boundaries of the individual that are central to western notions of truth, genius, and the life "form."

It is no coincidence, then, that the opening scene of Sierra making a mural evokes 1960s and 1970s artists of color whose work disrupted Eurocentric traditions of art—from the separation of aesthetics and politics to material choices and the hierarchy of forms. As artists of color pushed back against their exclusions from the museums and canons of art history, women artists of color also challenged the patriarchal cultural norms within their racial-ethnic communities that disapproved or denied them public roles and spaces to create art. Las Mujeres Muralistas, for example, a Chicana and Latina arts collective in San Francisco, produced eleven murals in the city's Mission District by 1977.[6] Chicana artist Yolanda M. López created works that inverted traditional representations of Chicanas and Latinas in mainstream and Latinx cultures. Sierra's artistic foremothers also includes Judith Baca, who revolutionized community muralism in Los Angeles during the late 1960s and 1970s, establishing the Social Public Arts Center (SPARC) to support community muralism. In recalling Sierra's location on top of scaffolding, Baca produced a set of instructions for "women artists on the logistics of 'working outdoors on a large scale,'" including how to "successfully construct such large objects as one- or two-story scaffolds" (Gaspar de Alba 121). By distributing *Women's Manual: How to Assemble Scaffolding*, Baca circumvented the sexist notion that "women were physically not able and politically not 'meant' to create murals, to build and climb scaffolding, to be on public display and withstand the comments of passersby" (Gaspar de Alba 121).

While Sierra literally stands on the art infrastructure built by women of color in the 1960s and 1970s, her immediate predecessor is Sandra Fabara, better known as Lady Pink, whose presence in the evolution of street art dovetailed with the rise of hip hop culture. Born in Ecuador and raised in Queens, Lady Pink painted subway trains between 1979 and 1985, and her public role as one of the only Latina artists amongst all-male crews of "writers" exemplifies the persistence of gendered exclusions in public art-making, despite earlier inroads made by women in the civil rights era.[7] Aware of the double bind of race and gender for female artists of color in the twenty-first century, Older addresses the exclusions by opening *Shadowshaper* with Sierra's conversations with Manny over her mural.

In fact, Manny's invitation to Sierra to make a mural on the Tower's wall is also permission for her to enter the Junklot, an androcentric space claimed by an older generation of men. When Sierra calls out to Manny to ask if he is absolutely sure that she can paint on the Tower's wall, he replies, "That's why we asked you to do it. We hate the Tower. We spit on the Tower. Your paint is our nasty loogie, hocked upon the stupidity that is the Tower" (2). The collective "we" is ambiguous, but it suggests that the Junklot is not discarded space to those who use it and, as readers learn, the male elders of the community who are the eyes and ears of the neighborhood.[8] Sierra's mural, alongside Papa Acevedo's memorial mural, is a community's response to an architectural "monstrosity" that represents more than an incompatible building in a longtime Afro-Latinx community. The Tower is the physical sign of encroachment, a marker of the vulnerability of a working-class neighborhood of people of color that is perceived by city officials and redevelopers as vacant, resonating with the fifteenth century's doctrine of discovery, and with seventeenth-century legal concepts like "terra nullius," which allowed European colonial powers to take control of land presumed uninhabited or that no other colonial powers had claimed (Fitzmaurice 302). Thus, Sierra's mural *strikes back*—marking the Junklot as a home-place, belonging to the people who use it, the community that knows it, and the diasporic memories it houses.

The importance of diasporic memory in the built environments of Afro-Latinx neighborhoods, to which Older alludes with the Junklot, echoes in the colonial histories of forced removals of indigenous and African peoples during the European formation of the "new world." It also resonates in the succession of urban renewal programs in the mid- to late twentieth century that pushed people of color out of their home-places, producing a collective trauma that clinical psychiatrist Mindy Thompson Fullilove calls "root shock" (quoted in Lipsitz 6).[9] Gentrification is not a natural or random result of a capitalist system with no connections to structural inequalities in the United States (Mirabal 16). Instead, it is calculated and predictable in who it effects, demonstrated by its historical patterns and repetitions. Following the devastating fires and razing of buildings that destroyed whole neighborhoods in the South Bronx in the early to mid-twentieth century and amid redevelopment plans for the Cross-Bronx Expressway, people of color reclaimed "the rubble-strewn lots where multistory buildings once stood" (Sciorra and Cooper 156). El Barrio (East Harlem), the Lower East Side, and Brooklyn also endured decades of urban "renewal." Communities responded in multiple ways, but a central response for Afro-Latinx residents was the construction of *casitas* in open lots.

A form of Caribbean vernacular architecture, *casitas* are associated with Puerto Rico's working poor and, in their materials and shape, recall the nineteenth-century rural countryside of Puerto Rico (Sciorra and Cooper 156–57). In the late twentieth century, *casitas* fostered place consciousness for Puerto Ricans and other diasporic peoples in New York City, as they held cultural celebrations, community meetings, and cultivated fresh food in proximity to *casitas*.

Casita culture, then, is "not merely a nostalgic lament for an idealized past but a form of community organization whereby control of one's immediate environment is achieved through the use of traditional expressive culture" (Sciorra and Cooper 158).[10] For Manny and "the other older guys," the Junklot is a space in which they express common bonds of a shared identity that is tied to the land—their neighborhood—linking the threat of immediate displacement to diasporic memories of forced removal. While Manny does not own the Junklot, he performs rights of ownership by inviting Sierra to paint a mural on one of its bordering walls. His gesture reveals that spatial relationships are more complicated than Eurocentric constructs of individual property rights, which are predicated on seventeenth-century doctrine that emerged during the transatlantic slave trade and the seizures of indigenous peoples' lands. This is an important point to make in reading Sierra as the New Mestiza with an alien consciousness because her ability to see her world differently is not only intuitive or spiritual; rather, it is performative and intergenerational, as elders like Manny pass on traditions of resistance to social-spatial encroachment.

"In theorizing 'alien' consciousness," Ramírez writes, "Anzaldúa draws a parallel between the splitting of the land and the splitting of the racialized, sexualized, and colonized subject (i.e., the queer *India/mestiza*) and for whom it is and was home" ("Cyborg Feminism" 389). Anzaldúa tracks the spatiotemporal succession of colonial rule to the nineteenth century, when "the Gringo, locked into the fiction of white superiority, seized complete political power, stripping Indians and Mexicans of their land while their feet were still rooted in it. . . . we were jerked out by the roots, truncated, disemboweled, dispossessed, and separated from our identity and our history" (29–30). The resonance with Fullilove's concept of "root shock" to describe the collective trauma of urban displacement in the twentieth century is palpable, as the images of indigenous and mestiza/o bodies ripped from the land extends to African slaves who were also dispossessed of their native heritages. These are two of the spatiotemporal locations in which Afro-Latinidad occurs and in which Sierra enters the serpent in the Anzaldúan sense, but in her case in a dragon mural, which comes into being as she begins to discern movement in the memorial mural of a recently departed community elder.

The Corporeality of Consciousness-Raising and the Intentionality of Chalk Drawing

The coloniality of power in the built environments of modern nation-states and the structural inequalities that they maintain for people of color converge in the colorism and gendered expectations and exclusions that Sierra encounters at home with her mother, aunt, and grandfather. While each encounter varies in degree of psychological harm, they are connected in the evolution of Sierra's alien consciousness, which Older describes through intimate details of Sierra's internal dialogue and sensory experiences. Sierra's confrontations with family elders maintains a level of tension in the novel that resonates in Anzaldúa's description of nepantla as a "space between two bodies of water, the space between two worlds. It is a limited space . . . where you are not this or that but where you are changing . . . it is very awkward, uncomfortable and frustrating . . . because you are in the midst of transformation" (237). While Sierra is not literally in a space between two bodies of water, she is near the Atlantic Ocean and specifically Coney Island. As an origin point for the African diaspora in the western hemisphere, the Atlantic Ocean is the site of rupture, fragmentation, and loss for Afro-Latinx peoples, whose histories are tied to the transatlantic slave trade. Meanwhile, Coney Island, which has undergone its own gentrification process, is where Sierra converges with the spirit world and reunites with Lucera, the mysterious female shadowshaper who Sierra learns is her grandmother.

Sierra's proximity to the Atlantic Ocean as a body of water that is key to her consciousness-raising is not the only catalyst of her transformation, however. She also confronts the cultural borders of Afro-Latinidad. The racism and sexism introduced to conquered peoples during colonial rule reverberate in the colorism and heteronormative gender norms of Sierra's family, which mirror the structures of power in the gentrified spaces of her neighborhood that are hostile to her racialized and gendered body. Yet within the matrix of social, spatial, and cultural borders, Sierra and her friends build an alternative kinship that restores their sense of belonging as they acknowledge and, really, love each other's differences. Her introduction to shadowshaping via Robbie, offers Sierra another way to continue building her alternative family that, eventually, will include her biological family. Learning to blur her vision in order to see differently and utilizing urban art strategies like chalk drawing, Sierra moves within and beyond the essentialist logic of gender and racial binaries.

When Sierra returns home from working on her mural to get ready for a party, she becomes self-conscious of her appearance when her mother María asks her, "Why aren't you changed?" and adds rhetorically, "I thought you were ready" (10). Looking down at herself, Sierra now feels *unready* as she rethinks the combat boots that she had "been painting in, and her fro [that] stretched magnificently around her in a fabulous, unbothered halo" (10). Her best friend Bennie, who has been waiting for her, interrupts the matriarchal disapproval. "I think you look great, Sierra!"

Bennie also comforts Sierra later in the novel, when Sierra encounters her Tía Rosa while helping her mother prepare *arroz con pollo* for dinner. At first, her aunt playfully teases Sierra about her new love interest, Robbie; but her joking quickly turns to an act of shaming when Rosa learns he is Haitian. "What did Tía Virginia used to say? . . . If he's darker than the bottom of your foot, he's no good for you!" (77). Rosa's articulation of the racist saying of another family elder reveals how colonial racism is passed down between generations. Admonishing Sierra for her interest in Robbie, Rosa next turns her attack on her niece, scorning her "wild and nappy" hair and leaving Sierra shaken as the words break the "force field" of her afro.

Descending into an abyss of memories in which her skin color was judged by others and that once even she described as "the color of coffee with not enough milk," Sierra distills the pain into a single message of not being enough as a person (79–80). She fights her way to the surface by staring in the mirror and declaring, "I am Sierra María Santiago. I am what I am. Enough" (80). Composed "enough" to leave the house and go see Bennie, Sierra arrives despondent. But Bennie, who earlier insisted on braiding Sierra's hair before her date with Robbie, soothes Sierra—telling her random gossip as she fixes her hair until Sierra is ready to talk (83). Benny's act is a decolonial one because it is not compulsory or transactional; rather it is a gesture of love and part of an expressive tradition (like preparing *arroz con pollo* for a family dinner) that restores Sierra through care and comfort.

In addition to Bennie's gestures of love to Sierra, their other friends, who include Izzy and Tee, a queer couple implicitly accepted by the social circle, tease each other about their appearances, as well as about Sierra's interest in Robbie, the "Weirdo McPainting Dude" and "Cartoon-Covered Haitian Sensation" (14). While their banter seemingly echoes the verbal exclusions of Sierra's mother and aunt, the playful rhetoric counters the exclusionary logic of the status quo and the colonial logic of Afro-Latinidad by establishing kinship through their perceived differences. "*Los atravesados*," Anzaldúa writes, "live here: the squint eyed, the perverse, the queer, the troublesome, the mongrel, the mulato . . . in short, those who cross over, pass over, or go through the confines of the 'normal'" (25). In listing the derogatory terms, Anzaldúa creates a textual space that, like the banter of Sierra and her friends, undoes the categories of exclusion as together they exceed the binary logic of what is and what is not "normal" through shared bonds of transgression.

In Sierra's navigations of the colorism and gendered expectations of her family, readers also learn how she became dispossessed of her knowledge of shadowshaping via her grandfather. Sierra begins to seek information from Lázaro, either in moments of his clarity or by scanning the photographs of community elders that adorn his walls. She learns that Lázaro originally welcomed anthropologist Jonathan Wick into the inner circle of shadowshapers and against the wishes of Lucera, who disappeared as Wick began to pursue her. Sierra also learns that her mother María is aware of shadowshaping but renounced it as young woman seeking mainstream acceptance and then denying any knowledge of it to Sierra—an act that pushed Lázaro to pursue only male successors, including Sierra's brother Juan.

Another male successor is Robbie, who Lázaro urges Sierra to find and ask for his help in completing her mural. "'Robbie from school?' Sierra said. 'Abuelo, how do you even know him?' Robbie was a tall Haitian kid . . . with a goofy grin and wild drawings covering every surface of his clothes, his backpack, and desk. If Sierra had been the kind of girl who gave a damn about boys and their cuteness, Robbie the Walking Mural would find himself somewhere on her top-ten list" (9). While the reference to the 1970s Chicana/o art collective Asco via the "walking mural" is, perhaps, unintentional by Older, it connects Robbie to civil rights-era art and positions him as a teacher of a particular mode of collaborative and performative arts-making. The title "walking mural" is one of several conceptual works that Asco enacted to push the boundaries of Chicana/o muralism through performative processions, anticipating the look and style of street art in the 1980s and 1990s.

But before Sierra learns the art of shadowshaping from Robbie, she endures a painful encounter with a "throng haint," created by Wick to hunt down shadowshapers and find Lucera. A "throng haint," Robbie explains to Sierra after her attack, materializes "when someone—someone powerful—uses binding magic to enslave a group of spirits and then fuses them together into a huge shadow" (128). The crisis the encounter causes Sierra—the restriction of movement and her inability to breathe, marks the critical turn described by Anzaldúa in her explanation of nepantla.

After visiting Club Kalfour with Robbie to check out his murals and witness the spirits dancing on the walls to the music of the club's Haitian band, Sierra is attacked on a "quasi-suburban enclave of stand-alone houses" in Flatbush (101). The attack follows Robbie and Sierra's encounters with two "corpuscles," or zombie-like entities that are the bodies of recently departed persons but possessed by a spirit under the control of Wick. When Sierra heads off in another direction from the corpuscule, she feels a different presence following her. Disoriented by her surroundings and exhausted from running, Sierra stops to confront the throng haint. Unable to see it, she hears shrieks of pain as the spirits wrestle with their binding and the chorus of voices demands to know where Lucera is. Ensnared in what feels like an invisible net, the supernatural force grabs her as "every cell in [her] body caught fire" while a "cool, horrible presence crawled under her skin" (104). As the darkness envelops her, Sierra collapses to the ground (104).

The sounds of the throng haint are also interspersed with other voices that are equally troubling to Sierra. These voices seem farther away to her as she languishes on the ground. They do not want to know where Lucera is but, instead, ask if someone has called the police or if anyone is going to help the young woman, to which another voice exclaims, "She must be another OD from that damn Dominican club over on Flatbush!" (105–6). The following night, after Sierra's brother Juan saves her from the throng haint's attack, Sierra's pain is compounded by the memory of these voices. Recalling her experience to Robbie, Sierra says, "The creature didn't hurt me, I don't think [but] I've never felt so close to death, so at the mercy of something so huge and terrible. And no one in that neighborhood would help; they just thought I was another drunk Puerto Rican from the club" (123). Sierra's distress includes her grief over the fact that no one helped her, which is part of the problem that gentrification causes. Along with changing the color and income of working-class neighborhoods, gentrification codifies racist assumptions of who belongs and does not belong in a neighborhood—the underpinning of which is who is and is not a human being.[11] The negation of her humanity in Flatbush causes an intellectual crisis that lingers for Sierra long after the physical assault by the throng haint ends.

Thus, while Older introduces supernatural elements in *Shadowshaper*, his story is not merely fantasy or dystopian science fiction. For Afro-Latinx communities, colonial appropriations of their cultures, forced removals from their land, and contemporary encroachments on their home-places is part of their historical experience and reality; but so is art as a form of resistance. Art has always been a valuable tool and a political weapon for colonized and oppressed peoples in their constant struggle to exist inside and *alongside* colonial modernity.

One of the art forms with which Sierra learns to resist Wick's destructive force is chalk drawing, an art form with deep roots in New York City. Although chalk drawing or "chalking" is now mainstream, and even considered mundane on college campuses and in suburban neighborhoods, its history as an intentional subversion of Eurocentric values of art and property rights continues in the twenty-first century. From the glowing baby symbols that Keith Haring chalked all over New York City's subway stations in the late 1970s and 1980s to Jean-Michel Basquiat and Al Diaz's moniker, "SAMO," for "same old shit," which they typically spray-painted but sometimes chalked on tenement walls, chalking also characterizes James De La Vega's public art in New York City. A Latino artist from El Barrio, De La Vega began chalking simple line drawings of fish and other figures with direct messages like "you are more powerful than you think" and "become your dream" on the sidewalks and streets of East Harlem in the early twenty-first century.[12] While De La Vega has publicly asserted that his chalk art is meant to inspire and uplift, he also knows that "words are weapons"—the consequences of which is the criminalization of artists who write and draw in public space (Ross).[13]

Chalking creates a different relationship to the built-environment by explicitly challenging the accepted boundaries of public space and private property, or who owns the sidewalks and streets, the abandoned walls, or subway stations and trains, all of which are considered transactional space or non-places—until someone marks them. Chalk art, then, gives pause to passersby, altering their experience of the city, which corresponds to the ontological shift that Sierra experiences when she heads out into the city under the cover of night with Robbie to learn how to shadowshape. Instructing Sierra to squint her eyes in order to see the spirits around her, Robbie makes a simple chalk drawing on the ground, explaining, "It doesn't have to be perfect, okay? You just want some semblance of what you're thinking" (134). Sierra pushes him for more information to understand the relationship between the spirit, the art, and herself: "'So it doesn't have to be, like . . . my dead relatives that go into my pictures, right?' 'Nah,' Robbie replies, 'it can be any spirit. Like I said, you'll attract likeminded ones with your *intentionality*'" (emphasis mine, 135). Heeding his instructions, Sierra lets "her vision blur and almost immediately saw a tall figure slow-stepping toward them" (136). Dropping to one knee, she "touched her right hand to Robbie's drawing," and braces for the "spirit to dive into her," as a "rush of coolness burst through her [and] streamed along her raised arm, past her chest and down to her right hand. Sierra's eyes flew open as the chalk man shuddered against the pavement and then scattered into nothing" (136–37).

In contrast with the physical restriction that Sierra experiences with the throng haint, the rush of coolness culminates in release, as her body serves as a conduit through which the spirit enters and then transcends her. But since the chalk drawing is not of her making, the connection between her and the form is lost. Concerned for the spirit's whereabouts, Sierra asks

Robbie what happened to it, and he explains that the spirit has moved on since it is not bound to the physical form, but that "it's an exchange. You give them form, they work for you—*with* you, ideally toward your goal" (136). The shared consciousness between the artist and spirit is key to the intention of shadowshaping, suggesting a mutualism that is unlike western notions of individual genius in art-making.

Trying again, Sierra takes a piece of chalk from Robbie and sketches "a girl in a ninja outfit." She then closes her eyes and reopens them halfway to blur her vision. A spirit glides across the path towards Sierra as she raises her left hand. "Just as the shadow reached her, she smacked her drawing with her right hand. The coolness slid through her faster this time, a rushing stream that burst out her fingertips" (137–38). As Sierra feels the spirits pass through her, she "erases the boundaries of identity and consciousness by experiencing others' physical sensations as if they were her own" ("Cyborg Feminism" 386). Shadowshaping is not an essentialist project, since Sierra is not drawing (on) her "dead relatives" or enslaving a spirit with binding magic, both of which suggest the confines of inherited knowledge and the limitations of individual desires. Rather, shadowshaping is a performative tool—an art form that is part of an expressive tradition and based on intentional exchanges between the past and present in service to a future world in which the New Mestiza uses her abilities to transcend the colonial limitations of race and gender.

Notes

1. Joe Austin explains that "graffiti" is known as writing in the urban art community and terms like "piece," short for masterpiece, include a writer's name in "elaborate, abstracted letter style characteristic of that particular writer" and a background of "urban landscapes" (37). In *Toward a People's Art: The Contemporary Mural Movement* (1977), Eva Cockcroft et al. characterize the 1967 *Wall of Respect* in Chicago as "not exactly a mural, nor was it simply a gallery in the streets. Its purpose was not to bring aesthetic enlightenment to an area too poor to support even a nominal art fair, but to use art publicly to express the experience of a people. It was a collective art, an event" (2–3). Unlike 1960s and 1970s community murals, street art in the late 1980s and 1990s did not center on collective action, but individual artists making names for themselves by marking space. I use the quote in a way not intended by authors to connect the two eras of urban-based art.

2. "Identity," Dolores Hayden writes, "is intimately tied to memory: both our personal memories (where we have come from and where we have dwelt) and the collective or social memories interconnected with the histories of our families, neighbors, fellow workers, and ethnic communities. . . . Decades of 'urban renewal' and 'redevelopment' of a savage kind have taught many communities that when the urban landscape is battered, important collective memories are obliterated" (9).

3. Crossing academic disciplines to account for Chicanafuturism, Ramírez maps a visual and performance art history in the sculptural and visual artwork of Marion C. Martinez, and performance art by Guillermo Gómez Peña, Roberto Sifuentes, and others to explore the impact of science, technology, and trilateral economic treaties on Mexican, Chicanx, and Latinx peoples. Ramírez also historicizes Chicanafuturism through Luis Valdez's *Los Vendidos* (1967), an acto (a short skit with an activist message) in which he presents a series of Chicano automatons to critique reductive representations of Mexicans and Mexican Americans in US mainstream culture ("Afrofuturism/Chicanafuturism" 189).

4. Ramírez frames her comparative analysis of Butler and Anzaldúa through the lenses of "essence" and "position" to account for both the unfixed identities of women of color as "cyborgs" and the histories that made them. She unpacks her assertion that "Butler's black heroines and Anzaldúa's queer mestiza subject differ from a more generic cyborg because they also emphasize very particular New World histories (African American and Chicana, respectively)" ("Cyborg Feminism" 394).

5. Anzaldúa also uses "extraterrestrial" in descriptions of the New Mestiza and Ramírez writes that to her knowledge, "few critics have scrutinized Anzaldúa's assertion that queer subjects connect different racial and national groups with 'extraterrestrials.'" ("Cyborg Feminism" 393).

6. Original members of Mujeres Muralista include Patricia Rodriguez. Graciela Carrillo, Irene Pérez, Venezuelan artist Consuelo Méndez, and later Ester Hernández (Gaspar de Alba 121).

7. Fabara's status as "the first lady of graffiti" disseminated beyond New York City's boroughs through her prominent role in Charlie Ahearn's *Wild Style* (1982), a film that documented and dramatized the graffiti and hip-hop ethos of the urban center in the 1980s. See Fabara's website: http://www.ladypinknyc.com/about/.

8. Manny is not only the domino king, but also "published, wrote, and delivered the *Bed-Stuy Searchlight*, churning out the three pages of local gossip and event updates from a little basement printing press over on Ralph Avenue" (4).

9. Lipsitz provides a relentless list of policies over the twentieth century, from the Federal Housing Act of 1934 to the implementation of redlining by the Federal Housing Agency, in order to upend the false but prevalent assumption in mainstream culture that racism is individual and not structural or government-subsidized, and therefore a thing of the past (2006, 2; 6; 20).

10. When New York City officials attempted to regulate the "illegal structures" in 1978 with the implementation of the GreenThumb program, Afro-Latina/o residents continued to build *casitas* and "in compliance with their own needs and aspirations" (Sciorra and Cooper 157).

11. The danger of being in the wrong neighborhood is broached earlier in the novel, when Older references a memorial mural to Vincent, Bennie's brother, who was killed by police (33). Death by gentrification is an ongoing problem for brown and black youth, as Alejandro "Alex" Nieto'a killing by San Francisco police made clear in 2014. The reference to Vincent's memorial mural also recalls Puerto Rican and African American aerosol murals in New York City in the 1990s, as documented by Martha Cooper and Joseph Sciorra in *R.I.P.: New York Spraycan Memorials* (1994).

12. In Los Angeles in the 1970s, chalking was advocated by various *centros* like the Centro Joaquin Murrieta, Karen Mary Davalos writes, "as an art form that did not rely on financial transactions by producing 'chalk-ins' in Belvedere Park" (69).

13. De La Vega was arrested in 2003 while painting a mural on the side of a Bronx warehouse and faced more serious charges because he had a prior conviction in 1999 for painting "Become Your Dream" on the side of a supermarket, which he had permission to do from the owner. See http://www.nytimes.com/2004/04/13/nyregion/a-jumping-fish-in-the -bronx-lands-its-creator-in-criminal-court.html.

Works Cited

Anzaldúa, Gloria. *Borderlands La Frontera: The New Mestiza*. 2nd ed., Aunt Lute Books, 1999.

Austin, Joe. "The Name and the City: Writing as an Illegal Art." *Public Art Review* vol. 8, no.2, 1995, pp. 36–37.

Cockcroft, Eva, John Pitman Weber, and James Cockcroft. *Toward a People's Art: The Contemporary Mural Movement*. 2nd ed., University of New Mexico Press, 1998.

Davalos, Karen Mary. *Chicana/o Remix: Art and Errata Since the Sixties*. New York University Press, 2017.

Fitzmaurice, Andrew. *Sovereignty, Property, and Empire, 1500–2000*. Cambridge University Press, 2017.

Ford, Ashley C. "Daniel José Older Creates Female Black Heroes to Make Fantasy More Real." theguardian.com, 25 Jun. 2015, https://www.theguardian.com/books/2015/jun/29/daniel-jose -older-black-heroes-ya-science-fiction?CMP=share_btn_link. Accessed December 15, 2017.

Fullilove, Mindy Thompson *Root Shock: How Tearing Up City Neighborhoods Hurts American, and What We Can Do About It*. 2nd ed., New Village Press, 2016.

Gaspar de Alba, Alicia. *Chicano Art: Inside Outside the Master's House, Cultural Politics and the CARA Exhibition*. University of Texas Press, 1998.

Hayden, Dolores. *The Power of Place: Urban Landscapes as Public History*. MIT Press, 1997.

Lipsitz, George. *The Possessive Investment in Whiteness: How White People Profit from Identity Politics*. Temple University Press, 2006.

Mirabal, Nancy Raquel. "Geographies of Displacement: Latina/os, Oral History, and the Politics of Gentrification in San Francisco's Mission District." *Public Historian*, vol. 31, no. 2, 2009, pp. 7–31.

Older, Daniel José. *Shadowshaper*. Scholastic, Inc., 2015.

Quijano, Anibal. "Coloniality of Power, Eurocentrism, and Latin America." *Nepantla*, vol. 1, no. 3, 2000, pp. 533–80.

Ramírez, Catherine S. "Afrofuturism/Chicanafuturism: Fictive Kin." *Aztlán: A Journal of Chicano Studies*, vol. 33, no. 1, 2008, pp. 185–94.

Ramírez, Catherine S. "Cyborg Feminism: The Science Fiction of Octavia E. Butler and Gloria Anzaldúa." *Reload: Rethinking Women + Cyberculture*, edited by Mary Flanagan and Austin Booth, MIT Press, 2002, pp. 374–402.

Ross, Barbara. "NYC Street Artist Says Apple Stole His Inspirational Slogan for iPhone 5 Ad Campaign." nydailynews.com, 12 May 2014, http://www.nydailynews.com/new- york/nyc -street-artist-apple-stole-slogan-article-1.1788402. Accessed February 12, 2018.

Sciorra, Joseph and Martha Cooper, "'I Feel Like I'm in My Country': Puerto Rican Casitas in New York City." *TDR*, vol. 34, no. 4, 1990, pp. 156–68.

Section 3

LatiNerds
and
Bookworms

7

The Smartest Girl in the World: Normalizing Intellectualism through Representations of Smart Latinx Youth on Stage

Roxanne Schroeder-Arce

Media and other forms of popular culture continue to provide negative stereotypes of the Latinx community in relation to intellectualism and education in the US. Scholar Ruth Enid Zambrana speaks to such stereotypes. "Media as a socialization mechanism conveys negative identity markers to Latino youth that is detrimental to their social and psychological well-being. . . . A transformation of the social constructions of Latino identity in both media and scholarly work is urgently needed to reverse the misinformed representations and omissions of positive benchmarks" (225). In other words, Latinx youth call for narratives that counter representations perpetuating stereotypical notions of their ethnic group. One such stereotype is that of the uneducated, stupid Latinx. Latinx youth need to see representations of Latinx individuals engaging with education, intellectual curiosity, and different ways of being smart. Other marginalized racial and ethnic groups experience similar marginalization and youth carrying these identity markers, often referred to as "at-risk," face like challenges in interrupting negative stereotypes. More plays centering Latinx and other marginalized racial and ethnic groups are being written, produced, and published, but the disparities in demographics and dramatic works depicting such characters remains. *The Smartest Girl in the World*, a new play for young audiences by Miriam Gonzales, which won the American Alliance for Theater in Education's Distinguished Play Award in 2019, offers such representations as Latinx youth navigate the US education system and seek to recognize themselves as intellectual beings capable and worthy of being educated while maintaining a sense of cultural awareness, pride, and connection.

In a 2017 interview, Gonzales speaks to her aims in writing *The Smartest Girl in the World*: "I'd like to sort of normalize difference." In the play, Lizzy and her older brother Leo are essentially on a journey to become the smartest children in the world. Unlike much US Latinx dramatic literature for youth, the play's Latinx youth are engaged with challenges beyond their racial and ethnic identity. In fact, the play does not paint the Latinx identity of the youth as a problem, nor does it reify stereotypes of undereducated, apathetic Latinxs. Rather, the play offers young people a look at youthful Latinx intellectuals who never question their smartness in relation to their identity markers. This chapter explores *The Smartest Girl in the World* as an example of Latinx dramatic literature that offers positive representations of Latinx characters and families and specifically Latinx youth who celebrate their smartness. Bringing together theory around identity development in Latinx youth, culturally responsive pedagogy, and audience reception, this chapter examines how *The Smartest Girl in the World* (as one specific example of TYA), and theatre for young audiences in general, may work toward positive identity development among Latinx youth. While this chapter's focus is not on the value of broader representation of Latinx characters on stage in particular, I acknowledge scholarship articulating the potential for positive identity development by brown children seeing positive images of brown bodies on stage. Here, I intend to build on that body of work and offer a bridge between such scholarship and that which focuses on how intellectually curious and academically invested Latinx youth can be at times ostracized by both non-Latinx peoples who may perceive them as trespassers and by the Latinx community, who see them as wanting to be something that they are not—something other than Latinx, essentially white.

Persistent Identity Challenges for Latinx Youth: A Need for Smart Representation

Theatre for young audiences is poised to offer positive representation of and to youth of color, representations that disrupt negative stereotypes often offered in other forms of media. A new anthology of Latinx themed plays, *Palabras del Cielo: An Exploration of Latina/o Theatre for Young Audiences*, compiled by José Casas and edited with Christina Marín, is a space for TYA companies to look for work to meet the need for such offerings. The book also includes scholarship, including Kelly Fey Prestel's chapter "They Don't Look Like Me Up There: A Look at Representation of Marginalized Populations in Theatre for Young Audiences (TYA) in the United States." Prestel asserts, "TYA as a cultural industry produces cultural products and artifacts that contribute to the identity construction of young people. Representation in cultural productions plays a critical role in identity construction. Continued negative or lack of representation contributes to the marginalization of certain groups, and such representations may prevent positive identity construction and perpetuate stereotyping and negative attitudes towards marginalized groups."

While perhaps obvious, and despite the data, the Latinx community remains underrepresented in TYA in the US. Prestel further laments, "Of all populations, the largest disparity in representation vs. youth population occurs in the 'Hispanic' population, with an 88.3% gap in 2014 and an even greater gap, 92.2%, in 2017. It was only one of two populations that saw a decrease in representation between 2014 and 2017. This trend is disheartening to observe as a member of the Latinx community." Certainly, beyond being represented is the need to disrupt the kinds of representation being offered. Latinx youth have long faced identity-based challenges of stereotypes and limited expectations of their intellectual potential from many sources, and perhaps most critically from the schools that are meant to educate them. Angela Valenzuela brought a swath of attention to the problem of assimilation nearly twenty years ago with her book *Subtractive Schooling: U.S.-Mexican Youth and the Politics of Caring.* She laments, "I came to locate 'the problem' of achievement squarely in school-based relationships and organizational structures and policies designed to erase students' culture. . . . Schooling is organized in ways that subtract resources from Mexican youth" (10). Despite such scholarship calling attention to the need for a more inclusive, culturally responsive education system that values Mexican American youth's heritage and lived experiences, assimilation has prevailed in our school system, and Latinx youth continue to struggle. Valenzuela offers more.

> Before dismissing urban, U.S.-born youth as lazy underachievers, it behooves researchers and practitioners to first examine the school's role in fostering poor academic performance. Bringing schools into sharper focus . . . reveals that [Mexican American] U.S.-born youth are neither inherently antischool nor oppositional. They oppose a schooling process that disrespects them; they oppose not education, but schooling. My research suggests that schools . . . are organized formally and informally in ways that fracture students' cultural and ethnic identities, creating social, linguistic, and cultural divisions among the students and between the students and the staff. (5)

A decade later, scholars continue to document how such biases still permeate our US schools and how our systems support such xenophobic practices. In

2007, Beth Hatt explained that a great deal of gatekeeping is practiced in US education systems, which supports a cycle of favoring youth from affluent, most often white families. Hatt posits,

> Artifacts such as grades, test scores, and college preparatory curriculum associated with smartness represent some of the gatekeeping mechanisms. The students who succeed in getting past the gatekeeping points are told that they have succeeded due to working hard and being smart. The students who fail to pass the gatekeeping points are told that they are lazy and/or not smart enough. In reality, who succeeds past these gatekeeping points is largely connected to race and class with wealthy, white students receiving the easiest passes through gatekeeping points. As a consequence, the status quo gets reproduced through these gatekeeping mechanisms. (152)

Latinx youth are often labeled incapable by gatekeeping policies and practices, while those who eek past such biased hurdles are also criticized for trying to be something that they are not, and they are often ultimately labeled by others as geeks.

Still, another decade passed with little change to US schools to support the success of Latinx youth. In fact, Latinx youth and other youth of color have faced more challenges even in instances when they have been able to tenaciously bypass gatekeeping practices that hold them back. Carrillo and Rodriguez introduced the term "smartness trespassing" in their 2016 article that examines "the politics of claiming a 'smart identity' as a student of color" (1237). The article chronicles the plight of a Latina high school student who "had much success in the classroom even amidst negative experiences due to her 'trespassing' into the areas deemed for 'intelligent' people who *are not supposed to look like her*" (1237). Essentially, Latinx youth are criticized no matter where they fall on the smartness scale that was created for youth who are often already perceived to be smarter and more hard working.

In her 2017 study on whites' attitudes towards the Latinx community, Celia Olivia Lacayo found that many white people view Latinxs as intellectually inferior to whites and other minorities whom they recognize as closer to assimilating to whiteness. Her study notes, "Although respondents were only asked about Latinos, they used other groups as comparisons to further make their case. Respondents attributed the 'model minority' narrative to Asians as a way of differentiating them from Latinos. They perceived Asians as being smart and capable of acquiring white American values while perceiving Latinos as incapable of doing so. Respondents thus used Asians to support their case that Latinos are inferior" (574). In other words, white culture is viewed as central and most smart, and any lack of assimilation on the part of non-white people equates to less smartness. Latinx youth's cultural knowledge and language are often viewed as deficiencies rather than additions to their intellectual capacities. Unfortunately, such racism and antisemitism are frequently internalized by Latinx youth and they begin to see themselves as deficient as well.

Media forms other than dramatic literature have responded to a need to disrupt the deficient narrative and offer more representation of smart Latinx youth. In her 2017 article "Soy Brown y Nerdy: The ChicaNerd in YA (Young Adult) Literature," Cristina Herrera illustrates how two young adult novels, through representation of two distinct young, smart Chicana/Latina protagonists, offer young girls a counter-narrative to the often-portrayed nerd as white and male. She explains,

> Classifying the two characters as nerds is not to suggest there is something unique or unusual about Chicanas who enjoy reading, writing poetry, or math. This logic narrowly frames ChicaNerds as outliers, as young girls who are not "supposed" to have these types of interests. Instead, we can find ways in which this nerd identity offers teenaged Chicanas an empowered subjectivity in stark contrast to the all-too familiar stereotypes of the fumbling, rejected (White male) nerd in popular culture. While these characters do not necessarily refer to themselves as nerds, they do, in fact, claim their right to intellectual curiosity and enthusiasm for "nerdy" school subjects, qualities we can read as nerdiness. (308)

Herrera notes that the book authors, like Gonzales, normalize Latinx smartness, offering Latina characters who love math and poetry. These young women have surpassed the gatekeepers and "by successfully battling the gender, racial, and class dynamics of their families and their communities, these protagonists learn . . . to accept and proudly claim their Chicana nerdiness" (308). More offerings like these novels that offer positive representations of smart Latinx youth are necessary to disrupt negative stereotypes and structural racism pressing on those who share these identity markers.

Smartest Girl as a Social Intervention

Staging representations of smart Latinx youth offers a similar though also very different kind of social intervention to that of young adult literature on the page. By viewing brown bodies on stage, youth collectively see representations of themselves while also witnessing others seeing them. Being seen in a positive light is critical to positive self-identity development. A few years ago, I reflected on an experience I had watching a Latinx play with my then nine-year-old bilingual daughter and her friend. I wrote of the experience, "I detected what appeared to be a sense of cultural pride in my daughter. It appeared that the bilingual, culturally specific story had offered an acknowledgement of her cultural capital with her white friend" (170). Too often, the cultural knowledge and lived experiences of young people of color goes unseen and unvalued by white gatekeepers who unknowingly dismiss cultural knowledge that they do not know and understand. The benefits of Latinx youth witnessing Latinx plays are clear; qualitative and quantitative data showing the need for such work is available, but the opportunities for young audiences to see Latinx stories and characters on stage have not risen. For some time, the field of TYA has collectively claimed that there is simply not a body of Latinx TYA from which to draw. Clearly, that is not now the case, but TYA companies continue to offer a disparaging number of Latinx plays across the country, despite the steady growth in Latinx young people in our schools and communities.

The Smartest Girl in the World is one such play in that body of work. While the play has been produced, it has not been picked up by TYA companies as much as one would expect or hope. Gatekeepers need to make this play more accessible to the young people who need to see it. The play premiered at Childsplay in Tempe, Arizona, in 2015 and has since experienced recent productions at Imagination Stage in Bethesda, Maryland, in 2017 and at Austin Playhouse in Austin, Texas, in 2018. The script was published by Dramatic Publishing. I was honored to direct the recent Austin production, a few hours from Gonzales' home town of Corpus Christi, Texas. Gonzales was able to come to the production, which afforded our company, family audiences, and students at the University of Texas at Austin where I teach the opportunity to talk with Gonzales following the opening performance. Much of the discussion revolved around how the play resonated in Austin with both the bused-in school audiences and the evening and weekend family audiences. Austin Playhouse conducted no formal research on the production, though the informal feedback was that the play was an important offering in Austin. The play certainly hit home with our all Latinx audiences. The five actors and I, as a white ally who has worked in Latinx theatre for over twenty-five years in Texas, could recognize the clear Texas Mexican American storytelling of Gonzales from the first read of the play. Some audience and cast members asked Gonzales about her motivation for writing the play, and again she referred to normalizing difference.

Through working closely with the text, I perceive that to normalize difference, Gonzales consciously introduces elements of the young people's culture in the play on their own ground, rather than in relation to the dominant, white culture. The characters speak in Spanish and English at different moments, reminiscent of the ways in which many Latinx peoples in South Texas speak. The play includes mostly young characters: Lizzy, Leo, their cousin Hector, Lizzy's best friend Cheryl, and game show contestants. The adult characters include Aunt Kid and a game show host. Lizzy and Leo's parents are not seen until they appear briefly in a dream sequence, though their voices are heard throughout. The young characters talk about school, Leo's health problems, and sibling rivalry without acknowledging their Latinx identity explicitly. The Latinx youth with whom I witnessed the production, however, including my twelve-year-old daughter, who identifies ethnically as Latinx and racially as white and indigenous, seemed drawn in by the bilingual nature of the play and by the brown actors on stage.

The young characters in the play articulate their idea of smartness influenced by notions that have been created by the dominant, western ideology of what it means to be smart and successful. In an early scene in the play, Leo informs Lizzy that they will need to be more academically smart in order to fulfill their dreams.

LEO: Lizzy. Look at me. We've been over this a hundred times. *I* have higher expectations for you. You. Have. To. Be. Smart—like me. One day we'll be *real* grownups—go to college, get big-time jobs. And, if we're smart, like Einstein smart—straight A's, speak 10 languages, invent stuff—we'll make money, tons of it, and *nothing* will stop us. We'll live in huge houses, with a hundred butlers, and all the candy we want all day. (16)

Like this Latina student, Leo is introduced as a smart young person, dedicated to his studies. Their cousin Hector finds Leo's interest in academics boring, and initially picks on Leo about it. Lizzy is less resistant to participation in Leo's study-games, like creating historical skits, his way of learning and playing at the same time. Because Leo has sickle cell disease, his parents do not allow him to participate in the game show of his dreams, and Lizzy decides to study hard herself and try out for the show. Leo is three times an outsider: as a descendent of Mexican immigrants living in the US, as a smart Latinx, and as a "sick kid."

Though Leo does not ever allude to his and his sister's racial and ethnic identities in relation to his goals, the economic challenges of the family are clear. We only hear the parents coming and going to work, and Leo often takes care of Lizzy because both parents are running to work in the evenings. Both parents are bilingual, though they speak more Spanish in the play than do the children. One can infer that living in a country that demonizes immigrants from the south, Lizzy's parents face challenges in finding work that can pay the bills. The children's father is clearly not getting enough sleep and the parents both seems to be running to different jobs. The youth dream of going to Hawaii with their parents, and winning the game show means this dream becoming a reality.

Recognizing and Highlighting Different Ways of Knowing

While *The Smartest Girl in the World* does at times account for smartness in terms of academic success, honoring the reality of the young people's perceptions based on their influences, the play seeks to disrupt internalized racism and honor other kinds of learning and knowing. The play ultimately invites young audiences, both Latinx and non-Latinx, to consider how to negotiate disparate notions of success that are coming at them by their families and communities, their schools, and by the mass media. In the end, Lizzy discovers many important lessons, which are not taught in typical US school systems, nor in the media. She begins to realize that there are many ways of knowing, and that one's own awareness of one's smartness and an appreciation of family connection are absolutely critical. She and her brother Leo begin to recognize that knowing facts may not lead them to happiness. The play ultimately offers criticism of a society focused on material success. Lizzy's Aunt Kid explains that as Lizzy seeks to win the game show, she must not lose sight of her reasons for investing in the competition in the first place. In a scene near the end of the play, Lizzy tells her aunt about why she is frustrated with her brother, and her Aunt offers Lizzy some wisdom about what really matters.

AUNT KID: Well . . . you *are* getting older, aren't you? . . . *Ay, mi querida.* You must remember *why* you did this—for your brother—for your family. (LIZZY tries to interject) No, no, no, wait, listen to me. *Listen.* (Takes a breath.) This has happened—in our family—already—to your *tía* Linda's son, Pedro, and his wife, Melly, and their children. I don't want the same thing to happen to you . . . and to Leo.

LIZZY: What—what happened?

AUNT KID: Nothing was more important to them than succeeding in this country. And . . . they did.

LIZZY: They did?

AUNT KID: Pedro and Melly worked hard, the children went to college. They became doctors, lawyers, bought fancy cars and clothes. But, then, some grew jealous of each other. And, then the worst happened.

LIZZY: What?

AUNT KID: They stopped talking to each other—forever. (41–42)

Through her story, Aunt Kid reminds Lizzy of the need to remember her values as she seeks success. The notion is not a dichotomy; rather Aunt Kid subtly teaches Lizzy that she can be academically smart while also maintaining a connection to her family and her culture. She can honor all kinds of smartness; she can value what she learns through her lived experience and also value what she learns through schooling.

Jimmy Noriega speaks to the body of plays represented in the *Palabras del Cielo* anthology in his article. He offers that the plays

> present their audiences with characters who are forced into unsettling situations, yet find a way to persevere in their search for home and belonging within the United States. What lies at the core of these plays, however, is a very necessary, yet fragile, call to action: one that seeks to empower Latina/o youth through performance by presenting them with characters that they can relate to and learn from as they develop their own ideas of the world and how they want to engage with it. These plays demonstrate the different strategies youth use to confront the challenges, frictions, and disappointments of living as a marginalized "other" within the US borders. They also demonstrate the importance of culture, family, history, and home in the formation of their identities, hopes, and dreams.

Latinx youth must see positive representations of their culture, family, history, and works that value them and portray them as important contributors who are at *home* in the US, as they are, not as the US would like them to be. The criticisms of subtractive schooling offered by Valenzuela twenty years ago can still be applied to US schools today, and I would argue that our historically white theatres often fall into subtractive practices when seeking to offer plays "for" marginalized communities. Our TYA companies must listen and learn from communities as much as they attempt to bring these communities into their institutions to teach them.

We will increase positive and primary inclusivity of racial and ethnic diversity in our programming. We serve a nation with a shifting tapestry of racial and ethnic diversity. We will reflect this tapestry of culture and race with respect and dignity on our stages. We will tell stories that celebrate culture, challenge marginalization and stereotypes, and amplify voices traditionally unheard. We will take steps to diversify our audiences in racial and ethnic representation. We will find new ways to engage with diverse populations to expand our core audience. We will maintain a welcoming environment for people of all races and ethnicities.

Normalizing Latinx Smartness

In the current US climate, Latinx young people are recognized and labeled as outsiders based on their ethnic and racial identity. Many assimilate to appear and feel less on the outside. By resisting assimilation, youth face criticism by the dominant culture; by assimilating, youth face criticism from other Latinx folks and at times the dominant culture as well. Ultimately, Latinx youth who express intellectual curiosity and seek academic success are further othered, seen as nerds, geeks, and freaks, who have no right to be so. I live with such a character. As my daughter grows, I watch and engage as she struggles to embrace and nurture her own intellectual yearning, based on societal expectations that shift as she moves through her world. Depending on the gaze of who watches her, her interest in learning is at times seen as posturing, and other times as selling out. I have seen her code switch as she has gone from a school of predominantly Latinx students and teachers to a school of predominantly ethnically white students and teachers. She speaks to the ways in which she has been viewed in each school and how she has learned to take cues from adults and peers and code shift to appear more or less academically interested and also more or less culturally affluent. Latinx young people, like my daughter, need examples of those who look and sound like them, who embrace their smartness, and who at the same time honor their common cultural practice of putting family and community before individual Western notions of success. *The Smartest Girl in the World* offers such an example. In the final scene, after Lizzy has gone onto the television game show and lost, Leo tries to cheer her up by showing her how she has inspired him to be brave and ask his parents if he can run for student council president:

LIZZY (pulls away): Leo . . . I . . . I didn't do so good today—on Challenge, I—

LEO: I watched you . . . on TV. You did great—really.

LIZZY: You watched?? Oooh nooo, it was soooo baaad.

LEO: No, it wasn't, you got a lot right.

LIZZY: I missed the Spanish question! Spanish! And then that horrible Hawaii one!

LEO: You got a little mixed up, so what. It happens. Lizzy, you were brave. You were on TV, and just as a *third grader*.

LIZZY: No, I lost. I'm not the smartest girl. You're right. I can't help. I never will.

LEO: Lizzy . . . you did help. I watched you today and I realized—if you can do that, I can talk to Mami and Papi about Student Council. (50–51)

Finally, we witness Lizzy helping her brother to move forward with asking for what he wants and needs. He acknowledges Lizzy's courage as a valuable key to success, as much as her knowledge of facts, and they move to address their parents as a unit, thus illustrating the family ties that often bind Latinx youth to one another, to their larger family units, and to their communities.

I am hopeful that more children's theatre companies and schools across the country will produce *The Smartest Girl in the World* and engage the work in an effort to inspire dialogue with young people about notions of Latinx identity, smartness, and labels that we use to put people in boxes. Representing and thus normalizing notions of Latinx intellectual curiosity is necessary and simply, well, smart.

Works Cited

Carrillo, Juan F., and Esmeralda Rodriguez. "She Doesn't Even Act Mexican: Smartness Trespassing in the New South." *Race Ethnicity and Education*, vol. 19, no. 6, 2016, pp. 1236–46.

Gonzales, Miriam. *The Smartest Girl in the World*. Dramatic Publishing. 2018.

Hatt, B. "Street Smarts vs. Book Smarts: The Figured World of Smartness in the Lives of Marginalized, Urban Youth." *The Urban Review* vol. 39, no. 2, 2007, pp. 145–66.

Herrera, Cristina. "Soy Brown y Nerdy: The ChicaNerd in Chicana Young Adult (YA) Literature." *The Lion and the Unicorn*, vol. 41 no. 3, 2017, pp. 307–26.

Lacayo, Celia Olivia. "Perpetual Inferiority': Whites' Racial Ideology toward Latinos." *Sociology of Race and Ethnicity*, vol 3, no. 4, 2017, pp. 566—579.

Noriega, Jimmy. "Latina/o Youth and Journeys of Transformation: Theatre of Migration, Exile, and Home." *Palabras del Cielo: An Exploration of Latina/o Theatre for Young Audiences*, compiled by José Casas and edited with Christina Marín. Dramatic Publishing, 2018.

Prestel, Kelly Fey. "They Don't Look Like Me Up There—A Look at Representation of Marginalized Populations in Theatre for Young Audiences (TYA) in the United States." *Palabras del Cielo: An Exploration of Latina/o Theatre for Young Audiences*, compiled by José Casas and edited with Christina Marín, Dramatic Publishing, 2018.

Schroeder-Arce, Roxanne. "The Américas Award On Stage: A Call for More Latin@ Theatre." *The Américas Award: Honoring Latino/a Children's and Young Adult Literature of the Américas*. Lexington Books, 2016, pp.169–80.

Straubhaar, Rolf, and Pedro R Portes. "The Social Construction of Latino Childhood in the New South." *Global Studies of Childhood*, vol 7, no. 3, 2016, pp. 266–77.

Valenzuela, A. *Subtractive Schooling: U.S. Mexican Youth and the Politics of Caring*. SUNY Press, 1999.

Zambrana, Ruth Enid. *Latinos in American Society: Families and Communities in Transition*. Cornell University Press. 2011.

8

"These Latin Girls Mean Business"[1]: Expanding the Boundaries of Latina Youth Identity in Meg Medina's YA Novel *Yaqui Delgado Wants to Kick Your Ass*

Cristina Herrera

In queer Chicana filmmaker Aurora Guerrero's first film, the critically acclaimed *Mosquita y Mari* (2013), the plot line initially appears to be a common tale: a straight-A student named Yolanda helps the street-wise Mari with her homework, and an unlikely friendship ensues. But as viewers know, the film is hardly a cliché, and as it traces the two young Chicanas' relationship from friendship into first love, what unveils is a tender and compassionate examination of urban, working-class, queer Chicana girlhood. While the film is crucial within the field of Chicana feminist studies for its insistence on recognizing and validating young girls' sexual desires,[2] I would add that it breaks ground for doing this while simultaneously expanding the boundaries of representation for young, urban Latinas. Yolanda (affectionately nicknamed "Mosquita" by Mari) and Mari are captivating characters precisely because of their differences, one being a "school girl," and the other street-smart and sarcastic. By no means are these kinds of Chicanitas unique, as we know; but in a refreshing move, Guerrero deems straight-A students *and* tough-talking girls worthy of their own story. In its unapologetic representation of young, queer Chicana love amidst the busy Los Angeles backdrop, *Mosquita y Mari* envisions many ways of being Chicana despite the overall absence of films about this demographic.

In my previous scholarship, I have examined the ways in which Chicana YA writers have challenged simplistic and narrow renderings of Chicana adolescence through the construction of the Chicana nerd, whom I've dubbed the ChicaNerd.[3] These writers demand that we make visible smart and studious Chicanitas, characters not unlike the fictional Yolanda/Mosquita, who must navigate her urban surroundings as well as her burgeoning queer desires and her parents' expectations of academic excellence. Yet despite the success of films like *Mosquita y Mari* that portray young Latina girls who fall outside the stereotypical "chola" aesthetic, we cannot overlook the recent re-emergence of the chola/homegirl in popular writings and the consistent pattern of media and popular culture's erasure of non-chola identities. In articles such as Andrew S. Vargas's in *Remezcla*, "A Look Back at the Movie That Taught America How to Dress Like a Chola," or Barbara Calderón-Douglass's *Vice* article "The Folk Feminist Struggle Behind the Chola Fashion Trend," as just a few examples, the chola (alternatively known as the homegirl) is described as a figure of Chicana feminist resistance, the epitome of cool toughness. Of course, one can hardly say the chola has disappeared, as she and her predecessor, la Pachuca, have been theorized by prominent Chicana scholars like Rosa Linda Fregoso, Marie Keta Miranda, and Catherine S. Ramírez.[4] These scholars draw attention to the ways in which Pachucas and cholas have challenged the gendered, raced, and classed confines of urban spaces that have traditionally limited Chicana mobility, important contributions to Chicana feminist scholarship.

But as this chapter questions, what can be gained by broadening the boundaries of Latina urban identity to include young Latinas who are not cholas? The Cuban American young adult novelist Meg Medina, in her unflinching examination of adolescent bullying and urban Latinidad in *Yaqui Delgado Wants to Kick Your Ass* (2013),[5] calls for an expanded representation of young, urban Latina womanhood that refuses to romanticize the chola. The novel's protagonist, the fifteen-year-old Piedad "Piddy" Sánchez, who dreams of being a wildlife biologist, is relentlessly bullied by a "tough" girl, the title's namesake, Yaqui Delgado, because of Piddy's perceived aloofness and her refusal to play by the school's problematic racial/color hierarchy. However, we should not read Medina's text as merely a scathing critique of the chola/homegirl who terrorizes Piddy. The text does give some context to Yaqui Delgado's violent nature, including stark poverty and her placement within the child welfare system. But even as the novel attempts a sympathetic understanding of the harmful consequences wrought by poverty and urban violence, the text also invites readers to examine the ways in which smart and ambitious young Latinas—outsiders within the "typical" urban high school setting—are themselves victims of bullying, violence, and identity policing that deems smart young women "not Latina enough."

This chapter will begin by re-visiting what can easily be regarded as the most familiar Latina urban identity, the chola, who has been the subject of a number of popular and academic studies, including films. It must be noted that most popular and academic studies I discuss have largely used terms like "chola" and "homegirl" beneath the identity marker Latina, though in fact the girls they examine are predominantly Chicana/Mexican American. Piddy Sánchez, the protagonist in *Yaqui*, is not Chicana, but is the daughter of a Cuban exile mother and estranged Dominican father. Yaqui Delgado is also Latina, but the specificities of her ethnic identity are absent. My discussion, then, not only challenges the seemingly natural alignment of cholas/homegirls with urban identity that erases and marginalizes other Latina girls, but it draws attention to the gaps in scholarship that have yet to be filled. I will then move to a discussion of *Yaqui*, a text that not only questions the idealization of the chola or tough Latina, but adamantly proposes more critical attention on urban Latinas who do not comfortably fit within the tough-girl paradigm. Moreover, this novel reclaims invisible Latinas like Piddy who are subsumed by the common popular script that reduces Latina adolescents to tough girl identities and little else.

The Charming Chola? Homegirls, Cholas, and "Tough" Urban Girls in Popular Culture

The urban Latina has been the subject of important feminist scholarship since at least the mid-1990s, with the publication of Chicana film scholar Rosa Linda Fregoso's seminal article "Homegirls, Cholas, and Pachucas in Cinema: Taking over the Public Sphere." Fregoso maintains that contemporary cholas and homegirls, along with their antecedent, la Pachuca, have historically been "characterized as a deviant in studies about adolescent girl gangs," and their "story remains untold and untheorized" (Fregoso 317). Much has changed since Fregoso's assertion of the invisibility of these urban Latinas, given that in the decades since her groundbreaking work's publication, a number of scholarly and cultural works have documented the chola's cultural significance. Her claim that cholas and homegirls have been largely understood as "bad" is supported by sociological work on girlhood, most notably research conducted by Meda Chesney-Lind and Katherine Irwin. In their important text, *Beyond Bad Girls: Gender, Violence and Hype*, the authors examine the sensationalist media attention paid to teenage girls, mostly beginning in the 1990s, which they trace to centuries-old constructions of all women as possessing a "duplicitous nature—appearing superficially 'innocent' and 'nice' while actually being manipulative, devious, and occasionally evil" (Chesney-Lind and Irwin 12). The success of popular films like *Mean Girls*, they claim, undoubtedly perpetuated the myth of the apparently "natural" bad tendencies found in adolescent girls, but additionally, young girls of color face real-life consequences as a result of the "mean girl" myth, such as harsher policing of their behavior within school settings and the criminal justice system (Chesney-Lind and Irwin 135). As Vera López and Meda Chesney-Lind add, "While the good, innocent, virginal girl continues to be an idealized image of womanhood associated with white females, it remains largely unattainable for young women of color, who are often characterized as hypersexual, manipulative, violent and sexually dangerous. The available gender scripts for girls of color, particularly Latinas and African Americans, emphasize their innate 'badness'" (López and Chesney-Lind 528). Although films such as *Mean Girls* feature white teen girls as the antagonists, the pervasive image of the "bad" or "criminal" girl in popular culture is aligned with African American and Latina girls, resulting in sexist and racist practices deemed necessary to "control" this demographic. In the case of *Mean Girls*, the white girls' bullying is one of the film's major sources of humor, which dangerously suggests that when white girls do bully, it is laughable, but girls of color who bully must be punished. For example, by universally marking young adolescent girls, especially girls of color, as a "problem" in need of solving, schools have created harsh anti-bullying programs that do little to address the systemic erasure of girls' unique experiences and needs (Chesney-Lind and Irwin 103). Perhaps more insidious is the historic tendency to "assign" the "moniker of violent . . . to girls of color" (Levy 46). The "violent" label is undoubtedly connected to the higher rates of incarceration of these women, although they are not more likely to commit violence than their white counterparts (Chesney-Lind and Irwin 184).

In response to racialized stereotypes of young urban Latinas as "bad," scholars have attempted to theorize cholas or homegirls as subversive figures representing working-class Latina feminist identities. In her discussion of Pachucas, Catherine S. Ramírez argues that these young women, in their "distinctly racialized, working-class, urban youth style" (Ramírez 2) represented a rejection of "white Americanness and middle-class comportment . . . [as well as] normative gender" roles (Ramírez 11). Because of their unique identity-construction that fell outside of prescribed mainstream and Mexican gender codes, Pachucas were viewed as dangerous and naturally violent. Although several decades have passed since the Pachuca's heyday, Chicana feminist scholars trace similar descriptors of the contemporary homegirl. But as Marie Keta Miranda argues in her study *Homegirls in the Public Sphere*, these young homegirls should not be so narrowly framed as "deviant," and their "exaggerated toughness and bravado" should instead be read as performative in their attempt to "create a presence in the public sphere" (Miranda 81–82). For Miranda, adopting "toughness" is not so much evidence of a "bad" disposition as it is a mode of surviving interlocking systems of racial, gender, and class oppression. Much as Fregoso and Ramírez interpret cholas and Pachucas as responding to gender and racialized practices that may restrict their visibility and mobility, so too does Miranda call for a more nuanced, feminist mode of understanding urban Latinas.

Without a doubt, this Chicana feminist recuperation project is significant for its response to decades of historical and cultural erasure of urban Latinas/ Chicanas. In addition, this resurgence of attention in recent popular writings has suggested there is something alluring or charming about the chola and her aesthetics. But what does it mean that this pervasive alignment of urban Latina adolescence and young womanhood with chola identity remains largely intact in popular culture, seen in films such as the *Fast and Furious* film franchise? Although non-cholas in fact do exist, seen in television series such as the immensely popular series *Jane the Virgin* and *Ugly Betty*,[6] the chola continues to be the most common urban Latina identity.

The question remains: how can we celebrate all forms of Latina/Chicana gender expression without privileging one above the rest? Cholas and homegirls *are* significant Latina feminist identities, as research argues, but contemporary Latina YA literature presents us with a much more diverse representation of young, urban Latina adolescence that stands in stark contrast to the tough chola.

Girls in the Hood: Latina YA Literature and the Case of *Yaqui Delgado Wants to Kick Your Ass*

Research on urban girlhood has noted the pervasive alignment of negative stereotypes with girls of color, which suggests that urban landscapes themselves are partially responsible for creating this supposed "badness." But to make such assertions overlooks urban girls' "remarkable strengths in the face of these adversities" (Leadbetter and Way 1). Indeed, it also suggests that urban girls, particularly urban Latina teens, comprise a monolithic identity of the chola/homegirl, or as Jillian Hernández adds, the "chonga," who is "often described by Latinas/os in South Florida as a low-class, slutty, tough, and crass young woman" (Hernández 64). Although the chonga is associated with this geographic zone, as Hernández explains, identity markers like chola/chonga/ homegirl "interpellate specifically marked bodies in primarily urban locations (Miami, New York, Chicago, Los Angeles)" and are "representative of 'bad' subjectivities" (Hernández 67).[7] The irony of ascribing the "bad" label to urban Latinas, of course, is that a combination of ethnicity, gender, and social class will always mark this demographic as "bad" regardless of their participation or not in overt or covert criminal behavior. Moreover, to narrowly ascribe one identity to urban Latina girls, the chonga/chola/homegirl, erases other urban youth identities that coexist with these "tough" girls. For example, in recent Chicana and Latina YA texts, such as Lilliam Rivera's *The Education of Margot Sanchez* (2017), Erika Sánchez's *I Am Not Your Perfect Mexican Daughter* (2017), and Gabby Rivera's *Juliet Takes a Breath* (2016), the teenage protagonists navigate their Chicago and Bronx neighborhoods in ways that depart from the usual chola script. Unlike their chola/chonga/homegirl counterparts, these young Latinas do not construct tough exteriors, instead choosing to create urban identities on their own terms, although this is also not without problems.

Cholas have been present in much Latina literature, for example in works by Mary Helen Ponce, Yxta Maya Murray, and Helena María Viramontes;[8] but more recent Latina YA literature broadens the representation of urban Latina girls in ways that challenge the "natural" alignment of urban settings with chola aesthetics. Rivera's novel *Juliet Takes a Breath*, while it traces Juliet's painful path of claiming a queer Latina self, also takes aim at the challenges faced by ambitious, college-bound Latinas: "*I need a break. I know that the problems in the hood are systemic . . . but damn if this place and the people here don't wear me down*" (Rivera, original italics, 4). Rather than renounce her barrio, Juliet wishes to see beyond the confines of New York City. However, lest we believe the novel simplistically advocates leaving the barrio as a solution to Juliet's struggles, the text honestly reveals Juliet's frustrations and vulnerabilities as a young queer Latina who feels she does not belong in her neighborhood. Leaving home for a summer in Portland, Oregon, to study under the guidance of a white lesbian scholar does not easily cure her sense of isolation either, and instead, Juliet must learn through a series of challenges and setbacks to carve her own path, which may not be understood by all but is authentic to her needs and desires. In recent Latina YA texts such as this, writers respond to popular culture's tendency to narrowly ascribe one identity, the chola, with young, urban Latina womanhood, by presenting us with characters like Juliet, born and raised in the hood, who feel constrained by the limited identity scripts surrounding them.

Yaqui begins in the protagonist Piddy's second year at a new high school she instantly despises because of its geographic distance from her previous high school, best friend Mitzi, and social network. But most important, Piddy immediately becomes a target, as her classmate Darlene informs her, "Yaqui Delgado hates you. She says you're stuck-up for somebody who just showed up out of nowhere. And she wants to know who the hell you think you are, shaking your ass the way you do" (Medina 2). As Piddy soon learns, her style of walk is read as overtly sexual, a threat to Yaqui's seniority in the school's problematic racial and gender hierarchy.

Although Piddy's confident walk is a result of harmless merengue lessons learned from her godmother, this style, combined with her lighter skin and bookish ways, marks her as an "outcast," someone unfit to sit with "the Latin kids" in the cafeteria:

> I spotted the Latin zone right away, but I didn't know a single one of them from any of my classes. As I got closer, a few of the guys grinned and elbowed each other, but none of the girls looked like they were going to make room. In fact, it was downright chilly how they stared at me. . . .
>
> So here I am at the corner table near the trash cans—the worst real estate in the cafeteria. . . . Our table is all the kids from our fourth-period science class . . . which I'm finding out is a breeding ground for outcasts here at Daniel Jones High School. (Medina 4–5)

Piddy's description of the high school's distinct social hierarchy echoes research that has examined the ways in which students who fall outside the "jock" or "cool" identities are often victims of bullying and ostracism (Kinney, Ortner). Beyond that, however, is Piddy's acknowledgment that although she may be a "Latin girl, too" (Medina 6), her lighter skin and good grades render her "not Latina" within a social circle that defines Latinidad along arbitrary markers of behavior and physical appearance, as she admits: "White-skinned. No accent. Good in school. I'm not her idea of a Latina at all" (Medina 6). Piddy quickly learns that within this narrow framing of Latinidad, her identity is reduced to that of "outcast," affirming scholar Sandra D. Garza's assertion that "skin color and the physical body largely mediate our relationships with society, marking insiders and outsiders in the global, national, and local arenas" (Garza 39). Piddy's academic achievement works in combination with her lighter skin to prevent her from claiming a seat in her school's "Latin zone." Within the high school's parameters, even coveted cafeteria seating is determined by one's perceived "Latinness."

Piddy's admission that she "didn't know a single one of them from any of my classes" also points to problematic educational policies like testing that separate students based on arbitrary indicators of ability. When her classmate Darlene challenges Piddy, she is left defenseless: "It's because those girls are a rougher bunch—nothing at all like Mitzi and me. . . . 'My last name is *Sanchez*, remember?' I finally say to Darlene. 'My mother is from Cuba, and my dad is from the Dominican Republic. I'm just as Latin as they are'" (Medina, original italics, 6). In fact, in Julie Bettie's research on girls of color, she notes the stigma some Latina girls face for doing well in school, most problematically, accusations of trying to "act white" (Bettie 158). Piddy's defensive response reveals her awareness of racial and gender constructs that have defined "roughness" as natural markers of Latina womanhood. No matter her ethnic heritage that designates her "just as Latin" as Yaqui and her friends, Piddy's behavior and habits as a "good girl" will always mark her as an inferior, lesser Latina. As a newcomer who does not yet understand the rules of her school's pecking order, Piddy is initiated through violent means.

This violent initiation, however, begins with Piddy's futile attempts to discard her reputation as a smart overachiever, an outsider, in the hopes that denying this part of herself will make her less of a target for Yaqui and her crew. One night when Piddy and her mother are walking home from the grocery store, Piddy spots Yaqui and her friends playing a game of handball in the neighborhood park. Although the sight of these girls immediately strikes Piddy with fear, it is her mother who utters her disgust.

> "*Son unas qualquieras,*" she mutters. Nobodies. No culture, no family life, illiterates, she means. The kind of people who make her cross to the other side of the street if she meets them in the dark on payday. They're her worst nightmare of what a Latin girl can become in the United States. Their big hoop earrings and plucked eyebrows, their dark lips painted like those stars in the old black-and-white movies, their tight T-shirts that show too much curve and invite boys' touches. The funny thing is, if I could be anything right now, I'd be just like one of them. I'd be so strong that I could stand without flinching if people pelted me with rubber balls. . . . Yaqui and me, we should be two *hermanas*, a sisterhood of Latinas. . . . We come from countries that are like rooms in one big house, but instead, we're worlds apart. (Medina 55–56)

According to Piddy's mother, Clara, it is the US's perceived lax attitudes on sex and dating that contribute to this "nightmare" of plucked-eyebrow, hoop-wearing Latinas, that is, cholas. Clara may indeed be outside of the white, middle-class mainstream, but her judgmental assumptions of the girls' families and home lives suggests that she has accepted such stereotypes of cholas as "cualquieras." However, Miranda's scholarship on homegirls argues that their distinct appearance reflects "an attainment of mastery in a masculinized sphere" (Miranda 81). Without a doubt, the barrio park has long been constructed as a male domain, especially the act of playing handball, as films like *American Me* would suggest, which explains Piddy's simultaneous fear and admiration of these girls' confident, even brazen body language and demeanor within an environment marked by gendered and racialized spaces. As scholar Raúl Homero Villa explains in his research on urban literature and culture, the barrio "is a complex and contradictory social space for its residents" (Villa 8).

This becomes apparent in Clara's seething words, as she recognizes the shared ethnic and class realities that make these "cualquieras" her neighbors. The barrio may indeed be "home" for Yaqui and Piddy, but their lived experiences starkly contrast despite their shared urban space and residence.

While Clara's accusations of these girls' lack of "culture and family life" mirror mainstream warnings of "bad" girls of color that must be controlled, it is important to note that even as Piddy fears Yaqui and her friends, she nevertheless recognizes the ways in which educational and social structures have served to distinguish between the "good" Latina and the "bad" Latina. "Good" Latinas look like Piddy; "bad" Latinas look like Yaqui. Her desire to be "just like one of them" is rooted in her understanding that although Yaqui and her crew are deemed "bad" by the likes of her mother and school administrators, this "badness" comes with a mode of self-protection and infamy that nevertheless does not challenge their belonging within Latinx culture. Within this troubling racial logic, "tough-looking" girls like Yaqui are easily classified as Latina, while shy and bookish girls like Piddy must prove themselves as "Latin girls, too." Undoubtedly we must call into question Piddy's belief that merely sharing an ethnic identity with her nemesis makes them similar and potential *hermanas* in arms, but her recognition that the two girls are in fact "worlds apart" points to the racist and classist educational system that segregates students like Yaqui from "higher-achieving" students like Piddy. If Yaqui is viewed by Piddy as a real Latina because of her toughness and appearance, then in contrast, Piddy's schoolgirl ways mark her as an inauthentic Latina because of deep-seated myths of under-achieving, troubled Latinas. Piddy's laments reveal the dangers of internalizing harmful myths that only contribute to the policing of identity in relation to skin color and even academic performance.

So ingrained is this myth of the under-achieving and therefore tough Latina, that when Piddy earns her very first failing score on an assignment, she feels both a sense of shame and "a little tough" (Medina 35). Within these troubling social constructions that narrowly determine who is Latinx or who gets to claim Latinx identity, Piddy grapples with her sense of self that marks her not only as an easy target but as someone whose identity is always already in question. Not long after she becomes the target of Yaqui's hatred, for example, she goes so far as to drastically alter her appearance by dramatically over-plucking her eyebrows and wearing a dark shade of lipstick: "I look expressionless and strangely vicious. If Ma walked by me, she might never recognize me at all. *That's not my daughter,* she'd think. And she'd be right. Maybe this is the new me I need to find. A girl tough enough to face Yaqui" (Medina 152). What Piddy learns from her school community is that being a tough girl makes one Latina, as if it is impossible to separate violence from Latinidad. Moreover, to look Latina requires an altering of appearance into what can easily be classified as the chola/homegirl aesthetic: plucked eyebrows, dark lipstick, stern facial expression. Within this logic, looking and being Latina actually means looking like and being a chola.

In the novel's bleak and realistic glimpse into the racial and gender politics of urban high schools, it offers as well a critique of Draconian school policies, particularly those that do little to guarantee that school environments are "bully-free zones." Instead, as Chesney-Lind and Irwin maintain, these anti-violent measures proposed in schools "involved school officials in the patrolling of the noncriminal behavior of girls in ways that could clearly be seen as part of a larger project of regulating girls' sexuality, deportment, and obedience to authority" (Chesney-Lind and Irwin 129). Nowhere is this more apparent than when Piddy herself is scrutinized by her school principal, Mr. Flatwell, when she is caught erasing an epithet that is scribbled on another school outcast's locker (Medina 100). Although she admits that she did not scribble the epithet but erased it in her attempts to shield and protect her classmate from seeing it, she is nevertheless sentenced to detention, evading the principal's questions when he asks her how she is liking her new school: "If I tell him about Yaqui, everything will just get worse. Being a narc means you're too weak to take care of yourself. . . . Where will that leave me? I'll be even more of a social outcast than I am now—open season for anyone to get after me" (Medina 101). In her deliberate choice of words that resembles language often used to describe prison politics and urban codes of honor, Piddy astutely understands that admitting to the bullying, while it may protect her temporarily, will not actually stop, much less prevent, this type of behavior from occurring in the first place. "Ratting" out her classmates, she suggests, will also further distance herself from the identity marker of Latina that she is anxious to maintain. "Authentic" Latinas do not rat out their peers. To her astonishment, her actions are determined to be "defacing school property" (Medina 103), and she soon learns that Saturday detentions are the same sentences given to students, such as Yaqui, who arrives the same morning as Piddy. A common form of school discipline, the detentions do little to protect students like Piddy and her classmate, Rob, who is also a target of bullying and whose locker is defaced. Moreover, in a large urban high school that is understaffed and underfunded, the novel offers a subtle but present critique on educational inequality that fosters violence.

For readers, Yaqui's eventual attack on Piddy is a challenging and painful passage to digest, particularly for the uncanny and precise language that paints a vivid picture of the brutal assault, which is recorded by Yaqui's friends and, in true twenty-first-century fashion, uploaded to YouTube: "Yaqui lunges again. I can feel the rage in each slap and bite; it's like I'm being devoured alive" (Medina 161). As a victim of such a horrific beating, Piddy compares this experience to being cannibalized, or perhaps more precisely, to being the sacrificial lamb who is mauled by the girls, whom she describes as "like a wolf pack organizing their hunt" (Medina 160). Although the animalistic language Piddy uses may be troubling for some readers, I would suggest that the passage detailing her assault be read as the novel's efforts to empathize with victims of violence for their refusal to follow problematic social hierarchies or for merely being in the wrong place at the wrong time. Indeed, Piddy herself struggles to make sense of her victimization and her painful acknowledgement that being a victim of violence transforms her into "this new girl with the pummeled face" (Medina 183). As she learns, she is no longer a Latina who does not fit in with her fellow Latinx peers; in addition, the violence she has suffered, along with the public display of her brutalization, remains a source of trauma even after she transfers to her previous high school to complete the academic year: "Everything else is the same, but I'm not" (Medina 255). Her traumatic experience, however, is used as a catalyst to at last vocalize what she has endured.

But perhaps most significant are the events proceeding the attack: the video's circulation, Yaqui's suspension, and Piddy's transfer to a science magnet school. These concluding events raise questions, undoubtedly intended by the author, about the effectiveness of the solution. For example, after the beating, Piddy's godmother, Lila, attempts to convince Piddy that divulging the details of the attack was necessary and moreover, Yaqui's attack proves that Piddy is "better" than the likes of Yaqui: "You're different," she continues. "You're going to be better than that, and that's what kills her, Piddy. *That's* what makes her burn with hate. She can already see you're winning. You're going to get an education and use your brain" (Medina, original italics, 220). Although Lila's words are intended to comfort her traumatized goddaughter, these remarks mirror Clara's earlier disdain toward Yaqui and the "cualquieras" belonging to her gang. Without a doubt, readers are intended to empathize with the battered Piddy as a victim of bullying, but Lila's words echo the Chicana/Latina scholarship that has theorized urban predecessors like Pachucas and cholas, who have been held with similar disgust within their respective barrio communities. While Piddy's admission to the prestigious magnet school essentially ensures her eventual college placement, the obvious question arises: what happens to Yaqui? Indeed, will the suspension address her propensity for violence? Will she ever change? I raise these questions in a chapter that examines the "outsider" urban Latina teen, but in doing so, I am also taking care in not vilifying the chola/homegirl/chonga character, Yaqui, whose suspension potentially foreshadows a life of more violence, poverty, and educational hardships.

Conclusion

In the Chicanx and Latinx studies courses I teach, one of the first class activities I assign is for students to log on to Google Images and type the word "Chicana," and later "Latina." I explain to my students that by no means am I suggesting that we take these images as hard fact; instead, I ask my students to consider what it means when the predominant image that appears on the screen is the cholafied Latina. While respecting the presence of the chola in our communities and offering feminist analyses of what she signifies in terms of gender, ethnicity, and identity, I also encourage my students to offer their own critiques, namely to question why this is the most common identity script that appears in popular culture and casual Google searches. Our class discussion then addresses "touchy" subjects like authenticity and hurtful comments my own students have faced about "not being down" because they do not dress like or look like cholas/os. I find this activity incredibly useful for confronting these myths to which they have been exposed, all while demonstrating the liberating possibilities of defining Latinidad on one's own terms, much like the character Piddy Sánchez.

Meg Medina's novel, with its graphic and stark glimpse into the life of a young Latina who is relentlessly bullied by a high school classmate, is an important text in the field of Latinx YA literature that addresses Latina youth identities but also tackles the pervasive problem of bullying. Unlike recent popular writings that have, perhaps inadvertently, described the charming and charismatic chola/homegirl as an urban figure to revere, *Yaqui Delgado Wants to Kick Your Ass* presents us with an alternative view of the chola. Like recent YA texts that feature urban Latina teens who do not look like, much less identify with, the chola/homegirl/chonga aesthetic, Medina's novel privileges the voice and experiences of Piddy Sánchez, a smart, ambitious, and lonely girl from Queens who is rendered an outcast, a nobody, and definitely not "really" Latina. Of course, young urban Latinas like Piddy populate large cities like New York, Los Angeles, Chicago, or Miami, but in the recent re-emergence of popular writings on cholas/homegirls, we may be left to believe that this urban identity script is the only one available to Latina teens.

What about the hippie Latina teens? The Goth Latinas? The athletic Latinas? The nerdy Latinas? The graphic tee and jeans-wearing Latina? The girls like Piddy who yearn to be biologists? A more poignant question to ask is why popular culture continues to define Latina adolescence, particularly urban Latina adolescence, along such narrow terms. Until more novels like *Yaqui* are published that dare to present Latina teens in all their complexities, we risk propagating the myth of urban Latinas as a monolithic group that erases other modes of living and thriving in the hood.

Notes

1. A line uttered in *Yaqui Delgado Wants to Kick Your Ass* by the protagonist's classmate Darlene, who warns her to stay away from the "Latin" girls in their class (6).

2. See Catrióna Rueda Esquibel's groundbreaking work on lesbianism in Chicana girlhood stories, as well as Marivel Danielson's examination of queer Chicana girlhood.

3. See my 2017 article, "Soy Brown y Nerdy: The ChicaNerd in Chicana Young Adult (YA) Literature" in the journal *The Lion and the Unicorn*.

4. See Fregoso, "Homegirls, Cholas, and Pachucas in Cinema"; Miranda, *Homegirls in the Public Sphere*; and Ramírez, "Sayin' Nuthin."

5. Hereafter referred to as *Yaqui*.

6. See Tanya González and Eliza Rodríguez y Gibson's important work *Humor and Latina/o Camp in Ugly Betty: Funny Looking.*

7. See, for example, the YouTube series "Chonga Girls," as well as the Facebook page of the same title, which subversively and humorously responds to the negative characterization of chongas as "low-class."

8. See, for example, Viramontes's collection of stories *The Moths*, Ponce's *Hoyt Street*, or Yxta Maya Murray's novel *Locas*.

Works Cited

Bettie, Julie. *Women without Class: Girls, Race, and Identity*. University of California Press, 2014.

Calderón-Douglass, Barbara. "The Folk Feminist Struggle behind the Chola Fashion Trend." *Vice*, 12 Apr. 2015, https://www.vice.com/en_us/article/wd4w99/the-history-of-the-chola-456. Accessed 10 July 2017.

Chesney-Lind, Meda, and Katherine Irwin. *Beyond Bad Girls: Gender, Violence and Hype*. Routledge, 2008.

Fregoso, Rosa Linda. "Homegirls, Cholas, and Pachucas in Cinema: Taking over the Public Sphere." *California History*, vol. 74, no. 3, 1995, pp. 316–27,

Garza, Sandra D. "Decolonizing Intimacies: Women of Mexican Descent and Colorism." *Aztlán*, vol. 39, no.2, 2014, pp. 35–64.

González, Tanya, and Eliza Rodríguez y Gibson. *Humor and Latina/o Camp in Ugly Betty: Funny Looking*. Lexington Books, 2015.

Hernández, Jillian. "'Miss, You Look Like a Bratz Doll': On Chonga Girls and Sexual-Aesthetic Excess." *NWSA Journal*, vol. 21, no. 3, 2009, pp. 63–90,

Herrera, Cristina. "Soy Brown y Nerdy: The ChicaNerd in Chicana Young Adult (YA) Literature." *The Lion and the Unicorn*, vol. 41, no. 3, 2017, pp. 307–26.

Kinney, David A. "From Nerds to Normals: The Recovery of Identity among Adolescents from Middle School to High School." *Sociology of Education*, vol. 66, no.1, 1993, pp.21–40.

Leadbetter, Bonnie J., and Niobe Way, eds. *Urban Girls Revisited*. NYU Press, 2007.

Levy, Melissa K. "'Boys Fight, Girls Fight': Adolescent Girls Speak About Girls' Aggression." *Girlhood Studies*, vol. 5, no. 2, 2012, pp. 45–64.

López, Vera, and Meda Chesney-Lind. "Latina Girls Speak Out: Stereotypes, Gender and Relationship Dynamics." *Latino Studies*, vol. 12, no. 4, 2014, pp. 527–49,

Medina, Meg. *Yaqui Delgado Wants to Kick Your Ass*. Candlewick Press, 2013.

Miranda, Marie Keta. *Homegirls in the Public Sphere.* University of Texas Press, 2003.

Murray, Yxta Maya. *Locas.* Grove, 1997.

Ortner, Sherry B. "'Burned Like a Tattoo': High School Social Categories and 'American Culture.'" *Ethnography*, vol. 3, no. 2, 2002, pp. 115–48.

Ponce, Mary Helen. *Hoyt Street.* University of New Mexico Press, 1993.

Ramírez, Catherine S. "Saying 'Nothin': Pachucas and the Languages of Resistance." *Frontiers: A Journal of Women Studies*, vol. 27, no. 3, 2006, pp. 1–33.

Rivera, Gabby. *Juliet Takes a Breath.* Riverdale Avenue Books, 2016.

Rivera, Lilliam. *The Education of Margot Sanchez.* Simon and Schuster, 2017.

Sánchez, Erika. *I Am Not Your Perfect Mexican Daughter.* Knopf, 2017.

Shepherd, Julianne Escobedo. "Chola Style: The Latest Cultural Appropriation Fashion Crime?" *The Guardian*, 15 Aug. 2014, https://www.theguardian.com/fashion/2014/aug/15/ -sp-chola-style-cultural-appropriation-fashion-crime.

Vargas, Andrew S. "A Look Back at the Movie That Taught America How to Dress Like a Chola." *Remezcla*, 19 Mar. 2015, http://remezcla.com/film/looking-back-at-the-movie-that -taught-america-how-to-dress-like-a-chola/.

Villa, Raúl Homero. *Barrio-Logos: Space and Place in Urban Chicano Literature and Culture.* University of Texas Press, 2000.

Viramontes, Helena María. *The Moths and Other Stories.* Arte Público, 1985.

9

Tomás Rivera: The Original Latinx Outsider

Tim Wadham

As a children's librarian in Arizona working with young Spanish-speakers, I saw firsthand how they identified as outliers, outsiders, and outcasts. Barriers of language separated them from even their own families as parents continued to speak Spanish at home while at school they were pressured to speak and read only English. Integration into American culture separated them from their own cultural traditions. Public libraries were an institution with which they were not familiar, or which they feared because of the need to provide legal identification, something they didn't necessarily possess. In my work I learned that for members of the Latinx community finding themselves characterized as "Other," to come into a place where they feel they didn't belong, they needed to be given *permission*. An experience I had while working as the Youth Services Coordinator for the Maricopa County (AZ) Library District demonstrated powerfully how this feeling can be seen in the Latinx migrant community. One of the branch libraries is located in the small town of Aguila, Arizona, about ninety miles west of Phoenix. Aguila is a very small agricultural outpost, closer to the California border than it is to Phoenix, and the majority of the residents are migrant workers. The branch librarian at the time was concerned that the adults, especially mothers, were not coming into the library. She asked me to come and speak to them. I prepared a program that included reading aloud a couple of picture books, including *Tomás and the Library Lady* by Pat Mora. I heard back from the librarian that the next day these women were waiting at the door of the library for it to open. They came in. The librarian was the one who provided this crucial insight: they came in because they had been invited. I realized that

I wanted to find a way to reach out to the Latinx community more broadly to welcome them to enter the library, and by association the larger world, and the answer first came in the book I had read to those mothers—*Tomás and the Library Lady.*]Then it expanded beyond my wildest vision through a stage adaptation that I commissioned from Childsplay Children's Theater based in Tempe, Arizona, which attracted the participation of playwright José Cruz González.

When one thinks of Latinx outsiders, a strong argument can be made for Tomás Rivera as the prototype (González, personal interview). Rivera is now known as the father of Chicanx literature (Magill 540). His work, . . . *y no se lo tragó la tierra* is the urtext of this genre and in 1971 won the first Quinto Sol prize given by the now-legendary publisher to the best fictional work by a Mexican American author. Quinto Sol's purpose was to recognize Chicanx writers, and for Rivera, this recognition led him to a remarkably successful—if relatively short because of his untimely death at age 48—academic career in which he rapidly rose up the ranks. However, long before Tomás Rivera became the first Latinx chancellor of the University of California at Riverside, he was an outlier, following the crops with his migrant laborer parents from his birthplace of Crystal City, Texas, on a trail that in 1944 led to Iowa. It was while in Hampton, Iowa that the young Rivera met "the Library Lady," which is how he always referred to her (he did not remember her name). This librarian clearly had a strong impact on Rivera. The fact that the "Library Lady" turned out to be a bilingual German American who spoke with an accent suggests that she empathized with Spanish-speaking Rivera as a fellow outlier—someone separate from the mainstream culture of Midwest America.

This chapter focuses on two key texts that interpret this story from Rivera's childhood for young readers and theater-goers. Rivera's story was first retold in 1997 by Chicana poet Pat Mora in the picture book,[*Tomás and the Library Lady*. Mora's story is about a little boy who wants to read. The book portrays the young Rivera gaining confidence in his ability as he reads books from the library out loud to his family] In 2006, playwright José Cruz González was commissioned by Childsplay to adapt Mora's book for the stage. His adaptation focuses on how Rivera's encounter with the Library Lady drove his development as a writer. Neither interpretation is wrong, as Rivera's story supports both narratives. Both texts justify the placement of Rivera as the prototype of the Latinx outsider/outlier, but it is González's text that shows more clearly how Rivera was able, through writing, to break out from the cultural stereotypes that isolated him and find through language—both as a reader and a writer—permission to belong.

The Library Lady—Bertha Gaulke

The trope of the "outsider" is not unique to Latinx literature, but is certainly a driving archetype in much, if not most, of Latinx writing. Tomás Rivera was one of the first to present the archetype of the Latinx outlier, partially because he lived the experience and was ultimately driven to write about it. Frank Pino writes that the familiar archetype of the outsider reflects the "sociological, psychological and ontological orientation of the Mexican-American" and sees the import of these orientations and others as "especially evident" in Rivera's writing (453). Pino provides a perceptive comment about the Latinx child as outsider, saying that the protagonist of . . . *y no se lo tragó la tierra* "is more than a Chicano boy growing up in a migrant setting, he becomes more than a symbol of a cultural group which is alienated from other cultures and from a part of its own culture. The youth is a human being who has come to understand he can live with himself in spite of 'the other' and should in fact do so, because that 'other' is himself" (458). Rivera himself said that he had come to recognize his "other" in Chicanx literature ("Fiesta of the Living" 439).

What follows is Rivera's own description of his encounter with the Library Lady taken from an interview with Juan D. Bruce-Novoa, who published a volume of interviews with Chicanx authors:

> In Hampton, Iowa there was a little old lady, tennis shoes and all, who helped me out. Every day I'd walk down to pick up the mail at the post office for my parents and pass the Carnegie Library. . . . I was about ten years old and it was the first time I had come into contact with a library. This lady must have noticed me passing every day, so she stopped me one day and invited me in. . . . She took me down into the basement and showed me all the periodicals. She'd ask me "What do you want to know about?" "This and that," I'd answer, and she would take out the newspaper where we could find it. Then she'd say "Let's go back to 1900" and she'd take out a newspaper from 1900. . . . Then she would say, "Here, you can take these books with you. Read them. Whenever you finish, return them." . . . Every day she had different readings for me, one or two books she thought I'd like, lots of sports books, especially. Then she introduced me to the mystery-type books. *Y así iba dándome todo eso.* Every summer we spent in Hampton, Iowa, I looked forward to going back to that library where she was waiting for me with all these books. I don't even remember her name. (142–43)

The Hampton library is small but imposing. In 1944 the main entrance was accessed by a large set of stairs that could very well have been perceived as intimidating to a young boy. Rivera describes himself "passing" the library daily until the Library Lady appeared and gave him permission to come in. This is how Rivera described the encounter on another occasion: "Because *carne* means meat in Spanish . . . I would wonder—a meat library? The [librarian] must have noticed that I used to stop to gaze at the library [because] one day she came out and invited me into the building. To my amazement, it was filled with books" (Baltes, "Dr. Rivera," 1). This is a key moment that mirrors the experience I had with the migrant mothers in Arizona.

While we don't have any substantive first-hand narrative from Rivera himself about his time with the Library Lady beyond the Bruce-Novoa interview, there is no question that Rivera felt like an outsider. His own writing illustrates the "educational and language barriers" that set him apart and with which he struggled as a child and young adult (Magill 548). In Rivera's book . . . *y no se lo tragó la tierra*, the semi-autobiographical narrator states, "He'd just stare and when they put me in the corner apart from everyone he kept turning to look at me, and then he'd make a gesture with his finger. I was mad but mostly I felt embarrassed because I was sitting away from everyone where they could see me better" (Rivera, Arte Público, loc. 1029). He describes, in third person, being punished for not speaking English. "He thought of how the teacher would spank him for sure because he didn't know the words" (Rivera, Arte Público, loc. 1765). Rivera did say that in the fifth grade he started speaking English "without translating" (Rivera, "Richard Rodriguez" 5). Rivera was born in 1934 and would have been ten years old and in fifth grade in 1944, the same year that he is known to have been in Hampton, Iowa. It is certainly conceivable that Rivera's experience with the Library Lady jump-started his facility with English.

If the Library Lady's influence on Rivera was so significant, who was she? While working on Childsplay's stage adaptation of Pat Mora's book with José Cruz González I had the opportunity to travel to Hampton, Iowa, to do research. I spoke with former Hampton Public Library Director, Judy Harper. She told me that Bertha Gaulke was well known as the librarian at the time that the Rivera family was in Hampton, which she believes was April through October 1944. Speaking of Gaulke and Rivera, Harper says in an interview published in the local newspaper that "they were kindred spirits. This was during World War II. Bertha was from a German family. They spoke German in the family. They were kind of outcasts. Then she met this little boy who also spoke a different language" (Baltes, "A Gift Never Forgotten"). As the migrant workers did not have the appropriate documentation for library cards, Gaulke checked out materials for Rivera with her own card. This is significant because typical public library rules would dictate that someone with no fixed address could not have a library card. Gaulke apparently broke protocol in letting Tomás take books from the library using her credential, risking the loss of the materials. However, this action demonstrates that Gaulke helped Rivera feel that he belonged. Harper further states, "I have heard that not only did she give him the books, and discarded newspapers to take home, they were also teaching each other languages. . . . She was teaching him German and he was teaching her Spanish" (Baltes, "A Gift Never Forgotten"). Ms. Gaulke was known for walking around town in tennis shoes, which is a detail that Rivera remembered. Interestingly, Gaulke wore tennis shoes when walking to and from the library, but not in the library when it was open. This is the primary clue that points to Gaulke as being the Library Lady. Gaulke may have seen the young boy looking at the library and invited him to come in. Another possibility is that she may have invited him in when the library was closed, and she would likely have changed into her tennis shoes. Harper reports that Gaulke "really liked children . . . she had story times for children. She was what every librarian hopes they will be during their lifetime" (Baltes, "A Gift Never Forgotten"). Rivera's comment that he and Gaulke went to the basement to look at newspapers indicates that this could have taken place when the library was closed to the public.

Why would Gaulke take an interest in this young Spanish-speaking boy? Gaulke was a German American who spoke accented English. In a community like Hampton during World War II, anyone with German ancestry would have been regarded with some suspicion. While she was accepted in her role as the town librarian, it seems logical that she would have felt like an outsider because of her accent alone. Hampton librarian Judy Harper said that she felt strongly that Gaulke took an interest in young Tomás Rivera because, like her, English was not his first language, he spoke with an accent, and as only a temporary visitor in the community, was an outlier (Baltes, "A Gift Never Forgotten"). It seems clear from Rivera's own recollections that Gaulke's focus was on helping him become a reader. Rivera would not have had the necessary identification to get a library card; nonetheless Gaulke provided him with books that she trusted he would return.

Pat Mora's Picture Book: Rivera as Reader

Pat Mora's 1997 picture book, with illustrations by Raul Colón, was a boon to school and public librarians and teachers. Here was a story of someone with brown skin who succeeded and was prodded on his way to success by a librarian through reading. What better message could librarians want to send? The reactions I saw when reading this book aloud to groups of children, including multi-racial and Latinx groups, was proof of the truly inspiring nature of Rivera's story.

Mora's book begins on the road with Tomás in a car with his family traveling to Iowa. Once in Iowa, his parents go to work in the fields. He's still too young for field work and spends his time playing soccer with a makeshift ball made from an old teddy bear sewn by his mother. In Tomás's family, the storyteller is Papá Grande, Tomás's grandfather. While walking downtown, Tomás discovers the library. He is greeted by the friendly Library Lady, who gives him a drink of water and asks what he wants to read about. "Tigers, Dinosaurs," answers Tomás (Mora). The books she gives him transport him into another world. She checks out two books for him in her name, and he runs home to share them with his family. We next get an episode at the town dump, where Tomás looks for books, while his brother Enrique looks for toys and his father looks for pieces of iron he can sell. Tomás returns to the library throughout the summer and teaches Spanish to the Library Lady. Then the crops are picked, and Tomás comes to the library with Papá Grande to give the Library Lady a farewell gift of *pan dulce*. The Library Lady gifts him a book of his own, which he cherishes and reads on the bumpy ride back to Texas.

The final page of Mora's book contains a photograph of Rivera as an adult, with a few sentences about his work as the first Latinx chancellor of a University of California campus in Riverside, where the library was named after him. Coming to the end of this story, showing children the photograph, and indicating that it was a true story at times provoked audible gasps from the young audience. It is important to understand that the majority of the children with whom I shared this book saw themselves as outliers or outsiders as well. In one small Phoenix suburb, the school administrator asked the county library to not add books in Spanish to their collection, as they insisted that they wanted their predominately Latinx student body to speak and read English. Cut off from the language that forms their culture, these children could easily identify with the young Rivera.

José Cruz González' Play—Rivera as Writer

Pondering Rivera's story and wanting to bring his story to as wide an audience as possible, I thought about the possibility of commissioning an adaptation of the story for the stage. Tiffany Ana López remarks on the power of "critical witnessing" in live theater (302). A theory that acknowledges the ability of the live theater experience to go beyond entertainment to inspire actual change in the lives of the audience, "critical witnessing" is a key to understanding why the story of Tomás would reach its full potential on the stage. In a contextual sense, the idea was that young Latinx audiences would see themselves in Tomás and that the play would influence them to see that they had potential beyond the boundaries of their current lives. Like Dallas Children's Theater Artistic Director Robyn Flatt, I saw that it was important for Latinx children as "the other" to "find something on the stage that resonates with them personally" and that they hear the "language and stories which their parents and grandparents may have told them" (Schroeder-Arce, "Dallas Children's Theater" 24–25). Like Flatt, it was clear to me that live theater with Latinx characters "validates who they are which translates into a sense of pride, ownership and belonging" (Schroeder-Arce, "Dallas Children's Theater" 25). This idea, along with the fact that many of the Latinx children we served had never seen live theater, made a stage adaptation the ideal way to share Tomás' story.

I had worked previously with Childsplay and their artistic director David Saar to provide booklists to accompany the teacher guides for their productions. Founded by Saar in 1977, Childsplay is known as one of the top children's theaters in the United States. In addition to performing live theater, they travel to schools in the greater Phoenix area introducing children to live theater. I approached David Saar with my idea, and he was immediately supportive. I obtained a grant through the Arizona State Library that would guarantee a substantial number of performances in local schools. Childsplay was able to leverage that grant to get a grant of its own to hire a playwright. It had worked previously with José Cruz González, and he was a natural choice to be tasked with the stage adaptation.

Now seen as the "godfather" of Latinx theater for young audiences, José Cruz González saw his first live theater when he was a first grader. Of the experience, he says that the play "opened up a strange new world to me. Impossible things are possible" (González, *Nine Plays* 3). Like Rivera, González is also the son of migrant farmworkers. Of his childhood, González is quoted as saying, "We grew up working with my mom and grandparents in the fields, canneries, and packing sheds in town" (*Nine Plays* 3). Like Tomás, González's Grandfather "regaled the family with stories and riddles (*Nine Plays* 3). González was first drawn to the theater through his experience seeing El Teatro Campesino and Luis Valdez's groundbreaking play *Zoot Suit* specifically. It was, he says, the first time he had seen his own ethnicity represented on stage. His goal became to work with them some day. He saw their work as a model and said that this is what he wanted to do—create a "mainstream work that tells the story of the other, the outsider" (González, personal interview). While not overtly political or as didactic as many of El Teatro Campesino's agitprop productions, González says that in his theater for young audiences he does indeed want to teach as well as entertain (González, personal interview). González was attracted to the commission to write *Tomás* because he felt it was important to write about a "dreamer who actually dreamed and made it happen" (González, personal interview). He was impressed by Rivera's "unending thirst to learn" despite the life that his parents lived (González, personal interview).

González's play follows the basic structure of Mora's picture book, with some important differences and additions that make use of theatrical convention to reach young audiences on a visceral and emotional level. The play is performed by a male and female actor who both serve as narrators and play all the roles. To make the play as simple as possible to facilitate potential touring productions, González envisioned the set as "a framed structure that serves as a projection area. At center is a small moveable structure that may serve as a bench, bookshelf, or table" (*Nine Plays* 127). The convention of the actors being narrators, or better yet storytellers, gives the play a sense of being something like a campfire or bedtime story told directly to the audience, with both actors saying together lines such as, "This is their story," and, "This is what they said," to demarcate the space between the narration and the action and the transformations that the actors make from one character to another. As the old truck carrying the Rivera family, shown as a shadow image on the screen, wends its way northward, Tomás sleeps. The conversation that González creates for the parents focuses on their desire for Tomás to gain a better education. Tomás has been tossing and turning in his sleep. González shows the audience what is troubling him in his dreams as Tomás opens a suitcase to reveal (via video footage projected on the screen at the back of the set) a "Nightmare Teacher" who berates Tomás for not speaking English. She threatens him and forces him to say, "I will not daydream, be lazy or speak Spanish!" (González, *Nine Plays* 129). This scene puts the focus on Tomás' status as an outlier because of his language. The Nightmare Teacher threatens Tomás that if he doesn't "say it," she will get him (Gonzalez, *Nine Plays* 129). Here González more clearly defines Rivera's status as an outsider as a result of the language barrier. Many Latinx outcasts have this in common. Either their lack of knowledge of English causes them to be the "other," shunted to the side, or more recently, their lack of knowledge of Spanish separates them from their grandparents, parents, and their culture.

Having the Nightmare Teacher appear in a suitcase to torment Tomás introduces the element of magical realism, a realm in which González often works and which comes from his own Latinx heritage. According to González, as he grew up there was always evidence of a world that you could not touch or see, but that he was positive existed. A door would creak open, and his mother would speak with his father, who had passed away years prior. "It was normal to feel a ghost in the house" (González, personal interview). The magical is commonplace in the world of the Latinx outsider. Gabriel García Marquez reinforces this view when he states that amazing and unexplainable things happen all around us, "but Western people can't see them because of their upbringing" (Mason 22). In an essay on González's work in the theater, Susan Mason directly connects the magical realism in González's plays with Tomás Rivera's view of the Chicanx relationship with nature, quoting Rivera as saying that the Chicanx "knelt upon the land . . . and gave it life" (22). What this suggests is that while Rivera may have felt like an outlier among other people, the land accepted him. Pat Mora's book has no examples of magical realism, and when Raul Colón's illustrations depict scenes from the books Tomás is reading, they are the boy's imagination and not something real. This is a key to why González's play is able to more effectively depict Tomás as an outsider. As Mason points out, live theater is an "ideal medium" to portray magical realism, as the "dramatic dimensions of the world on stage are flexible and limitless" (26).

A feature of González's play that further makes use of this idea of limitless dramatic dimension is the portrayal of Tomás' grandfather, Papá Grande, as a moustache moving on the video screen. In her discussion of the play, scholar Roxanne Schroeder-Arce describes taking her ten-year-old daughter Genevieve to a Texas production of the play. Genevieve reported that her favorite part was "when Papa Grande was snoring and his moustache was moving on the screen. When the moustache wiggled, it was really funny" (Schroeder-Arce, "*Tomás and the Library Lady*"). Papá Grande says, "Some say that *artistas* are *locos*, but I say they are touched with God's own brilliant madness" (González, *Nine Plays,* 130), a statement all the more surreal coming from an animated moustache. In one scene, Papá Grande tells a campfire-style story about a man riding on horseback through a forest on a stereotypically windy, dark, and stormy night. Something grabs the man, and we think it must be an animal, or perhaps a Chupacabra, but the culprit is just a thorny tree holding the rider fast. Mora includes this story in her book, but it takes on a more meaningful vision metaphorically when told by Papá Grande, signified by only his moustache projected on the video screen. Rivera was strongly influenced by the storytelling he heard as a child, which he called "remembering, narrating and retelling" (Rivera, "Chicano Literature: Fiesta of the Living" 440). Many of the stories he heard included supernatural characters or spirits. Here González elevates the storytelling from the realistic portrayal in Mora's book to something more like myth and legend "carried in memory and transmitted from one generation to another through storytelling" (Mason 26). González uses theatrical magic like this to bring children to a place where no one is an outsider.

Tomás is definitely influenced by his grandfather's storytelling. When he discovers the library and the Library Lady invites him in, she introduces him to the books and gives him one he can borrow and take home. He tries haltingly to read the English and the Library Lady helps him. He goes home and tells the story of his adventure to his Amá. Tomás continues to visit the library throughout the summer, reads lots of books, and learns more English from the Library Lady. He reads stories to his brother Enrique, and his head fills up "with new words in English" (González, *Nine Plays* 145).

The play also includes the detail of Tomás finding a copy of *Don Quixote* in Spanish (which he would keep for the rest of his life) and a tattered book called *In Darkest Africa*, while in the Hampton town dump with his father. *In Darkest Africa* became a very influential text in Rivera's real life. At the dump, Tomás looks at the map in the Africa book with Enrique and begins imagining Africa in imaginative play with his brother. The map opens Tomás's eyes to a larger world and he picks up a piece of paper and starts writing. Enrique asks Tomás why he isn't drawing pictures, but Tomás explains that "now I can describe a picture with words" (González, *Nine Plays* 148). This line forms the emotional climax of the play and of Rivera's journey in González's dramatization.

In his visits with the Library Lady, the two playfully teach each other their own languages. What is important for González is how the language games that Rivera and Gaulke play together build Rivera's confidence in English, and also how their association sparks Rivera's love for language, which is quite apparent when reading his works. As Gaulke taught Rivera German and he taught her Spanish, Rivera truly learned how to "describe pictures with words."

Prior to the final scenes of the play, Tomás has one last visit from the Nightmare Teacher, but this time he triumphs. He shows her that he can read and understand English, and that he is not afraid of her. She melts away like the Wicked Witch in *The Wizard of Oz*. He can understand the teacher now. She doesn't have to treat him like an outcast. Language, the thing that kept him on the outside, is now his ticket to belonging. Of course, his ethnicity still makes him one of the "others," but his English makes him less so. Genevieve Schroeder-Arce focused on this as the primary message of the play. "I think the message of the story is that you should confront your fears" (Schroeder-Arce, "*Tomás and the Library Lady*"). It is insightful that this idea is what would stand out for a ten-year-old child after seeing this play. There is definitely a sense of fear in being an outlier—the fear inherent in not being able to understand someone else, not knowing what is going on, and potentially being ostracized because of this.

But it is language that allows Tomás to face and overcome his fears. Papá Grande, once again via his mustache on the video screen, and Tomás pay one last visit to the Library Lady, acknowledge what she has done to build Tomás' linguistic confidence and teach her one last word in Spanish: *Adiós*. Goodbye. Here González deliberately changes Mora's version of the narrative and imagines Gaulke giving Rivera a blank book, rather than a library book, to read. This is the clearest indication of his vision of Rivera as a writer. The Library Lady tells him that he might grow up to be "a great writer with your very own books in the library" (González, *Nine Plays* 152). In the final scene of the play, Tomás opens his composition book and begins to write. The male actor then transforms into the adult Tomás, reciting some lines from one of Rivera's commencement speeches, while the female actor tells of Rivera's success in academia, and the library named after him, all because he "was encouraged to read by a library lady in Iowa" (González, *Nine Plays* 153).

In analyzing how González transforms Rivera into a prototypical Latino outlier it is important to also acknowledge the transactional relationship between the live audience and the actors and the story being presented on the stage. Like song lyrics, a dramatic script is dependent upon an additional element to realize its intended purpose. Lyrics need music, and theater needs a stage and performers bringing the words to life. And the fact that some of these words were Spanish was inspirational to young audiences, one of whom wrote a thank you to Childsplay saying "I am bilingual, just like Tomás."

But as González points out, words are just one part of the equation. On a sabbatical trip to see international children's theater in Europe, González's primary takeaway was that in the best works he saw, language was not necessary (González, personal interview). This is an important idea when considering the impact of González's imagining of Tomás Rivera's encounter with the library lady. González has made it clear with the addition of the Nightmare Teacher that language was a major factor that contributed toward Rivera feeling like an outsider. In the play, this thing that has separated him from the mainstream world is what draws him and the library lady together. Finding someone to whom he can teach Spanish makes him able to feel as if by sharing his culture, he can create a world where he is no longer an outsider, but can exist as an equal with others as they all share cultural traditions.

Receiving Permission

González's play concludes with words from the adult Rivera delivering a commencement speech that González found in the UC Riverside Rivera archives: "On behalf of the many Chicano parents who have aspired for generations that their children be educated but do not know what the education system is . . . on behalf of the Chicano writer who hungers for community and justice" (González, *Nine Plays* 153). In his speech, Rivera says that there is a hunger for community among Chicanx artists. Language creates community, but exchange of and respect for differing cultural traditions also does. González's insight about the strongest plays being ones where language was not necessary provides a key to creating cross-cultural communities. Bertha Gaulke was an example of someone reaching out and embracing an outsider like herself even though verbal communication was difficult, as they tried to communicate in a language that for neither was their native tongue. Out of that desire to communicate and create community, however, a shared language emerges. Bertha Gaulke died in 1974, never knowing the impact that she had on the young Rivera.

González's conception of Rivera becoming a writer hits closer to the heart of why Rivera is the prototype of Latinx outliers. Rivera realized that he wanted to be able to tell stories—*his* stories of migrant laborers like his parents, including the children of these migrants, who hoped that words, education, and knowledge would help them rise above their parents' station and not have to endure what they had endured. The goal of these parents was for their children to no longer be outsiders, but to fit in. Tragically, this might mean loss of the cultural nuances that come with fluency in the Spanish language, and the loss of some traditions like *Día de los Muertos* or Cinco de Mayo, which in the United States has become a day to drink margaritas and enrich Mexican food restaurants, with no connection at all to the actual origins of the observance itself.

While Rivera began life as an outlier, he transcended that status by taking the tools that being an outsider had given him and turning them into a way to express his otherness. It is through his writing that he became the prototype of the Latinx outsider. It is no surprise that Rivera wrote in Spanish. It is no surprise that in interviews, such as the one with Bruce-Novoa, that he switched between English and Spanish. Tomás Rivera found a way to give himself permission to belong by articulating his own experience of being on the outside as a writer whose works would present the migrant experience in a truthful and honest narrative accessible to everyone.

Note

1. For more on critical witnessing, see Trevor Boffone, "Performing Eastside Latinidad: Josefina López and Theater for Social Change in Boyle Heights."

Works Cited

"About Us." *childsplayaz.org*, http://www.childsplayaz.org/index.php/about/history. Accessed 7 July. 2018.

Baltes, Ray. "A Gift Never Forgotten." *Hampton Chronicle*. 6 April 2005, pp. 1.

Baltes, Ray. "Dr. Rivera Recounts Story of Hampton Librarian." *Hampton Chronicle*. 6 April 2005, pp. 1, 3.

Boffone, Trevor. "Performing Eastside Latinidad: Josefina López and Theater for Social Change in Boyle Heights." PhD diss., University of Houston, 2015.

Bruce-Novoa. *Chicano Authors: Inquiry by Interview*. University of Texas Press, 1980.

González, José Cruz. Personal interview. 21 March, 2018.

González, José Cruz. *Nine Plays by José Cruz González: Magical Realism and Mature Themes in Theatre for Young Audiences*. Edited by Coleman A. Jennings. University of Texas Press, 2008.

González, José Cruz. "Tomás and the Library Lady." In *Nine Plays by José Cruz González: Magical Realism and Mature Themes in Theatre for Young Audiences*, edited by Coleman A. Jennings. University of Texas Press, 2008, pp. 122–55.

Grajeda, Ralph F. "Tomas Rivera's '. . . y No Se Lo Trago La Tierra': Discovery and Appropriation of the Chicano Past." *Hispania*, vol. 62, no. 1, 1979, pp. 71–81.

Herrera, Cristina. "Soy Brown Y Nerdy: The ChicaNerd in Chicana Young Adult (YA) Literature." *The Lion and the Unicorn*, vol. 41, no. 3, Sept. 2017, pp. 306–26.

Herrera, Juan Felipe. *Portraits of Hispanic American Heroes*. Penguin Young Readers Group, 2014.

Mason, Susan Vaneta. "The Playwriting of José Cruz González." in *Nine Plays by José Cruz González: Magical Realism and Mature Themes in Theatre for Young Audiences*, edited by Coleman A. Jennings. University of Texas Press, 2008. pp. 20–27.

Masterpieces of Latino Literature. Edited by Frank N. Magill. HarperCollins, 1994.

Pino, Frank. "The Outsider and 'El Otro' in Tomás Rivera's *. . . y No Se Lo Tragó La Tierra*." *Books Abroad*, vol. 49, no. 3, 1975, pp. 453–58.

López, Tiffany Ana. "Suturing Las Ramblas to East LA: Transnational Performances of Josefina López's *Real Women Have Curves*." In *Performing the U.S. Latina and Latino Borderlands*. Indiana University Press, 2012, pp. 296–308.

Rivera, Tomás. "Chicano Literature: Fiesta of the Living." *Books Abroad*, vol. 49, no. 3, 1975, pp. 439–52.

Rivera, Tomás. "Richard Rodriguez' Hunger of Memory as Humanistic Antithesis." *MELUS*, vol. 11, no. 4, 1984, pp. 5–13.

Rivera, Tomás. *Short Stories by Tomás Rivera: Bilingual Edition*. Edited by Julian Olivares. Arte Publico Press, 1989.

Rivera, Tomás. *. . . y no se lo tragó la tierra*. Quinto Sol, 1971.

Rivera, Tomás. *. . . y no se lo tragó la tierra*. Kindle edition, Arte Público, 1987.

Schroeder-Arce, Roxanne. "Dallas Children's Theatre Walking the Walk!." *Incite / Insight*, vol. 2, no. 1, Oct. 2010, pp. 24–26.

Schroeder-Arce, Roxanne. "Tomás and the Library Lady: Framing an Expert's Review." *HowlAround*, http://howlround.com/tom-s-and-the-library-lady-framing-an-expertsreview. Accessed 7 July 2018.

4

Non-Cholos in the Hood

10

Young, Gay, and Latino: "Feeling Brown" in Emilio Rodriguez's *Swimming While Drowning*

Trevor Boffone

At the beginning of Emilio Rodriguez's debut play *Swimming While Drowning*, protagonist Angelo Mendez takes the stage of a poetry lounge. His poem explains how when things break, we must fix them. As Angelo searches for something to fix *him*—to help him come to terms with his sexuality—he finds it in an unexpected place: Mila, his roommate at an LGBTQ teen homeless shelter. With Mila having entered his life and left in a flash, Angelo longs for the connection of first love, even if he has grown to accept himself for who he truly is. Angelo declares, "From an early age we learn / That once you break something / You're supposed to fix it / But fixing is not the same / As un-breaking / And un-breaking is not the same / As never having been broken at all / So now I find myself / Trying to press repeat / On the moments between us" (Rodriguez 2–3). Rodriguez's play then shifts to the present to tell the story of two gay Latino boys who come together in the unlikeliest of places: an LGBTQ homeless shelter.

Although *Swimming While Drowning* touches on themes of race, ethnicity, class, and gender, the play principally sheds new light on queer Latinx sexualities. Simply put, Rodriguez emphasizes outsiders—gay Latino teens—within an already marginalized community.

In what follows, I engage with queer Latino playwright Emilio Rodriguez's 2017 play *Swimming While Drowning*.[1] In general, cultural production by, for, and about the queer Latinx population has been "underestimated, overlooked, and undervalued," making theatre such as *Swimming While Drowning* especially ripe for critical inquiry (Pérez 141).[2] I focus on the unpublished playscript while taking into account performances of the play. After discussing the core issues leading to queer youth homelessness and the lived realities of this often-forgotten demographic, I turn to Latinx theatre—in particular Theatre for Young Audiences (TYA)—to demonstrate the ways in which Rodriguez's work forges a new space to stage and demystify queer brown youth identities. Though not explicitly written for young audiences, the play focuses on gay Latino coming-out and coming-of-age narratives. As such, the play has been well received by young adult audiences. In many ways, *Swimming While Drowning* is a revolutionary play for how Rodriguez gives subjectivity to outsiders within already marginalized communities. The play's two protagonists, Angelo and Mila, grapple with their race, ethnicity, gender, and sexuality in ways that are not typically represented in popular culture and theatrical production. Rodriguez's play breaks ground for not only dramatizing homeless youth, but also for the ways in which the play portrays queer Latino boyhoods in a multi-faceted way.

Whereas *Swimming While Drowning* is fundamental to Latinx theatre for its inclusion of gay teen narratives of sexuality and desire, I add that Rodriguez's play does this while also broadening the confines of representation for queer boyhoods. As such, I argue that Rodriguez's play creates a new identity marker within Latinx cultural production: the homeless queer Latino teen. Although these urban youths wrestle with the expectations of masculinity, they both actively reject the major identity script of Latino urban identity: the cholo, which has all-too-often become the stereotypical image of Latino men.[3] While this predominant identity script continues to receive widespread exposure in contemporary mainstream media, works such as *Swimming While Drowning* demonstrate the ways in which Latinx playwrights push against this stereotype of Latino urban youth identity, subsequently broadening the identities of young Latinos. Both Angelo and Mila struggle with preconceived expectations of masculinity and toughness that are so closely linked with how cholos are viewed in the mainstream. That Mila is a tough, street-smart teen only adds to the nuance with which Rodriguez dramatizes this world of youth homelessness. In light of this, I engage with Latinx cultural theorist José Esteban Muñoz's theory of "Feeling Brown" to explain how Rodriguez's play establishes a typography of queer Latino youth identity that pushes against preconceived notions of Latinidad. While both Angelo and Mila "feel brown," or like a problem, they demonstrate the resilient bonds that queer teens have when faced with issues of living up to societal expectations and (un)belonging. As homeless teens, they feel like they simply don't belong or have value. Ultimately, Emilio Rodriguez's *Swimming While Drowning* renders being—and feeling—brown *and* queer visible, thus forging new space in Latinx Theatre for Young Audiences for queer Latino boys to be represented.

Swimming While Drowning from Page to Stage

After moving to Detroit to work for Teach for America, Emilio Rodriguez began researching the challenges facing queer youth of color and LGBT homeless shelters. To further enter this community, he volunteered at an LGBT homeless shelter and an LGBT resource center in Detroit and interviewed several queer people who had lived in shelters. One woman explained to Rodriguez "the reality that many teens feel they have to lie about their upbringing in order to secure a spot in the shelters, which are almost all underfunded and have very limited capacity" (Rodriguez quoted in Enriquez). Inspired by these experiences, Rodriguez wrote *Swimming While Drowning* about queer youth feeling like they must lie about their lives to stay at shelters, which seldom have space and are oftentimes underfunded. In an interview on the 50 Playwrights Project, Rodriguez adds,

> I also wanted to write authentic teenagers who are flawed and learning just like I was when I was 15. So not everything they say is something I agree with, but I do think the controversial moments create discourse for the audience. When we hear something "upsetting" or "problematic" we can ask "What situations would someone have to be in to say that? What experiences have they had that differ from mine?" That's how empathy is created and that's what theatre is for. And I think that allows us to reflect on how our experiences and education shape our beliefs. Ignorance is tolerance waiting on knowledge. (Quoted in Boffone)

To do this, *Swimming While Drowning* focuses on two gay Latino teens living in a homeless shelter in Los Angeles. Angelo Mendez leaves his home out of the fear of not living up to his homophobic father's expectations. At the shelter, his roommate Mila helps Angelo find his authentic voice. The play is not plot-driven per se, but instead is dedicated to character and thematic development. Rodriguez offers a series of vignettes between the two boys that highlights their friendship while also weaving in issues of (un)belonging, race, ethnicity, sexuality, and the ever-increasing familial and societal expectations both Angelo and Mila face. At its core, *Swimming While Drowning* is about survival. What must each boy do to survive their homelessness, their losses, their youth, and, ultimately, their sexuality? How can Angelo and Mila help each other survive? In the end, Angelo learns how to cope with heartbreak through writing and performance.

The gay teens in *Swimming While Drowning* struggle with love. Both want to love and, perhaps more importantly, want to be loved. As queer teens, however, love oftentimes feels like an impossible dream. In an interview with

Amy J. Parrent, Rodriguez notes how in an early staged reading of the play, several spectators noted how "people never get to see LGBT people of color in a relationship. I never thought about how rare that is in theater, but I couldn't pinpoint another play that did." Even though *Swimming While Drowning*'s primary focus is not on Angelo and Mila's romantic relationship, the resilient bonds that the two boys form with each other are nonetheless the heartbeat of the play. As outsiders within both their Latinx communities and as people of color in the shelter, Angelo and Mila must find each other in order to navigate what will only become rockier terrain. Although there are certain commonalities in each boy's journey, their different identity markers lead them to having incredibly disparate experiences and outlooks on how queer Latinos can find a place in this world.

Feeling Brown: Staging Queer Latinx Youth Identities

While Angelo and Mila's identity markers and personalities often clash with each other, ultimately they find solace in their commonalities. As gay Latinos, they share what José Esteban Muñoz calls the condition of "Feeling Brown," or feeling like a problem in a society that values whiteness (and heterosexuality). In "'Chico, What Does It Feel Like to Be a Problem?': The Transmission of Brownness," Muñoz argues that identity is a problematic term when it is applied to Latinx peoples because these groups do not adhere to specific definitions of race, nationality, language, or other traditional markers of difference. This is most clearly seen in *Swimming While Drowning* through class, racial, and linguistic differences. By feeling like a problem, Latinx individuals often find a link that functions to help them belong within a society that openly and frequently discriminates against them. Angelo and Mila's condition of Feeling Brown is marked by what they have in common and what unites them, *lo común* and *la unidad*. According to Muñoz: "Feeling Brown is feeling together in difference. Feeling Brown is an 'apartness together' through sharing the status of being a problem. . . . Brownness is a value through negation, the negation projected onto it by a racist public sphere that devalues the particularity of non-Anglo Americans" ("Chico" 444–45). "Feeling Brown" is in conversation with anthropologist Turner's notion of communitas if we look at both phenomena as the communal pleasure of sharing common experiences (Turner 2). It is necessary that these individuals come together to construct a mode of belonging achieved through the concept of community, in this case happening within the walls of a homeless shelter for LGBTQ teens.

Moreover, the notion of "Feeling Brown" builds on other more well-known theories centered on outsider Latinx identity formation, most notably Muñoz's notion of disidentification: a theory to explain how racial outsiders mediate the dominant culture by transforming it for their own benefit rather than adhering to the dominant culture's mandates for appropriate forms of Latinx identity. Muñoz states that disidentification "is about cultural, material, and psychic survival. It is a response to state and global power apparatuses that employ systems of racial, sexual, and national subjugation. . . . Disidentification is about managing and negotiating historical trauma and systemic violence" (161). In this way, the marginalized individual can utilize processes such as disidentification and the condition of "Feeling Brown" to navigate systems of power and enter into the mainstream as a strategy and act of survival.

Although Muñoz's theories specifically speak to the lived realities of communities of color, they are also ripe for analyzing the troubles facing queer teens at large. While queer teens of color certainly face the added challenges of racial and ethnic oppression, LGBTQ youth in general must contend with many challenges unknown to their straight counterparts, as is evidenced in *Swimming While Drowning*. Queer teens, as well as those questioning their sexual orientation, are at higher risks for depression, drug use, suicide, and school difficulties. For many reasons, school climates have profound influence over the quality of life of queer middle and high school students. According to medical social scientist Michelle Birkett et al.'s research findings on middle school students in the Midwest, LGBTQ youth face higher levels of bullying and homophobia than heterosexual youth (989). Students who question their sexual orientation report even higher percentages of these negative effects. What is more, queer youth face higher rates of suicide attempts than straight teens. In a study of 31,852 eleventh grade students in Oregon (4.4 percent of whom identified as LGBT), sociomedical scholar Mark L. Hatzenbuehler found that queer youth were more likely to attempt suicide compared to straight teens by a 21.5 percent to 4.2 percent margin (896). According to Hatzenbuehler, the risk of attempted suicide increased by 20 percent in unsupportive private and public social environments (896). Hatzenbuehler's study only reiterates the fact that LGBT youth face greater challenges with mental health. In conclusion, he advocates for developing policies and programming that will help to reduce the disparities in suicide attempts based on sexual orientation. Notably, this study excludes trans teens.[4]

Naturally, the difficulties facing queer youth only compound when they encounter the additional realities of homelessness. LGBTQ youth are overrepresented among homeless youth. Although LGBTQ youth only make up about 7 percent of the total youth population, they make up about 40 percent of the youth homeless population (Durso and Gates 2). LGBTQ youth experience homelessness at higher rates and more extended periods of time than cisgender heterosexual youth (Abramovich 1485). In myriad ways, queer homeless youth are vulnerable to threats beyond their control.

Notably, there are few plays that focus on queer youth of color. Even though LGBTQ youth have gained attention from playwrights such as Philip Dawkins (*Charm*), Tira Palmquist (*And Then They Fell*), A. Rey Pamatmat (*Edith Can Shoot Things*), David Pumo (*Auntie Mayhem*), and Pia Scala-Zankel (*Street Children*), queer Latinx youth narratives such as Cherríe Moraga's *Giving Up the Ghost* have been seldom staged up to this point. As Chicanx theatre scholar Jorge Huerta notes in *Chicano Drama*, there were few plays about gay Latinxs until the 1990s and, even so, these plays were rarely published (12). When *Chicano Drama* was published in 2000, there was still a noticeable scarcity not only of queer Latinx plays, but even more so of scholarship about these works. Aside from the landmark volume *Out of the Fringe: Contemporary Latina/Latino Theatre and Performance*, LGBTQ Latinx theatre has historically been an outlier. Yet queer Latinx playwrights have always existed and have subsequently used dramatic writing as a tool to expand homogenous notions of Latinidad. In the present, Millennial Latinx playwrights such as Benjamin Benne, Josh Inocéncio, Christina Quintana, and Emilio Rodriguez have taken to the stage to pen nuanced depictions of queer youth Latinidades.[5] With regard to homeless youth in Latinx theatre, Migdalia Cruz's *Salt* has received the most critical acclaim and scholarly attention. An adaptation of John Ford's *'Tis Pity She's a Whore*, *Salt* follows a family of child prostitutes to comment on how the city and politics have the potential to crush children. Focusing on child sex workers, *Salt* exposes survival sex among homeless youth, not unlike *Swimming While Drowning*. Beto O'Byrne's *You're Not Alone (anymore)* comments on New York City's homelessness epidemic and features issues of LGBTQ homeless youth, although they are not the play's central story. These plays remain crucial to exploring the intersections of queer identity and homelessness. Even so, a gaping hole in dramatic literature persists, especially as it pertains to the United States' ever-growing Latinx population. For these reasons, Rodriguez's work remains a vital outlet for representation within this community.

As *Swimming While Drowning* demonstrates, the intersections of race, ethnicity, and sexuality render queer Latinx homeless youth vulnerable to their surroundings. They live as outsiders within an already marginalized group and therefore constantly face issues of belonging and unbelonging. As there are so few representations of LGBTQ Latinx youth in popular culture, individuals such as Angelo and Mila find it more difficult to gain a sense of belonging in their communities (Reck 228–29). First and foremost, queer Latinx youth often face a higher likelihood of parental rejection and emotional neglect, leading to LGBTQ youth having higher rates of homelessness. According to scholars Laura Durso and Gary Gates, 68 percent of LGBT homeless youth cited family rejection as the main reason they fled or were ousted from their homes. The difficulties queer youth endure only increase when one factors in marginalized ethnic and racial identities. According to clinical social workers Caitlin Ryan et al. in "Family Rejection as a Predictor of Negative Health Outcomes in White and Latino Lesbian, Gay, and Bisexual Young Adults," queer Latinx youth reported greater parental rejection than white, ethnic majority queer youth (346–52). Given that family influences are essential to the ways in which youth develop their identities, parental rejection can lead to negative mental and physical effects such as depression, substance abuse, and unprotected sex (Ryan et al. 346).

"He Looked at Me like He Wished I Was Never Born": Negotiating Queer Latinx Youth Identities

Swimming While Drowning's two protagonists—Angelo and Mila—show how race, ethnicity, and sexuality conflate in relation to homelessness. Having been displaced, they struggle with (un)belonging, "Feeling Brown," and being perpetual outsiders. As "Feeling Brown" is closely associated with "shame and isolation as its general conditions," it is consequently "the affective rebound of constrained gender expression and sexual desire" (Wargo 177). While Mila struggles with these negative repercussions in more visible ways, Angelo's journey demonstrates the ways in which gay Latino boys can develop invisible scars because of their sexuality and these feelings of inadequacy. Angelo finds himself in the homeless shelter because of neglect and rejection from his family. As social workers Geofrey Ream and Nicholas Forge note, family conflicts are one of the main causes of homelessness among LGBTQ youth (10).

Cultural values saturated in homophobia in traditional households motivate certain families to spurn their queer children, even going so far as to disown them and kick them out of the house. Notably, Angelo is in the shelter because he claims that his dad beat him when he came out. "He beat the shit out of me until I bled. The neighbors had to call the cops when they heard the screaming. They found me in a pool of my own blood. The best part: My dad made a smiley face out of the blood on the ground" (Rodriguez 24). After Mila is beat up by a group of guys, he seeks comfort and advice from Angelo. In this moment, Angelo reveals that he was lying—his father never beat him. Angelo explains the pain he felt when he came out to his father: "If you could've seen the look in his eyes . . . It was worse than a beating. He looked at me like he wished I was never born. . . . He gave me THAT look for sixteen seconds; he sucked the air out of the room. . . . That was no stare. Staring is something *humans* do. *This* was something else. *He* was something else" (Rodriguez 60). Even if Angelo has never suffered physical violence for being gay, his experience speaks to the hardships that emerge out of familial relationships for queer youth. Although he was not kicked out of the house, his father's reaction encouraged him to run away and seek housing in a gay homeless shelter. Because space is so limited in the shelter, Angelo lies about having been beat up by his father so that he won't be turned away. Lying becomes a survival tactic. In any case, Angelo can vividly imagine the possibility of violence, which suggests how queer youth of color are always potential victims.

Contrary to Angelo's middle-class (and sheltered) upbringing, Mila has faced added struggles from the ways in which his sexuality conflicts with his class, racial, and ethnic identity markers. For instance, as an Afro-Latino, he is routinely identified as just "black," while his Latinidad is unrecognized and undermined. When the two boys meet, Angelo questions how Mila can be Latino and not speak Spanish (Rodriguez 20). Later, Angelo asks Mila about his use of the word "nigga" (Rodriguez 39). Rodriguez writes:

ANGELO: How come you can say the n word, but I can't?
MILA: Because, I'm black, nigga.
ANGELO: I thought you said you were Latino.
MILA: I'm both, stupid.
ANGELO: How's that possible? (39)

Mila's experiences as an Afro-Latino reiterate the ways in which anti-black racism pervades the Latinx community (Jiménez Román and Flores 2). Adding to this, his inability to speak Spanish makes him feel not "Latino enough" and not a productive member of the ethnic group. As Latinx studies scholars Miriam Jiménez Román and Juan Flores state in *The Afro-Latin@ Studies Reader*, Afro-Latinx folks must contend with "the historical location of Blackness at the bottom of the racial hierarchy and the Latin@ propensity to uphold *mestizaje* (racial and cultural mixture) as an exceptionalist and wishful panacea" (3).

In addition to the problems that arise from upholding mestizaje as the benchmark for Latinidad, Mila's struggles only increase when his sexuality is factored in. Although Mila accepts his attraction to men, he distances himself from all things "gay." While the two boys are discussing Angelo's poem, Mila refers to the poetry as "gay" (Rodriguez 44). The exchange that follows reveals the power of words and labels:

ANGELO: Why are you so ashamed of who you are?

MILA: I'm not. I just don't wanna be dancing around like some faggot all the time.

ANGELO: Don't call me a faggot, faggot.

MILA: Hold up, I'm not a faggot. You ain't about to call me no faggot.

ANGELO: You're gay. That's why you live in a gay homeless shelter. You're a faggot.

MILA: I ain't a faggot, alright? (Rodriguez 44)

Mila never once identifies as gay, even going so far as to admit his fear of being identified as a "faggot," or "a little bitch who can't stand up for himself. A little boy who wants to be a girl. Wears dresses and shit" (Rodriguez 44). As jotería studies[6] scholar Daniel Enrique Pérez claims, "Typically being a maricón is associated with an effeminate role that demoralizes men" (143). In this way, identifying as a "faggot," or the Spanish equivalent "maricón," disrupts hegemonic notions of masculinity. Put simply, to engage in same-sex activities or to be labeled as such destabilizes the ways in which youth such as Mila experience their Latinidad. As Mila states, "You can be gay, you just can't show it. You gotta fool people or else they'll destroy you, you know?" (Rodriguez 44). Mila's struggles reveal the ways in which queer youth of color are more sensitive to conflicts and confusion about their identities. Under an intersectional lens, Mila's struggles reveal the triple jeopardy that one faces being gay, black, *and* Latino. Overall, this increases the likelihood of both physical and psychological trauma (Page 24).

Given these premises, Mila's journey demonstrates the ways physical and psychological abuse negatively affect queer brown youth. Notably, Mila was sexually abused by his aunt's boyfriend when he was a young boy. While talking with Angelo about the abuse each boy has faced, Mila reveals, "I bet you had yo ass knocked to the floor . . . because your tía's boyfriend . . . decided he liked you better than he liked your tía. . . . No?" (Rodriguez 61). According to social workers Gerald P. Mallon and Peg McCartt Hess, homeless youth who have a history of sexual abuse by adults are more likely to engage in survival sex because they seek familiar relationship patterns (237). Even though the connection between Mila's current state and his previous experiences of sexual abuse is unclear, his desire for attention and appreciation is almost certainly a driving force explaining why he partakes in sex work.

Abuse has been a mainstay in Mila's life and is something that he clearly continues to struggle with while in the shelter. Although the details surrounding what happened to Mila regarding his tía's boyfriend are cloudy at best, what is evident is that his aunt's boyfriend sexually abused him in some capacity, an experience that has marked his life through adolescence.[7] In this instance,

Rodriguez offers a fundamental perspective on how trauma and violence can affect marginalized individuals. In "Not Outside the Range: One Feminist Perspective on Psychic Trauma," psychologist Laura Brown examines the ways in which trauma is often defined within a narrow framework "constructed within the experiences and realities of dominant groups in cultures" (102). In this way, Mila's narrative allows spectators a window into how queer brown boys navigate trauma. By situating personal experience as a point of departure for critical inquiry, we can begin to understand how these traumatic events do not affect Mila in a vacuum. For example, the violence Mila suffered served as a catalyst for him to leave home. This brings him to his current reality. To Mila, living on the streets and in shelters is a more viable option for living a fulfilled live. As Latinx theatre scholar Tiffany Ana López notes, there is a "spectrum of processing trauma, which includes how people come to define themselves not just as victims, but also as survivors, and eventually as those simply living" (185–86). For Mila, simply living is enough.

Mila's struggles peak when he turns to survival sex, a practice whereby he exchanges sex for money. Driven by financial benefits in addition to the desire to feel self-worth, LGBT homeless youth view transactional sex as a viable option to build their future. In a study from the Urban Institute, results show that "41 percent of homeless youth had last exchanged sex for money and/ or material goods during the last week and 26 percent had last traded a few weeks to a month before the interview" (Dank et al. 21). According to social workers N. Eugene Walls and Stephanie Bell, "homeless LGBT youth between the ages of 1 and 25 years are 70% more likely than homeless heterosexual youth to engage in survival sex," which they differentiate from other types of prostitution since its main purpose is to trade sex for money, food, and shelter (424–36). For a number of reasons, the effects of emotional and financial insecurity must be viewed in conversation with each other. For queer homeless youth, the lack of material support fosters insecurity about their future, such as their ability to find employment and their perceived self-worth. For youth such as Mila, a high-quality education is not a viable reality. They regard prostitution, therefore, as a feasible means to support themselves. In addition to the financial benefits of survival sex, homeless youth partake in the practice to feel valued; young people's desire for emotional and sexual attention is an added motivation. When Angelo asks Mila about sex work, Mila responds, "It is not as bad as you think," because the men he has sex with "talk to him differently" (Rodriguez 51). These men make Mila feel "special" (Rodriguez 51). In this case, Mila does not want to see himself as a victim. Being a victim, to Mila, is akin to being gay, which is a term he rejects. Throughout *Swimming While Drowning*, Mila makes it clear that he does not realize his self-worth; he isolates himself and continually creates barriers between himself and Angelo, seemingly the only person in his life who sees the beauty in Mila.

Conclusion

In the final moments of *Swimming While Drowning*, Mila and Angelo each take the stage alone to tell us how their time in the shelter has influenced them and how they changed each other (even if they likely will never see or hear from each other again). After sneaking out of bed and packing up his belongings in the middle of the night, the lights shift, focusing solely on Mila. "I got the guard of a soldier when he's under attack / You took the rhythm out of me but I don't want it back / Cuz I gotta lotta bags I wanna unpack / Leave the old me behind no more circles on the track" (Rodriguez 85). As Mila's poem reaches its climax, the sounds of a bus approaching are heard. The lights shift, Mila is gone forever, and the sounds of a bus leaving fill the theatre. In the near future, Angelo takes the stage at a poetry lounge in New York City to perform "Swimming While Drowning," a poem dedicated to love and the longing to reconnect with Mila. As Angelo professes, the presence of Mila helped him survive the shelter. "This is not a poem / This is a thank you / To the man who made / The weight of the world / Just a little bit lighter. . . . This is not a poem / This is an ode / To the man who / Took the words inside me / And created a writer" (Rodriguez 87). With Mila gone, Angelo now recognizes how sharing space and intimacy with another queer Latino boy enabled him to not only accept himself, but gave him the confidence to achieve his dream of becoming a writer. Although the two boys will likely never see each other again, Rodriguez makes it apparent that they will be in each other's lives far beyond what we see in *Swimming While Drowning*. In the end, Emilio Rodriguez's play establishes a typography of queer urban Latino youth identities that actively rejects stereotypes such as the Cholo. As outsiders, these two young teens wrestle with societal expectations of who or what a Latino male should be, ultimately finding community in each other through their shared feelings of brownness and disidentification. The result is a nuanced portrayal of gay Latino boyhood that, while outside the margins, forges new space in theatre for young audiences for underrepresented identities to flourish.

Yet stories such as Angelo and Mila's often go unnoticed in Latinx young adult literature and theatre for young audiences. Even the landmark 2011 critical anthology *Gay Latino Studies*, edited by Michael Hames-García and Ernesto Javier Martínez, does not consider the uniqueness of young adulthood. There is an overwhelming absence of discussion about how queer Latinidad and Latino masculinities apply to teenage boys. Even so, queer Latinx creative expression centered on youth identities has only expanded in the twenty-first century. The benchmark 2012 collection *Queer in Aztlán: Chicano Male Recollections of Consciousness and Coming Out*, edited by Adelaida R. De Castillo and Gibran Guido, features a vast array of creative writing exploring the intersections of Latinidad, queerness, and coming-of-age. Notwithstanding, scholarly production has not caught up with cultural production. As the expanses of Latinx theatre for young audiences continue to grow, we must ask ourselves who is being represented. When there are gaps, we must fill them. As this chapter has shown, now is the time for us to recognize gay Latino homeless youth, on our pages, on our stages, and in our communities.

Notes

1. *Swimming While Drowning* received a staged reading at the Activate Midwest Festival at Western Michigan University, a workshop reading under the direction of Alex Meda at the Latinx Theatre Commons' Carnaval of New Latina/o Work in 2015 at the Theatre School at DePaul University, a production at Theatre Nova under the title *Spin*, various informal readings, and finally a world premiere production directed by Francisco García at Milagro (Portland, Oregon) in February 2017.

2. Even though LGBTQ+ themed Latinx YA novels such as Benjamin Alire Sáenz's *Aristotle and Dante Discover the Secrets of the Universe* have received significant mainstream success in both young adult literature and literary circles at large, Latinx theatre exploring queer themes has not received the same exposure. Despite the fact that Latinx Theatre for Young Audiences (TYA) is thriving with new works by Karen Zacarías, José Cruz González, José Casas, and Georgina Escobar, and the landmark publication of *Palabras del Cielo: An Exploration of Latina/o Theatre for Young Audiences* by Dramatic Publishing in 2018, queer stories are often absent from this conversation. It seems that mainstream theatre and publishing are not ready to highlight stories that foreground the double marginalization of being both Latinx and queer. For many theatre companies catering to young audiences, producing a play by a Latinx playwright or one that centers Latinidad remains a reach. Likewise, for queer TYA, programming is more or less non-existent. Plays with LGBTQ themes geared towards young adults are by and large viewed as too controversial.

3. Also known as the homeboy, the cholo has been visible in films such as *Colors*, *American Me*, and *Cheech and Chong*, to name only a few. Although there are variations, popular culture has depicted the homeboy/cholo as a young male in baggy pants and flannel who may or may not drive low rider cars.

4. Public Health practitioners Greta R. Bauer et al.'s study fills these gaps by focusing on factors related to suicide risk in transgender people. Bauer et al.'s study focuses on trans people in Ontario, Canada, to identify the primary factors (social inclusion, transphobia, and sex/gender transition) that are associated with suicide attempts. Their research shows that in the United States, Canada, and Europe, anywhere from 22 percent to 43 percent of trans people report a history of suicide attempts. These numbers entirely factor in trans youth; Bauer et al.'s study only includes those aged sixteen and older.

5. In many ways, Benne's *Querencia: An Imagined Autobiography about Forbidden Fruits* is in conversation with that of Emilio Rodriguez. Benne's work is a memory play about Milo, a thirteen-year-old Latino who is struggling to understand his sexuality. As in *Swimming While Drowning*, Benne's play shows how resilient bonds between teenagers can ease the coming-out and coming-of-age processes. In addition to Benne and Rodriguez's plays, Josh Inocéncio's *Purple Eyes* and Christina Quintana's *Azul* are noteworthy plays about queer youth identities.

6. Jotería studies is the study of queer Latinx identities and communities.

7. For LGBTQ homeless youth, familial abuse is an all-too-common contributor to their homelessness; 54 percent of queer homeless youth report abuse by family members as a reason for leaving home (Durso and Gates).

Works Cited

Abramovich, Alex. "Understanding How Policy and Culture Create Oppressive Conditions for LGBTQ2S Youth in the Shelter System." *Journal of Homosexuality*, vol. 64, no. 11, Mar. 2016, pp. 1484–1501.

Bauer, Greta R, et al. "Intervenable Factors Associated with Suicide Risk in Transgender Persons: a Respondent Driven Sampling Study in Ontario, Canada." *BMC Public Health*, vol. 15, no. 525.

Birkett, Michelle, et al. "LGB and Questioning Students in Schools: The Moderating Effects of Homophobic Bullying and School Climate on Negative Outcomes." *Journal of Youth and Adolescence*, vol. 28, no. 7, 2009, pp. 989–1000.

Boffone, Trevor. "FAQs: *Swimming While Drowning* by Emilio Rodriguez." *50 Playwrights Project*, 4 Apr. 2017, 50playwrights.org/2017/04/04/faqs-swimming-while-drowning-by- emilio-rodriguez/.

Brown, Laura. "Not Outside the Rage: One Feminist Perspective on Psychic Trauma." *Trauma: Explorations in Memory*, edited by Cathy Caruth, Johns Hopkins University Press, 1995, pp. 102–12.

Dank, Meredith, et al. "Locked In: Interactions with the Criminal Justice and Child Welfare Systems for LGBTQ Youth, YMSM, and YWSW Who Engage in Survival Sex." *Urban Institute*, 2015, https://www.urban.org/research/publication/locked-interactions-criminal-justice-and-child-welfare-systems-lgbtq-youth-ymsm-and-ywsw-who-engage-survival-sex.

Durso, Laura E, and Gary J Gates. "Serving Our Youth: Findings from a National Survey of Service Providers Working with Lesbian, Gay, Bisexual, and Transgender Youth Who Are Homeless or At Rick of Becoming Homeless." *The Williams Institute*, UCLA School of Law, July 2012, williamsinstitute.law.ucla.edu/research/safe-schools-and- youth/serving-our-youth-july-2012/.

Enriquez, Maria. "Cafecito: Emilio Rodriguez." *Café Onda: Journal of the Latinx Theatre Commons*, 20 Oct. 2015, howlround.com/cafecito-emilio-rodriguez.

Hatzenbuehler, Mark L. "The Social Environment and Suicide Attempts in a Population-Based Sample of LGB Youth." *Pediatrics*, vol. 127, 2011, pp. 896–903.

Huerta, Jorge. *Chicano Drama: Performance, Society and Myth*. Cambridge University Press, 2000.

Jiménez Román, Miriam, and Juan Flores. "The Afro-Latin@ Reader: History and Culture in the United States." *The Afro-Latin@ Reader: History and Culture in the United States*, edited by Miriam Jiménez Román and Juan Flores, Duke University Press, 2010, pp. 1–14.

López, Tiffany Ana. "'Stunned into Being': The Practice of Critical Witnessing in Lorna Dee Cervantes's *Drive*." *Stunned into Being: Essays on the Poetry of Lorna Dee Cervantes*, edited by Eliza Rodríguez y Gibson, Wings Press, 2012, pp. 177–95.

Mallon, Gerald P., and Peg McCartt Hess. *Child Welfare for the Twenty-First Century: A Handbook of Practices, Policies, and Programs*. Columbia University Press, 2005.

Muñoz, José Esteban. "'Chico, What Does It Feel Like to Be a Problem?' The Transmission of Brownness." *A Companion to Latina/o Studies*, edited by Juan Flores and Renato Rosaldo, Blackwell Publishing, 2007, pp. 441–51.

Muñoz, José Esteban. *Disidentifications: Queers of Color and the Performance of Politics*, University of Minnesota Press, 1999.

Page, Michelle. "Homeless LGBT Youth of Color & the Runaway and Homeless Youth Act." *Northwestern Journal of Law & Social Policy*, vol. 12, no. 2, 2017, pp. 17–45.

Parrent, Amy J. "Left-Coaster Turned Mitten-Stater: A Rising Start in Theater World." *Pride Source*, 3 Dec. 2015, http://www.pridesource.com/article.html?article=74328.

Pérez, Daniel Enrique. "Entre Machos y Maricones: (Re)Covering Chicano Gay Male (Hi) Stories." In *Gay Latino Studies: A Critical Reader*, edited by Michael Hames-García and Ernesto Javier Martínez, Duke University Press, 2011, pp. 141–46.

Ream, Geofrey L., and Nicholas R. Forge. "Homeless Lesbian, Gay, Bisexual, and Transgender (LGBT) Youth in New York City: Insights from the Field." *Child Welfare*, vol. 23, no. 2, March 2014, pp. 7–22.

Reck, Jen. "Homeless Gay and Transgender Youth of Color in San Francisco: 'No One Likes Street Kids'—Even in the Castro." *Journal of LGBT Youth*, vol. 6, no 2–3, 2009, pp. 228–29.

Rodriguez, Emilio. Swimming While Drowning. N.d.

Ryan, Caitlin, et al. "Family Rejection as a Predictor of Negative Health Outcomes in White and Latino Lesbian, Gay, and Bisexual Young Adults." *Pediatrics*, vol. 123, no. 1, 2009, pp. 346–52.

Turner, Edith L. B. *Communitas: The Anthropology of Collective Joy*. Palgrave Macmillan, 2012.

Walls, N. Eugene, and Stephanie Bell. "Correlates of Engaging in Survival Sex among Homeless Youth and Young Adults." *Journal of Sex Research*, vol. 48, no. 5, 2011, pp. 423–36.

Wargo, Jon M. "At the Risk of 'Feeling Brown' in Gay YA: Machismo, Mariposas, and the Drag of Identity." *Affect, Emotion, and Children's Literature: Representation and Socialisation in Texts for Children and Young Adults*, edited by Elizabeth Bullen, Kristine Moruzi, and Michelle J. Smith, Routledge, 2017, pp. 175–90.

11

What Can We Learn from Cool Cats?
Chillante Pedagogy, Gary Soto, and the Chato Series

Elena Avilés

When he asks what we can learn from cool cats, Gary Soto means, of course, what can readers learn from the right of Chicanxs to define themselves on their own terms. A cool cat is a term that describes a hip, progressive, high-tech urban male subject. A cool cat represents what is modern and fashionable, often invoking an avant-garde style. A hip dude that moves with the times, the image of the cool cat fashions an attitude and behavior that shifts in accordance with what is in vogue. Cool cats may be literal images, symbolic representations, or archetypal figures in popular culture. Their entity has come to signify an expression, a response by historically marginalized social groups to their invisibility and constant erasure in dominant and mainstream society.

As a Chicanx and Latinx children and Young Adult (YA) writer, Soto expands thematic discussions on the history of cool cats as an apparatus of cultural capital imperative for young Chicano male readers and for their education. How are boys of color supposed to learn about positive identity formation if narratives about them, and on their own terms, are nonexistent? The twenty-first century's modern history, from the killing of Trayvon Martin (2012) and Michael Brown (2014) to Stephen Clark (2015), illustrates the imminent danger young males of color face in articulating a sense of self amidst the shifting apparatus of white supremacy and neoliberal control via violence, oppression, discrimination, and racist practices meant to erase their humanity. What are the ramifications men of color face for being "cool?"

In *The Greenwood Encyclopedia of African American Folklore*, which defines the identity politics associated with the word "cool" in relation to

African American or US black masculinity, David Todd Lawrence discusses the emergence of "cool" or "cool pose" to express a performative stance. He claims it serves as a "mechanism used by black men to help shield them from the harsh humiliation of their everyday existence in a world that, at the very least, undervalues them as human beings" (264–65). Noting that the term evolved into a folk icon and references black folkloric performance, Lawrence explains how models of "cool" behavior demonstrate a form of authenticity that is produced by US black masculine culture.

Within US black expressive culture, "The term denotes an attitude; a way of being in the world exemplified by a calm demeanor—a kind of casual smoothness and quiet confidence—accompanied by an impeccable sense of style meant to signify profound dignity and pride in the face of extreme oppression" (Lawrence 264). Symbolically and metaphorically speaking, cool cats earn respect through street credibility. Because hegemonic society constantly displaces male bodies of color, the immediate spatial environment men inhabit becomes the terrain where a positive sense of belonging manifests. Gary Soto's book series on Chato, a cool cat, engages with public notions of male-of-color identity by altering the pressures to ascribe to constructions of hypermasculinity such as being violent, hard, insensitive, and domineering. Building on contributions by Ybarra Frausto on *rasquachismo*, Amalia Mesa-Bains' *domesticana*, and Marci McMahon's "domestic negotiations," a Chicanx analysis of the cool cat as an archetypal reference of what it means to be Chicano, or *chicanidad*, reveals a precisely crafted storyline that offsets the salient negative stereotypes of Chicano bodies and neighborhoods while expanding conversations about gender. The extension of Frausto's scholarship into what I term *chillante* pedagogy, elucidates the radical attitude, stance, and performance of the Chicano politics as constructed by Soto in literary terms, with the visual compliments of Susan Guevara as illustrator.

Soto describes the performance of Chicano masculinity in connection to street credibility that consists of the sets of societal conditions where Chato's interests and opinions matter, where male of color performance results new interpretations of Chicano masculinities. In the series, hypermasculinity is dismantled with male protagonists in caring relationships with peers, males participating in community. The characters are outsiders of a Chicano masculinity that boxes males into gangsters in communities of color. By teaching young boys about how cool it is to just be yourself, to enjoy yourself, to love, to express emotion, to be in community, Soto's non-cholo male figures illustrate a barrio aesthetic that curbs hypermasculinity while preserving the tradition of the significance of the cool cat stance. Chillante pedagogy reveals how Soto honors the cultural legacies of Chicanismo by embodying non-cholos as cool cats.

Cool Cats and Hipness: A Genealogy

While the development of the cool cat image as we know it today has origins in black aesthetic practices, its image transcends racial lines. During the mid-twentieth century, cool cats made reference to the underground, youth subculture of communities of color, in particular that of African and Mexican American communities that were beginning to define themselves through homegrown aesthetics. The American Beat Generation of the 1960s, pulp fiction, and hippie culture are typical examples of the counterculture movement that started in the 1960s and came to fruition in the 1970s, a moment in time that transformed the figure of the cool cat into an accepted symbol of savviness. Jazz and the boogaloo[1] are two examples of such homegrown aesthetics originating from marginalized communities during the early twentieth century.[2]

While often used to convey negative messages about communities of color in urban spaces, the cool cat's figure, image, and representation changed over time, becoming ever more present in mainstream culture through the zoot suit,[3] also known as pachuco style in Chicanx culture, which has evolved into an accepted and venerated form of marking identity parallel to the hip hop style of today. Looney Toons, for example, cemented modern notions of the cool cat figure as an urban subject through the fictional character "Cool Cat."[4] From cartoons to music, the figure of the cool cat operated as a powerful mechanism on modernity and revolution in mainstream popular youth counterculture.[5] The cool cat figure incarnated a gendered, cultural, and social shift of values meant to challenge mainstream representations and imaginings about and by men of color, while for others it provided a mode of resistance to the status quo. Another change dealt with gender; over time a cool cat became a descriptor for women.[6]

Musician Lalo Guerrero is an example of a Chicano cool cat. He embodies Chicano male subjectivity and expression. He was known as "the original Chicano hepcat," "hep" being a historical variation of "hip." Through music, Lalo Guerrero captures the operative values of a subculture challenging, defying, and opposing hegemonic perspectives. His song "Los Chucos Suaves" (Cool Dudes) expresses the rhythm, sounds, and language of Mexican Americans during the 1940s and 1950s.[7] Guerrero's Zoot Suit-era music enacts the pachuco style rhythm, especially in the title of the song, which expresses Chicanx vernacular. "Chucos" is an abbreviation of "pachucos." A pachuco describes a Chicano zoot suiter, who was seen as an urban transgressor. The digital exhibit "American Sabor: Latinos in U.S. Popular Music" features an entry titled "Pachuco Boogie,"[8] which illustrates the dress, speech, and mannerisms that youth adopted in response to oppression and misrepresentation. Pachuco history is predominantly linked with the history of East Los Angeles because of the Zoot Suit riots of 1943. During the Chicano Movement, the pachuco became a Chicano archetype, according to Juan Bruce Novoa in *Retrospace: Collected Essays on Chicano Literature Theory and History* (1990). Luis Valdez's *Zoot Suit* (1978) and its adaptation to film in 1981 depicted the pachuco as a cool cat from East Los Angeles.

The representation of East Los Angeles cool cats in Soto's Chato Series covers the genealogy of Chicano cool cats in order to teach young readers about these mainstream outsiders, called hoodlums, thugs, and miscreants in mainstream society because to adopt the cool cat style implied being against the norm, against what is American. But how does one begin to tease out and see the complexity of masculine studies and the contributions of various aspects of the Chicanx culture of East Los Angeles to the United States and abroad in the Chato Series: *Chato's Kitchen* (1995), *Chato and the Party Animals* (1998), and *Chato Goes Crusin'* (2004)? What if one is a true outsider to Chicanx culture? How is a mass audience supposed to understand Chato or why he matters?

Chato is a cool cat, a figure embodying the latest trend in Chicanx style, as does the secondary protagonist, Novio Boy. The strengths of Soto's texts are the manners in which he fashions a male identity that engineers a representation of these modern-day cool cats as non-cholos meant to debunk mainstream stereotypes about East Los Angeles. The interpretation of Chato as a cool cat empowers disenfranchised neighborhoods like East Los Angeles, known as barrios or *colonias*, because it teaches children to celebrate Chicanx heritage and cultural legacy, while for ingroup children, even if impoverished, it teaches them about their cultural capital.

Soto's series on Chato deserve further scholarly analysis because for Chicano, Latino and Hispanic males, their criminalization is unfortunately less recognized than of African American men. According to the study "Why Neighborhoods Matter in Deaths by Legal Intervention: Examining Fatal Interactions between Police and Men of Color," by the Fatal Interactions with Policy Study (FIPS),[9] Hispanic men face a higher risk of police-related fatalities in highly segregated neighborhoods with little diversity than do other groups. In "Young Hispanic Men May Face Greatest Risk from Police Shootings," Gerry Everding reports two key findings in one FIDS study, that "Hispanic males were over 2.6 times as likely as others to be killed by officers from agencies with relatively higher percentages of Hispanic officers" and that "in neighborhoods with high levels of income inequality, such as poor areas undergoing gentrification, all males of color face a higher risk of being killed during interactions with police. Hispanic men face an even higher risk than black men in these settings." Against the backdrop of today's cultural politics and outright attack on bodies of color, Soto's book series about Chato reads as an oppositional stance that echoes some of the current social injustices of today: that not all men of color are gangsters and therefore suspect, and that men of color do matter as seen in the Black Lives Matter Movement.

Soto's construction of protagonists as non-cholos while being cool cats reveals his ability to weave past, present, and future knowledge production for young readers. He creates bridges from oral forms of storytelling in Chicanx communities into literature. The fashioning of Chicano male identity as non-cholos challenges readers to face hidden biases about males from historically disenfranchised communities. Thanks largely to the Hollywood industry, which has criminalized the modern Chicano body, the phrase "boys from the hood" often generates a monochromatic and negative image of males as gangsters.[10] Chicanx synonyms include the term pachuco, as already discussed above, as well as cholo, vato, and homies.[11] Within Chicanx linguistic expression, also known as caló, vato and homies express endearment, which is contrary to default gang affiliations as seen in stereotyped images of Chicanos in the United States. But the saliency of the pachuco cool cat and its evolution into the hip hop urban cool cat cannot be ignored as a key symbol, metaphor, and allegory for Chicano male synthesis and declaration of identity. This is what Soto conveys to all readers, young and old.

As such, in Soto's narrative world, cool cats transgress conventions about outsiders and their representation within children's and YA literature. The significance of his series rests in thematic and theoretical discussion of Chicanxs as outsiders. The links between Chicanxs and Latinxs and the notion of being outsiders are many: On the one hand, the cool cat figure represents the Chicanx individual as an outsider in relation to mainstream culture, which parallels African American struggles for visibility and participation. By bringing the reader into Chato's community, where his dress, speech, and mannerisms are culturally framed and contextualized, Soto channels a barrio logic of Chicanxs who cease to be outsiders in America. Through literature, he debunks mainstream ideologies of Chicanxs as "foreign," "alien," and "dangerous" by repudiating negative stereotypes about East Los Angeles—one of Los Angeles's oldest neighborhoods—as "poor," "lacking," "deficient," "uneducated," "linguistically inferior," and "crime infested," or as Oscar Zeta Acosta's book title acutely captures, *The Revolt of the Cockroach People* (1973).

On the other hand, Soto teaches children within and outside of mainstream culture about Chicanx sets of knowledge to demonstrate that every generation fashions the taste and style of what it means to be cool cats. Chicanx cool cats operate within cultural, social, political, gender, linguistic, literary, and visual subjective positions. Soto does not represent a single interpretation of the "cool pose" that defines Chicanx expressive culture, but rather traces the roots and influences fashioning Chicanx gendered identity within US politicized race and class categories. The characters of the book depict intergenerational notions of manhood and the diversity of the performance stance of male identity that reflects what Frausto calls a "bicultural sensibility" (6).

Revising Male of Color Masculinity: The Chato Series

Soto's series is a dexterous response to the absence of books on male-identified adults, teenagers, and children of color in children's and YA literature: it is textually and visually complex, while at the same time culturally responsive and thought provoking. In fact, many online comments on the Chato Series fail to understand the specificities of its Chicanx expressive practices. Judgements about its supposed inadequacies—the hidden transcripts—denote the internal workings of a Chicanx text and images decolonizing children's minds. Perhaps for those harsh critics who do not grasp Soto's play on culture, the interdisciplinary methods and approaches of *chillante* pedagogy may help them engage in critical and decolonial thought.

Soto also decolonizes the Latin American judgment of "otherness" and "less than" mentality that degrade Chicanxs. These offset the legacies of internal colonial models of transnationalism in Chicanx culture. The Chato Series channels a new pedagogical perspective about males of color in their communities, revealing that there is a difference and diversity in the performance of Chicano masculine culture and the fluidity of gender, sex, and sexuality that accompanies identity. In this respect, the series is a response to Spanish and US American colonialism. A playful narrative about cats communicates a powerful gendered lesson: literature and art can become an outlet for men of color to affirm a self-generated style. Soto's cool cat becomes a bodily metaphor of visibility, presence, and self-definition.

Representations of Chicano males as non-cholos challenge biases about who Chicanos are, and where and how they live. Soto honors the archetypal development of the pachuco as described by John Bruce-Novoa, but also interrogates Chicanxs themselves to check their internal colonial projections about cool cats. In *Chato's Kitchen*, for example, a prism of contemporary male figures and expressions exist: Chorizo's Chicano brown beret and UFW button evoke Chicano militant subjectivity, Novio Boy represents the modernized pachuco, Chato expresses the hip hop look, while Mr. Ratoncito (Papi) adheres to the traditional Texas cowboy look, the *vaquero* cowboy indicative of the leather belt, blue jeans and cowboy boots. Soto's Papi character is not hypermasculine or an overly sexualized male reminiscent of the Papi chulo stereotype. He is literally a Papi, a father. This chapter applies *chillante* pedagogy and *chillante* aesthetics to enact Chicanx critical perspectives on Gary Soto's writing and Susana Guevara's illustrations. *Chillante* pedagogy maps modes to teach and learn about Chicanx sensibilities within the landscapes of Chicanx and Latinx children's and YA literature. *Chillante* pedagogy may be inclusive of additional US Latinx experiences as *chillante* aesthetics present a way of understanding content that reflect US Latino artists and writers' activism in bridging past, present, and future knowledge production. In Chicanx children's and young adult literature, image and text communicate Chicanx aesthetic practices, often working together at the discretion of the reader, but which is also dependent on the reader. The interrelationship, synergy, and synthesis of *chillante* pedagogy is a calling aesthetic, like its root verb *chillar*: it screams and yells for your attention, in the same way that a text for young readers must be visually and textually calling. *Chillante* pedagogy provokes an *enfrentamiento*, a calling for an encounter, confrontation, and engagement. Chillante pedagogy is the child's adventure into the world of Chicano *rasquachismo*.

Mesa-Bains' expansion of *rasquache* sensibilities into the feminine and feminist realm offers a long-ignored element in Chicanx culture, the intimate and sacred contributions of women's actions. Mesa-Bains' theory helps readers to understand the cultural value of East Los Angeles and shows how everyday practices by individuals reference the behavioral survival social practices of family largely defined by a female and feminist sensibility. *Domesticana* reciprocates *rasquachismo,* but "domestic negotiations" uncloak Guevara's visual praxis.

Chillante aesthetics and pedagogy advance the development of Chicanx visual and literary *modus operandi* and the contributions of the scholars mentioned above, but within Chicanx/Latinx Young Adult Literature.[12] *Chillante* aesthetics is a practice and politics of expressive culture that is uniquely Chicanx. *Chillante* aesthetics enables a nuanced reading of text and image's interactions in shaping critical perspectives in children's literature. *Chillante* aesthetics and pedagogy illustrate the dignified moments Soto creates of urban and barrio expression, and of positive male-of-color identity. *Chillante* pedagogy reveals the coded sensibilities of barrio strategies of affirmation and resistance across text and image, and the decolonial cultural acts remixing notions of outsiders or outliers.

Chillante Pedagogy: A View of Barrio Aesthetics

Chillante pedagogy is about how cultural production teaches Chicanx sensibilities. *Chillante* pedagogy may be inclusive of US Latinx experiences, as *chillante* aesthetics present ways to bridge past, present, and future knowledge production. Within the realm of Chicanx children's and young adult literature, image and text intermix to communicate Chicanx aesthetic practices. *Chillante* aesthetics enables a nuanced reading of the interaction of text and images in shaping discourses, meaning, and logic in children's literature. Soto's interpretation of East Los Angeles's literary, visual, and linguistic sensibilities echoes *chillante* pedagogy's practice of a style, stance, or act. The Chato Series is a way of "looking" like cool cats, literally, metaphorically, allegorically, and symbolically. The series generates an oppositional stance, resonant of a "methodology of the oppressed" (Sandoval). The use of vernacular language, street words, and Spanish in all three books is an expression of Chicanx linguistic opposition. Soto eases monolingual concerns by including a glossary at the end. Like a true sociolinguist, he captures the linguistic diversity of the barrio, which he simply translates "the neighborhood." It's powerful for barrio children of ELA to see their homes defined as a neighborhood without the attachment of negative adjectives.

Soto creates a context for the emancipation of diverse linguistic registers that would otherwise not make it onto the pages of children's literature under the confines of language hierarchies. For example, in *Chato Goes Cruisin'* (2005) he challenges Spanish speakers who hear US Spanish speakers and perceive that these speakers are destroying the language by speaking Spanish in addition to the perception that US Spanish speakers don't know how to speak Spanish or English. The use of the terms "lonche, "órale," and "no problema" are some examples.

Soto disrupts these forms of linguistic violence by placing equal value on false cognates, borrowings of words between English and Spanish, legitimizing code-switching, and language variation. In the same vein, he also challenges myths about Chicanxs by English speakers. Some invalid thoughts about Chicanx English include the idea that Chicanxs speak bad English because they are Spanish speakers or that Chicanxs are all Spanish speakers, that Chicanx English has no structure and therefore exhibits incorrect grammar, and that Chicanx English is spoken by gang members and the uneducated. In *Chato and the Party Animals*, Soto writes, "Oh no! ¡Qué tonto! I think I forgot to invite him!" "*Pues*, let's go round up that party cat," "He was such a *suavecito*," and "Too bad this *vato* is gone," not to irk or to ridicule but rather to capture aspects of barrio life, especially for those who live outside it. By showing the way non-cholos speak, Soto debunks the idea that words like *simón* and *carnal* operate only within a gang member's lexicon. Through a *chillante* pedagogical reading of *Chato and the Party Animals*, Soto's ability to synthesize barrio cultural norms irrespective of expectations and context teaches readers about the variability and creativeness of Chicanx linguistic expressions.

The opportunity for young readers to engage with barrio aesthetics through counter storytelling, which Frausto defines as narratives of "*los de abajo*" or the underdogs, reveals Soto's countercultural influence and his commitment as a Chicano writer to using literature as a means to bring socially marginalized voices to the center (6). Reciprocal to Art Speigelman's *Maus: A Survival's Tale* (1980–1991), the graphic novel genre and the use of mice as metaphorical representations of *los de abajo* become powerful mechanisms by which Guevara also channels visual counter stories. Soto is a pioneer in being inclusive of the graphic form as seen in *Chato Goes Cruisin,*' a narrative not about lowriders but about taking a vacation on a cruise ship.

By writing about diverse Chicanx experiences, Soto stays true to the philosophy of what makes one a cool cat and also the core principles of the Chicano Movement with its links to the counterculture movement. The main protagonist is Chato, a cool, low-riding cat from East Los Angeles. Chato is a cool cat who reflects the style of his time: hip hop's emergence into the mainstream in the 1990s. A snapback, a jersey, and colorful shorts signify styles of urban male fashion. During the last decade of the twentieth century, a snapback (a cap worn backwards) was seen as rebellious.[13] In *Chato Goes Crusin,*' Chato wears a short sleeve button shirt that is green and orange, typical of hip 1990s fashion.[14]

For mainstream culture, hip hop's urban style was aggressive, unruly, and menacing, especially if worn by men of color. Chato's hip hop identity points out the richness of barrio culture through the transmission of insider knowledge. Hip hop was a creative movement of artistic expression coming from barrio communities. The absence of associations between crime and violence on Soto's part or its visual correlation to hip hop by Guevara nullifies the "thug life" stereotype about men of color. It teaches children about hip hop in what Frausto refers to as strategies of appropriation, reversal, and inversion in his description of Chicanx *rasquachismo*, or the underdog perspective as describes art critic Tere Romo (Ybarra-Frausto, *Chicano Aesthetics* 5).

The construction of communities of color, also known as barrios, as hip social spaces of lively non-cholo interaction molds readers to debunk Chicanxs and Chicanx spaces as perils. The figure and representation of Novio Boy, also a cat, explores the compendium of imaginings of cool cats in barrio communities. He wears a bandana, an oversized flannel shirt, and baggy pants. He carries his boombox over his shoulder. Novio Boy is a mimesis of the mainstream's contemporary barrio subject: the gangster, cholo, a vato. Novio Boy's identity disrupts hegemonic perspectives of people of color by debunking stereotypes of Chicano bodies in barrio communities. The fact that Novio Boy dresses in a gangster manner does not mean he is in a gang; rather what Novio Boy express is the performance of Chicano masculinity in a US context. He is not a criminal or a menace to society; he does not do drugs or commit crime. This parallels Chato, who also decriminalizes hip hop styles as he negotiates his identity as an outsider to Los Angeles, a world Mecca of fashion. The book also allows readers to think about the racialization of style and taste: is it the same thing to be a man of color in hip hop attire walking in the streets of Los Angeles as it is for anyone else doing the same? Chato and Novio Boy decolonize urban consciousness meant to teach children to not judge people by the way they look, especially during the 1990s at the height of heated racial tensions and incidents in Los Angeles amidst nativist political agendas.

Additionally, Soto "runs the gamut" of representations that exist about cool cats from an insider's and outsider's subjective position through the figure of Chorizo. Chorizo is, historically speaking, another type of cool cat in the series. But unlike Chato and Novio Boy, he is not a cat at all but a canine. Chorizo is a Chicano cool cat from the past, a Chicano militant, referencing the history of the brown berets, the Chicano Moratorium, and the Chicano Movement. He wears a red beret featuring a United Farm Workers logo and what seems to be a *zarape*, also known as a poncho or serape, which summons a sense of cultural pride because it is a garment that invokes the cultural traditions of Latin America with the lively colors of *la causa*.[15]

Aside from the image of the cool cat, Soto presents a diversity of identities that decolonize the monolithic representation of barrios. The mouse family debuting in *Chato's Kitchen* and reappearing in *Chato and the Party Animals* and the presence of Sharkie, Pelón, Blanca, and Coquetona in *Chato and the Party Animals* debunk the singular and derogatory typecasts of East Los Angeles citizens as poor and dirty or *cholos* and *cholas*. Soto also teaches readers how "looking" like a cool cat encourages readers to appreciate additional realities that exist in barrio communities. Names, for example, reference a form of positive tone of endearment—*barrio cariño*, where name-calling is not exercising abusive language or insult but rather what Chela Sandoval terms a "hermeneutics of love."

Soto decolonizes the barrio by giving presence to what the show *Stranger Things* (2016) has made acceptable and popular in mainstream culture today: the upside-down world or phenomenological experiences outside the logic of Western thought. In *Chato and the Party Animals,* the angels, folkloric images, dreams, and the images of La Virgen de Guadalupe communicate the mestizo sensibilities and transcendental survival of indigenous realities that abound in East Los Angeles. The use of Mesa-Bains' theory of *domesticana* allows us to understand the feminine and feminist contributions of Guevara's illustrations. Building on the visual practices of glamour as a radical expression with *domesticana,* McMahon's concept of "domestic negotiations" permits a new reading of "the domestic space" in Chato's series (51). An adaptation of McMahon's sense of "domestic" as a referent of the household and of the nation to Guevara's illustrations articulates a visual language where identities negotiate traditional gender, racial, and class roles.

Likewise, the interpretive theoretical framework for approaching the imaginative world of Chicanx heritage across a text-image medium in children's and young adult literature is *chillante* pedagogy and can also be applied to the visual practices. In relation to the visual field, decolonizing barrio communities while honoring the use of expressive color marks the visual traditions of Chicanx visual practices and their connection to Latin American art. Soto and Guevara reiterate these fundamental trans-American links defining the *chillante* aesthetics of the Chato narratives. Like Frausto and Mesa-Bains, *chillante* pedagogy does not dismiss transnational elements of Chicanx culture and in fact must be examined to understand the trans-American connections between Chicanx culture and the world not as some new global phenomena but as a continuation of the intangible heritage of Chicanx communities.

The *chillante* aesthetics in Soto's Chato Series presents the notion of community, *convivencia,* from a barrio system's view. Again, the literal definition of *chillante,* a word in the Spanish language, offers an adjectival dimension to the role of color. *Chillante* means a color that is lively, bright, what in Spanish is described as *muy vivo.* It offers a decolonial methodology for rethinking systems and how Chicanx artists color them with meaning. The practice of *chillante* aesthetics within children's literature continues the literary and artistic renaissance of the Chicanx movement. The infinitive verb form of *chillante* is *chillar,* which means to shout, yell, or brawl. An artist's visual, textual, and aural praxis is an expression of *chillante* aesthetics in Chicanx children's and YA literature. Because Chicanx children's and YA literature is relatively new, their visual expressions are colorful cries for social justice that references the *grito,* the cry, of the Chicano movement and are as significant as the actions of early Chicanx history.

In *chillante* aesthetics, the use of colors is a visual shout and brawl working toward a new vision of storytelling in literature, outsider ideologies coloring new imaginings of how books can educate children. Frausto, Mesa-Bains, and McMahon's scholarship draws largely from society's value system and how Chicanx styles affect literary production. The same holds true for Guevara, who illustrates what barrio sensibilities look like. In *Chato and the Party Animals,* Guevara represents the barrio communities as they are: storefronts are colorful, bright, and when not advertising what they are—*mercado, panadería, farmacia, librería y discoteca*, or a restaurant—they become the barrio's museums. Aside from the murals outside store fronts, Guevara also includes iconic Chicanx murals, creating an intertextual visual reference of Chicanx history. In *Chato and The Party Animals*, the mural "We Are Not a Minority" (1978) speaks about the contributions of community-based art practices of Chicanx culture. Similarly, the inclusion of a Virgen de Guadalupe and a "Sí se puede" mural points to the curricular significance of the interaction between verbal and nonverbal perspectives in *chillante* aesthetics as complex.

To understand the power of color and the operational use of color as a form of renegotiation and creativity in Chicanx expression is to see the Chicanx visual practices of *chillante* aesthetics. But often it may not be easy to detect, as is the case with the expression of "domestic negotiations" and a *domesticana* traditions in the Chato Series. McMahon's discussion of Fabiola Cabeza de Baca's "linguistic and domestic power" as a form of "feminine power in the public sphere" is helpful to illustrate how Guevara makes cultural critiques through art (McMahon 88). In *Chato's Kitchen*, Guevara depicts a large bowl of fruits and vegetables with beans, tomatoes, corn, and bananas. The banana's product sticker reads "Sangre de Honduras," or "Blood from Honduras," communicating the history of bananas, specifically the United Fruit company, the Banana Republic, and Honduras. The bowl of fruits and vegetables may be an image overlooked as insignificant, but through *chillante* aesthetics the bowl enforces the refinement of feminine domestic practices, in this case pottery.

Second, the bowl references foods and food practices of the Americas, but connotes US-Latin American relations, historical and contemporary such as the North American Free Trade Agreement (NAFTA). Third, the bowl itself may represent a decolonized diet, such as in the use of guacamole, which is a plant-based food. It also speaks about the relationship between food and health, which Mesa-Bains and McMahon would argue are feminine and feminist realms that in the context of family allow women to express a sensibility of their own. From *salsa* to *tamarindo*, the fact that the majority of the action takes place in the kitchen, the "domestic negotiations" in Guevara's visual narrative work to channel core Chicanx art practices of *rasquachismo* as a pedagogy.

Furthermore, when we think about the gender diversity Soto introduces in the series—males cooking, women being out in the public space, males working in the domestic space, males breaking gendered roles, equality among gendered subjects—the figure and expression of the Chicano "cool cat" expresses what McMahon calls domestic power. The non-cholo figure in a narrative about East Los Angeles is an oppositional style guiding the imaginations of readers toward a complex elaboration of self-fashioned identity. Children may not be able see how the text is imbued with references of how race, class, and gender categories work to criminalize men of color and their bodies in the nation-state discourse of America, but adults will, provoking adults to also interrogate the limitations of cool cats. Soto prescribes a barrio aesthetic that cancels the pressures of US notions of hypermasculinity and the trap of violence it creates for men of color. For example, hypermasculinity is suspended to teach young boys about how cool it is to strive for your own version of "cool" as men of color articulated through the cool cat entity in non-dominant society like East Los Angeles.

The audio and digital versions feature the voices of Willie Colón, Cheech Marín, and Luis Guzmán. These virtual formats offer readers a visual experience enhanced by audio that values the speech acts of Chicanx/Latinx barrio communities as an educational tool. Whether it's the voice of the Chicano actor from *Born in East Los Angeles* (1987), Cheech Marín, or the voice of Puerto Rican born, Lower East Side-raised Luis Guzmán, known for his wide roles as a pan-Latino thug, policeman, and comrade in film, or the sonorous and melodic vocalization of Nuyorican born, South Bronx-raised Colón, the series transmits, in an audible form, *chillante* pedagogy.

In the study of Soto's works as influenced by technology, *chillante* aesthetics extends to another field, the audio, as sounds can call attention like radiant color schemes or a robust lexicon. *Chillante* pedagogy also is about the ways coded sensibilities of barrio strategies of affirmation and resistance across text and image function as decolonial linguistic acts that transgress the limits of who are outliers. The translanguaging acts embedded throughout the textual words and images that composite Chato's universe are understood as moments, sites, and acts of voicing masculinity that ruptures insider and outside stereotypes of the *macho*. From Chicanx epistemologies on gender, sex, and sexuality, Soto leaves male-to-male identity open to diverse imaginings.

Chato and Novio Boy serve as metaphors of Chicano subjectivity outside mainstream stereotypes. Chato and Novio Boy's male-to-male relationship also redefines heterosexual kinship[16] As best friends, they show love and respect for each other. Their friendship thus serves as a metaphor for a more egalitarian and decolonial view of males in relation. One cat is not trying to outdo the other; there are not catfights, there are no top dogs or underdogs. Positive heterosexual male representations that fall outside hypermasculine stereotypes as well as representations referencing boys of color are additional revolutions Soto generates across the series. Chato is friendly, treats everyone equally and with respect. Novio Boy is also caring. He may dress like a vato, but dressing like a vato may reflect his taste for fashion and not a fossilized identity. In other words, Soto challenges the reader to analyze their own projections of Novio Boy.

Conclusion

The Chato Series expands the discussion surrounding Chicanx identity from its historical roots to scheming new imaginings that transgresses historical representations through children's literary expression. As a collective, the Chato Series generates positive and powerful images of subjectivity by engaging with the figure of the cool cat as an outsider of Chicanx and Latinx children's literature. In other words, the most powerful messages of the Chato Series are the ability of the cool cat figures to work toward new visions of barrio communities and of Chicanx culture as belonging to the greater umbrella of US Latinx children's and YA literature. Because narratives of barrio communities such as East Los Angeles are seldom seen in children's literature, the importance of expounding on taboo subjects as not taboo for children transforms historically disenfranchised communities of color like East Los Angeles.

Soto's series explores place as common and quotidian but echoing decolonized and avant-garde modes of thinking illustrates the moments when Soto and Guevara enact *chillante* pedagogy. The author-artist duo offsets stereotypes about East Los Angeles by showing the rich culture of this geographical region that aligns itself with the struggle for self-determination, self-affirmation, and cultural pride, the core values of the Chicano Movement defining *chillante* pedagogy in the Chato Series and teaching readers to answer to a call to themselves on their own terms.

Notes

1. A modern dance to rock-and-roll music.

2. Felix the Cat is an early twentieth-century example of the cool cat.

3. A zoot suit is a form of dress where a man's suit is not tailored. It characterized by a long loose jacket with padded shoulders and high-waisted tapering trousers. Under the normative standards of dress in the 1940s, the zoot suit was deemed an exaggerated style. The capitalization of Zoot Suit refers to the Zoot Suit riots.

4. Cool Cat is a "hep" tiger character who appeared in a series of cartoons in the late 1960s. In contrast to most of the other Looney Tunes characters, what separated Cool Cat was that he was a product of his time. Depicted in his shorts, he wore a green scarf and usually a matching beret (although in the last two cartoons he starred in, he was without his beret), spoke 1960s-style beatnik slang, and acted like the typically mellow, '60s adolescent ("Cool Cat," n.p.).

5. The 1958 song "Three Cool Cats" by the Coasters, and its re-recording by the Beatles in 1962, made the cool cat a powerful mechanism of new urban identities.

6. Cool cat varies in relation to gender. Consult Ramirez's *The Woman in the Zoot Suit*.

7. The first two stanzas of the song capture the new style of the pachucos, whose roots reference subculture. Spanish original: "Carnal póngase abusado / Ya los tiempos han cambiado

/ Usted está muy agüitado Y está buti atravesado / Antes se bailaba swing / Boogie-woogie jitterbug / Pero esto ya torció / Y esto es lo que sucedió." English translation: "Cuz get ready to be blown away / the times now have changed / you're too bummed out / and you're pretty much taken aback / Before we danced swing / boogie woogie, jitterbug / but that switched now / and this is what came next."

8. Pachuco boogie was a Mexican American dance music that alternated between African American and Afro-Caribbean styles ("Pachuco Boogie," n.p.).

9. The Fatal Interactions with Police Study (FIPS) database includes details on about 1,700 fatal interactions with police that occurred in jurisdictions across the United States during a twenty-month period from May 2013 to January 2015.

10. Some films include *Zoot Suit* (1981), *Stand and Deliver* (1988), *American Me* (1992), *Blood In, Blood Out* (1993), and *Mi Familia* (1995).

11. A linguistic variant, only in terms of spelling, for *vato* is *bato*. Homey is used interchangeably with the word homes.

12. Some language about *chillante* pedagogy and aesthetics appear in earlier publications by the author listed in the bibliography.

13. The sitcom *The Fresh Prince of Bel Air* displays the ways caps were a fashion statement in US popular urban expression.

14. Like *The Fresh Prince of Bel Air*, the comedy series *In Living Color* illustrates the vibrant use of colors.

15. *La causa*, or the struggle, was a term used during the Chicano Movement.

16. Through the name Novio Boy, Soto introduces queer identities, realities, and experiences to readers. If indeed Chato and Novio Boy are more than friends, a subtle queer tale of love and acceptance emerges within in alignment with barrio aesthetics' ability to foster marginal cultural expression. This may be a powerful read for children who may identify as queer but may not have the language to name it. Soto's inclusion of a queer possibility also makes it a normal and natural event of barrio communities, which also teaches children who may come from more traditional or colonized histories a way to think differently. I touch on this issue, acknowledging it merits additional scholarly attention.

Works Cited

Acosta, Oscar Z. *Revolt of the Cockroach People*. Vintage, 1989.

Avilés, Elena. "Chillante Pedagogy, 'She Worlds,' and Testimonio as Text/Image: Toward a Chicana Feminist Pedagogy in the Works of Maya Christina Gonzalez." *Voices of Resistance: Interdisciplinary Approaches to Chican@ Children's Literature*, edited by Laura Alamillo, Larissa M. Mercado-López, and Cristina Herrera, Rowman & Littlefield, 2018, 123–36.

Avilés, Elena. "Reading Latinx and LGBTQ+ Perspectives: Maya Christina Gonzalez and Equity Minded Models at Play." *Bilingual Review/La Revista Bilingüe*, vol. 33 no. 4, 2017, 34–44.

Bruce-Novoa, Juan, *Retrospace: Collected Essays on Chicano Literature Theory and History*. Arte Público, 1990.

Everding, Gerry. "Young Hispanic Men May Face Greatest Risk from Police Shootings, Study Finds." https://source.wustl.edu/2018/03/young-hispanic-men-may-face-greatest-risk-from -police-shootings-study-finds/

Fregoso, Linda. "La Onda Latina: The Chicano Movement Today." http://www.laits.utexas.edu/onda_latina/program?sernum=000535498&term=

Guerrero, Lalo, and Sherilyn M. Mentes. *Lalo: My Life and Music.* University Arizona Press, 2002.

Hernández, Lisa. "Soto, Gary." *The Oxford Encyclopedia of Latinos and Latinas in the United States,* edited by Suzanne Oboler, Oxford University Press, 2005, 143–45.

Lawrence, David Todd. "Cool." *The Greenwood Encyclopedia of African American Folklore,* edited by Anand Prahlad, Westport, 2006, 264–65.

Looney Toons Fandom TV Community. "Cool Cat." http://looneytunes.wikia.com/wiki/Cool_Cat

McMahon, Marci R. *Domestic Negotiations: Gender, Nation, and Self-Fashioning in US Mexicana and Chicana Literature and Art.* Rutgers University Press, 2013.

Mesa-Bains. "Domesticana: The Sensibility of Chicana Rasquachismo." *Chicana Feminisms: A Critical Reader,* edited by Gabriela F. Arredondo. Duke University Press, 2003, 298–315.

Ramírez, Catherine S. *The Woman in the Zoot Suit: Gender, Nationalism, and the Cultural Politics of Memory.* Duke University Press, 2009.

Smithsonian Institute. "Pachuco Boogie." http://americansabor.org/musicians/styles.

Soto, Gary, "Gary Soto." http://garysoto.com.

Soto, Gary, and Susan Guevara. *Chato and the Party Animals.* G. P. Putnam's Sons, 1998.

Soto, Gary, and Susan Guevara. *Chato Goes Cruisin'.* G. P. Putnam's Sons, 2004.

Soto, Gary, and Susan Guevara. *Chato's Kitchen.* G. P. Putnam's Sons, 1997.

Valdez, Luis. *Zoot Suit.* Mark Taper Forum, 1978.

Ybarra-Frausto, Tomás. "Rasquachismo: A Chicano Sensibility." *Chicano Art: Resistance and Affirmation, 1965–1985,* edited by Richard Griswold del Castillo, Teresa McKenna, and Yvonne Yarbro-Bejarano, Wight Art Gallery, 1991.

Ybarra-Frausto, Tomás. "Rasquachismo: a Chicano Sensibility." In Chicano Aesthetics: Rasquachismo Exhibit Catalogue, MARS, Movimiento Artiscico del Rio Salado, 1989. 5–8.

12

The Coming-of-Age Experience in Chicanx Queer Novels *What Night Brings* and *Aristotle and Dante Discover the Secrets of the Universe*

Carolina Alonso

I write to record what others erase when I speak, to rewrite the stories others have miswritten about me, about you.
GLORIA ANZALDÚA[1]

In 1982, Nancy Garden published the groundbreaking YA novel *Annie on My Mind*. The importance of this publication goes beyond the love evolving between two teenage girls. The most significant element in Garden's story is that it has a happy ending. It is impossible to ignore how literature, cinema, and television have exploited the "bury your gays" trope throughout the years. That is to say, the few lesbian and gay[2] characters and romances we do find in books, movies, and TV series, rarely survive the entire storyline or experience what could be described as a happy ending.[3]

Garden's novel digressed from this trope more than three decades largely because of the author's own experience. In the commemorative edition of *Annie on My Mind*, Garden explains how growing up as a lesbian, it was hard to find literature to which she could relate. The few books she could find that were clearly about lesbians "usually ended with the lesbian character dying in a car crash, being sent to a mental institution, or turning straight" (243).

Although the book suffered from censorship[4] in certain sectors of the country, it remains as one of the pillars of LGBTQ YA literature. Representation matters, and as Garden stated in an interview, "Kids in every minority need to see people like themselves in books; that's an acknowledgment of their existence on this planet and in this society" (Leitich Smith).

In present times, Chicanx youth have been exposed to racist and homophobic discourses from the most hierarchical sectors of the United States government.[5] Although more books are being written and published for queer young readers, specifically about gays and lesbians, there still remains a lack of Chicanx publications that center queer coming-of-age issues. With this current political and social context, the importance of telling these stories is more pertinent than ever. It is crucial for these young people to be represented, in a positive way, not just within the media but also in literature. It is also important that academics analyze and promote both the study of the texts that diverge from heteronormativity and explore published Chicanx queer coming-of-age books.

Hence this chapter analyzes the YA novel *Aristotle and Dante Discover the Secrets of the Universe* (2012) by Benjamin Alire Sáenz and the novel[6] *What Night Brings* (2003) by Carla Trujillo. These two writers have validated the Chicanx queer coming-out experience by placing two social outcasts, and queer characters, as their protagonists. These characters break from gender binaries and gender stereotypes, but are both still outsiders who endure different types of violence. Through their works of fiction, Trujillo and Sáenz also demonstrate that it is possible for young Chicanxs to explore queer desires through friendships while challenging the expectations of heterosexuality as the only possible sexual identity. And although these two prize-winning novels show the difficulties that can arise when the characters question their identities, the endings are encouraging. *Aristotle and Dante Discover the Secrets of the Universe* and *What Night Brings* are paramount in validating the queer experiences of Chicanx young adult readers.

Chicanx Coming-of-Age Genre

Stories about young Chicanxs coming-of-age are not a novelty. Both Trujillo and Sáenz are following the tradition of Chicanx authors as they write about young people in the quest for their identity. In fact, one could say that the foundation of Chicanx literature centers on coming-of-age stories. That is to say, during the time of the Chicano Movement, this genre had a fundamental role in promoting a Chicanx consciousness and nationalism, sought out by an organized collectivity, which would differentiate them from the hegemony. As Benedict Anderson and Eric J. Hobsbawm have pointed out, there is a fundamental relationship between literature and the process of creating a nation (López 204). In this sense, literature has frequently been used as an artifact to establish a national identity in individuals who share specific characteristics and who coexist in the same community.

The coming-of-age genre provides the author with the path to develop the subjectivity of the protagonist through personal growth, in which it is possible to make a critical and sagacious examination of the society and the environment that surrounds them. *What Night Brings* and *Aristotle and Dante* problematize the heteronormativity set as the norm in the canonical novels published after the Chicano Movement.[7] The protagonists in these two books struggle with similar issues exhibited in the canonical texts such as religion, violence, and the search for individual and collective identity, but they are also accompanied by the question of sexual identity. Thus, the coming-of-age process of these protagonists cannot be completed without them also having achieved an awareness of their sexual identity. Although the protagonists of *What Night Brings* and *Aristotle and Dante* embark on a path of uncertainty and violence, in recognizing their queerness, they are led to a positive ending, which asserts all of their identities.

What Night Brings tells the story of Marci Cruz, who along with her sister, Corin, has to endure the violence of their father and the indifference of their mother, who is more concerned with retaining her husband than with the well-being of her daughters. From the beginning of the story, Marci asks God for two things: for her father to disappear, and for God to turn her into a boy. The eleven-year-old protagonist believes that having a phallus will allow her to be with other women, which is her biggest yearning. With a high degree of humor, tenderness, and at the same time violence, Carla Trujillo developed a story that became a finalist for the Lambda Literary Award, which acknowledges her impact within mainstream LGBT literature. *What Night Brings* also presents an important story in Chicanx and Latinx literature in general, which has earned her the Mármol Prize and the Latino Literary Foundation Latino Book Award, among other recognitions (The Robert Giard Foundation).

Benjamín Alire Sáenz' *Aristotle and Dante* introduces us to Ari, an introverted boy who lives in El Paso, Texas, and who struggles to understand his identity. While trying to decipher the secrets that surround him, he meets Dante, a boy that contrasts with him in every aspect, but who quickly becomes his best friend. *Aristotle and Dante* has been very successful since its publication, winning important awards within LGBTQ literature such as the Lambda Literary Award and the Stonewall Book Award, in addition to the Pura Belpré Award, which "is presented annually to a Latino/Latina writer and illustrator whose work best portrays, affirms, and celebrates the Latino cultural experience in an outstanding work of literature for children and youth"

(Association for Library Service to Children). The success of the book has been such that in 2015 Editorial Planeta published the Spanish version, and its English audio book is narrated by the multi-awarded Puerto Rican figure Lin-Manuel Miranda.

Friendships and Queer Desires

The protagonists of *What Night Brings* and *Aristotle and Dante* experience queer desires in spaces that are generally considered, by a heteropatriarchal society, as normative. This is achieved through the affective relationships they establish with friends, which are developed in places that at first sight do not represent a social threat. These moments are decisive for the characters' construction and the development of their subjectivity. That is to say, it is because of these queer-erotic moments that they are able to contest an expected heterosexual adulthood.

My reading of these relationships and desires is based on the theories of Catrióna Rueda Esquibel about lesbian friendships. In her groundbreaking book *With Her Machete in Her Hand: Reading Chicana Lesbians* (2006), and specifically in the chapter "Memories of Girlhood: Chicana Lesbian Fictions," Esquibel analyzes girlhood, friendships, and comadrazgo.[8] She states that "in Chicana contexts, girlhood is a space and time before the imposition of normative heterosexuality and, as such, provides a site for texts to stage lesbian desires" (Esquibel 94). In *What Night Brings* and in *Aristotle and Dante Discover the Secrets of the Universe*—I argue this also occurs in this novel through the friendship of the two boys—friendly relations between the protagonists and people of the same sex allow them to question and ratify their sexual identity.

As Esquibel indicates, female friendships are socially perceived as inoffensive and innocent; thus they "provide a space, however restrictive, for lesbian desire" (Esquibel 125). In *What Night Brings*, Marci experiences this through her brief but significant friendship with her neighbor, Raquel. Marci feels a great attraction for her, but Raquel seems not to pay much attention to the girl until one day she invites her to see her garden. Raquel then gifts Marci with different products, and Marci confesses, "Each time she put something in my arms I wanted to grab and kiss her just like the people on TV. But all I could do was look at her and smile like an idiot. I left Raquel's house happy. And I felt good because I got to be with her" (Trujillo 43).

This exchange gives Marci the possibility to be close to the girl she desires and for whom she wants to become a boy. One could also presume that there is a mutual feeling of interest as Marci describes how Raquel "looked at me with eyes that went straight into mine, and down in my stomach" (Trujillo 42). When Marci returns home with the products, she explains to her mom that she was at Raquel's house, and the mom mutters a simple "Hmmmm" (Trujillo 44). As Esquibel points out, the expectation that female friendships are sexless and innocent prevents Delia from considering that her daughter could desire Raquel.

However, Marci makes a clear distinction between her love for Raquel and the way in which Eddie looks at her. In this regard, Cristina Herrera points out in "'The Girls Our Mothers Warned Us About': Rejection, Redemption, and the Lesbian Daughter in Carla Trujillo's *What Night Brings*" that:

> Her admiration for Raquel, although tinged with burgeoning sexual desire, is not voyeuristic and oppressive, that positions Raquel as an object of a (male) gaze. In fact, Marci is disgusted at the way her father stares at Raquel "like she was the star of a dirty movie" (39). This passage demonstrates Marci's critique of a social, sexual hierarchy that grants males the right to a visual gaze to exploit women as objects for sexual gratification. (28)

Marci, on the other hand, expresses having deep feelings for Raquel and admiring her for her garden and plants. At this point of the narrative, Marci wants to become a boy to have a romantic relationship with her neighbor.

Nonetheless, in that same conversation Raquel explains that she is waiting to leave and start her own life, something she accomplishes later by running away with a guy. Esquibel states in *With Her Machete in Her Hand* that in a heterosexual society, "Implied is the idea that this lesbian adolescence must come to an end, must be replaced by adult heterosexuality" (116). For Raquel, the only way to escape her family and patriarchal oppression is to flee with a man. But before leaving, Raquel leaves a note to Marci telling her not to give up her dreams (Trujillo 174). This scene is significant since not only is Raquel empowering her with her words, but also at this point Marci realizes that her path will not be like Raquel's. When Eddie finds out that Raquel has run away, he warns Marci about not doing the same thing: "'Leave for that low-life S.O.B.. I swear to God I'll kick your little asses to hell and back if you and Corin ever do that to me.' 'Don't worry,' I said" (174). Marci's response implies that she will not follow Raquel's way out; she will not need a man to escape.[9] In fact, at the end of the story Marci finds a new friend, Robbie. This friendship will allow Marci to develop her queer identity even further.

In *Aristotle and Dante* the friendship between the protagonists provides Ari with a space to experience a queer desire. While it is true that social rules and expectations are different for male and female adolescents—while girls are seen as passive and almost asexual, boys are assigned and even promoted an active sexual role—sexuality and desire are still expected to be heterosexual. In this sense, Esquibel's theories are still significant when analyzing a young male-to-male friendship, since it is implicit that within Chicanx culture friendships between men do not represent a risk for the heteropatriarchal hegemony.

One of the most notable examples of an erotic moment in this novel is when Dante gives Ari a sponge bath, which happens when he is convalescing after saving Dante's life. Ari keeps his eyes closed and describes the episode the following way: "I felt Dante's hands on my shoulders, the warm water, the soap, the washcloth. . . . He made me feel fragile as porcelain (Sáenz 144). When he opens his eyes, he sees Dante crying. "Dante had a look on his face. He looked like an angel" (Sáenz 144). However, instead of acknowledging any attraction or desire, Dante describes feeling rage. It is important to highlight that Ari constantly polices himself to not feel any attraction towards Dante. Esquibel points out that for the Chicanx characters she analyzes, "behaviors, identities, and desires are mediated by the heteronormativity of the worlds in which they live. Love and desire are constituted in relation to heterosexuality" (125). Throughout the novel, Ari tries to figure out his identity, which he believes should not be a queer one. He clearly specifies, "I don't kiss boys" (248). He is in a constant state of denial.

Nonetheless, later in the story, Dante, who already knows he wants to date boys, convinces Ari to experiment and see if maybe he would like kissing boys too. Although Ari claims he does not want to do it, he ends up kissing Dante back. "I don't know why I did it, but I did it. I stood up. And then he stood right in front of me. 'Close your eyes,' he said. So I closed my eyes. And he kissed me. And I kissed him back. And then he started really kissing me. And I pulled away. 'Well?' he said. 'Didn't work for me,' I said" (255). While Ari experiences this erotic moment, he denies enjoying it, a lie that he disclaims later. It could be said that Ari might be projecting the anxieties that Chicano queer men can feel when contemplating a possible family rejection because of their sexual orientation, especially considering that the novel takes place in 1985. In his widely cited article "Chicano Men: A Cartography of Homosexual Identity and Behaviors," Tomás Almaguer proposes to analyze the identity, desire, and homosexual practices of Chicano men. The article states that one of the most difficult issues to overcome for Chicano homosexuals is that of family pressure.

Although at the end of the story Ari's parents accept and encourage his sexuality, he does fear a possible rejection from his family. Ari has more siblings; however, the age difference and the circumstances surrounding his older brother make him feel like he is an only child. At the beginning of the book he states, "I didn't like the fact that I was a pseudo only child. I didn't know how else to think of myself. I was an only child without actually being one. That sucked" (13). This pressure can be one of the reasons why he tries not to disappoint his parents and continues to reject his feelings for Dante. Nevertheless, even when he states that kissing Dante did not "work for him," at the end of the novel he admits the truth: "I lied" (358). The same-sex friendships that Marci and Ari have with Raquel and Dante, respectively, allow them to experience feelings that society could otherwise completely restrict. Both Trujillo and Sáenz expose the importance of these friendships, validating the relevance they have for young queer Chicanxs and their coming-of-age process.

Discovering Silences and Secrets

In addition to the friendships and desires, the coming-of-age process of the characters is influenced by the relationships they have with traditional institutions. Both characters are surrounded by silences and secrecies, and they fight hard throughout the narratives to uncover them. Marci has many questions, but she is always punished or scolded when she shows curiosity[10] about gender and sexuality issues. One of the first examples of Marci being asked to remain silent is within the church. The mother superior reprimands Marci for the questions she constantly asks during catechism. The scolding comes to such a degree that the nuns plead with Marci to not ask another question again: "Mother Superior sat down. Then, with her hands folded together, told me I wasn't allowed to ask any more questions in class, of any kind. Ever" (21). But Marci, who thinks her questions are valid, insists on knowing the reason for the censorship, to which the mother superior responds, "Your questions do no one any good. They only make the other children doubt what we teach them . . . if you truly believed in God, you wouldn't be asking these kinds of questions" (Trujillo 21).

Marci decides to comply with these orders because she is afraid of the sisters. Before leaving the nun's office, she has to promise that she will never ask a question again, and she is dismissed, but not before being reminded that God would be watching her. In her edited collection *Chicana Lesbians: The Girls Our Mothers Warned Us About* (1991), Trujillo explains how Chicana lesbians have to negotiate religion and family: "For our own survival, Chicana lesbians must continually embark on the creation or modification of our spirituality and familia, usually implying alteration of the traditional, since these institutions, by their very nature, profess to be antithetical to the Chicana lesbian experience" (x). Both institutions, religion and family, were fundamental in the construction of the Chicanx nation and ideology and continue to be highly relevant within the community. However, as Trujillo explains, the intrinsic bases of these are incompatible to the lesbian and/or queer identity.[11] Cristina Herrera points out that both Marci and Corin realize the impact of the Catholic Church as they observe Delia's reverence to Eddie. This shows "Trujillo's critique of the Catholic Church's (or any religious institution's) power to shape and mold women's thoughts on familial power structure" (29).

Once, Marci questioned one of the nuns about who her husband was, and Delia censures her: "My mom told me her husband was Jesus, and that I shouldn't have asked her that because 'it wasn't nice'" (19). But she then questions how all the nuns could share one husband and who slept with them at night to what the mother replies: "Ay! Marcía. Malcriada! You and your nasty questions" (19). The adjectives that Delia chooses to silence and reprimand her daughter, "malcriada" and "nasty," are significant. She depicts the curiosity of her daughter as something disgusting, which also makes her a malcriada. The restlessness of knowledge that Marci exhibits deems her a naughty girl, and one lacking a good education at that.

In this way, Delia not only silences the voice of the protagonist but at the same time uses language as a weapon to discourage Marci's knowledge process. Just as it occurs in the other institutions, within the family Marci is reprimanded for questioning things that according to her superiors (all of them women who reinforce patriarchy)[12] are unquestionable. In *Borderlands/ La Frontera: The New Mestiza*, Gloria E. Anzaldúa talks about the measures used by society to silence women. In "How to Tame a Wild Tongue," she specifically mentions how when a woman questions the rules of her community she is labeled in different ways than men: "I remember one of the sins I'd recite to the priest in the confession box the few times I went to confession: talking back to my mother, hablar pa'trás, repelar. Hocicona, repelona, chismosa, having a big mouth, questioning, carrying tales are all signs of being *malcriada*" (76). Again, we see how the word malcriada is associated with the silencing processes used in patriarchal systems.

Furthermore, two of the secrets that Marci desires to uncover are about queer people: her uncle Tommy and her cousin Raylene. Her uncle Tommy was having an affair with a priest, Father Chacón. Eddie, who often bullies his brother because of his sexuality, calls him "jotito" and "queer," and when Marci questions what these words mean, Delia replies, "Nothing . . . It's a dirty word" (83). In addition, Marci's cousin Raylene is intersex, something that Delia briefly mentions and Marci tries to understand. With no answers, Marci is left wondering "what she looked like, and if she still acted like a boy" (26). She also starts speculating about Raylene's sexuality and gender identity. "I wondered if she was going to like girls like me. It's not fair, they should have let her keep her birdy. She might want it later "(26). Marci does not obtain answers for this or for most of her questions, so this quest for answers becomes fundamental in her coming-of-age adventure.

On the other hand, in *Aristotle and Dante* there is Aristotle, a lonely boy who seems to enjoy the idea of not having many friends, and one of the least popular kids at school. Ari does not feel that his personality and behavior align with other boys of his age, especially when it comes to girls. He reflects on this after listening to some lifeguards' conversation about girls: "See, the thing about guys is that I didn't really care to be around them. I mean, guys really made me uncomfortable. I don't know why, not exactly. I just, I don't know, I just didn't belong" (16). Although Ari, by and large, does not fit in because of his introverted personality, he is constantly haunted by the atmosphere of silence that surrounds his family and his house. Just like Marci, Ari is perpetually trying to unravel the very silences that prevent him from understanding and recognizing who he is.

The secrets of the universe to which the title refers include discovering his queer identity, but also uncovering what happened to his older brother, Bernardo, the eldest son of the Mendoza family, as well as his aunt's hidden lesbian identity. All that Ari knows is that his brother is in prison, and throughout the story he tries to discover the reasons behind the incarceration. For the rest of the family, Bernardo seems to not exist, and everything related to him is a secret. There is also Ari's father, who seems to wander through life like a ghost. Ari makes constant references to his father's silence, as well as the reserved attitude that he seemingly developed after returning from Vietnam: "Why couldn't he just talk? How was I supposed to know him when he didn't let me? I hated that" (23). However, the protagonist recognizes that he shares characteristics with his father and that unlike Dante, who is a social and extroverted boy, he also hides his feelings.

Another of the secrets of Ari's life shows similarity with Marci in that it had to do with a queer relative: his aunt Ophelia, who took care of him while his mother recovered from Bernardo's imprisonment. Ari did not find out Ophelia was a lesbian until she died and additionally, discovered that she had been rejected by her family so she had to move to Tucson, Arizona: "She'd lived a life separate from the rest of the family for reasons no one had ever bothered to explain to me" (276). None of her relatives but Ari's family attends her funeral. She is exiled from her family for not following the norms. In *Borderlands,* specifically in the section "Fear of Going Home: Homophobia," Anzaldúa explains, "For the lesbian of color, the ultimate rebellion she can make against her native culture is through her sexual behavior. She goes against two moral prohibitions: sexuality and homosexuality" (41). It was after her death that Ari's parents told him the story of Ophelia and her lover, which can be interpreted as a way for Ari's parents to honor her life by stating the truth. This confession led to his parents opening up and finally explaining his brother's crime, a transphobic-violent act.

Homophobia, Family and Violence

Marci and Ari are surrounded by violence, and both of them internalize it to the degree of reproducing or wishing to reproduce it. In *What Night Brings*, Eddie constantly beats Marci and her sister, Corin. He does not only inflict physical violence on his daughters; he also does it to his wife, displaying a superiority granted by his gender. Only uncle Tommy can physically defend himself and fight back. However, his hidden homosexuality prevents him from putting a stop to his brother's aggressions. And although Marci wants to become a man to be with other women, her desire would also grant her the possibility to fight back and stop the constant physical and mental abuse to which she is exposed. On one occasion, Marci dreams that she faces her father, who challenges her, emphasizing precisely the power that the phallus gives him.

> "Your daddy here's the one with the balls." He pointed to his birdy. "And he ain't scared of nothing. Nothing! You hear me? And I'm going to tell you something else; he's got the big Peter here to back up these huevos, too. You, girl," he pointed at me, "ain't got shit down there except a little piece of tail. And that little hombre," he got up from his chair, "is all you'll ever have." (Trujillo 144)

This type of reference to the sexual organs as representative of power helps us to understand one of the reasons why Marci considers it necessary to become a man.

Marivel T. Danielson references specifically in her book *Homecoming Queers* (2009) that this event, which occurred in one of Marci's dreams, shows that the correlation between power and the phallus is internalized (80). This is viable taking into account the relationship of power and subjugation to which the protagonist is exposed in her family nucleus. In "'If I Turn into a Boy, I Don't Think I Want Huevos': Reassessing Racial Masculinities in *What Night Brings*," Lisa Marie Cacho explains Eddie's violent personification the following way: "Marci's refusal to perform conventional femininity and respectable domesticity often underlies or prefigures her father's violent outbursts, which are partly provoked by his desire for a household with heteropatriarchal hierarchies" (73). Since the beginning of the story Marci navigates beyond the boundaries of the normative gender expression and therefore jeopardizes the hierarchies of power in which Eddie, as a straight man, is placed higher than the rest of his family.

Violence is also present in *Aristotle and Dante*. One of the crucial moments of the story happens when, in an act of homophobia, some guys brutally beat Dante after they find him in a street kissing another boy. It is important to reflect on the place and time of the story. As I have mentioned before, this story takes place in 1987 in El Paso. Thus, the hate crime against Dante occurs at a time where gay men were being targeted both by the mainstream culture and also within their own community. We know that the boys who attacked Ari are from their same neighborhood and that they are probably Chicanos.

After Dante's assault, Ari decides to avenge his friend by brutally beating one of the guys who attacked him. These acts of violence motivate Ari's parents to finally confess the full story of his brother, who murdered a prostitute when he realized that she was transgender, and then subsequently killed a man while in prison. The parents' fear that Ari perpetuated the violent actions of his brother encouraged them to ask him to stop fleeing his instincts and feelings. This is not something Ari can do easily, even when his parents show solidarity. In fact, Ari constantly shows what we could call an internalized homophobia.

Caroline T. Clark and Mollie V. Blackburn analyze violence and sex in LGBT YA novels and point out that—just like Marci—Ari daydreams of violent reactions. "Ari resists feelings of love between Dante and him, and when he is unable to do so by disassociation, he instead imagines a more forceful separation, that is one of violence" (874). They give the example of Ari wanting to hurt Dante after he gave him the sponge bath mentioned earlier. Another example of Ari imagining violent things is when he repeatedly dreams that he is riding his truck with a girl and runs over Dante because he is not paying attention. These dreams or thoughts in which Ari makes a violent action towards Dante can be interpreted as an internalized homophobia, which extends to the degree of wanting to hurt the person he loves and attack his own emotions. The environment that surrounds Ari and the time in which he lives do not allow him to consider the possibility of feeling a homosexual attraction without involving a sort of violence.

Safe Spaces and Queer Coming-of-Age

As stated in the beginning of this chapter, the protagonists cannot come of age until they have come out, in Ari's case, or realized it was acceptable to like other girls, as in Marci's situation. It is not until she moves in with her grandmother, after Corin shoots Eddie, that Marci realizes that she is not alone. Eddie's violence is what allows the protagonist to finally move in with her grandmother in New Mexico and find a space where she can express and accept her condition as a queer individual. Among the people who make up this new community are the grandmother, her sister, and a new neighbor, Robbie. When Marci confesses to her neighbor her attraction to other girls and realizes that Robbie also feels the same, she discovers that there is no reason to feel guilty about it. Robbie asks if she thinks that the secret they share is a sin, and Marci responds "no," and the novel ends with the two girls kissing.

In Ari's case, he also needs to leave his city, although momentarily, in order to completely accept his identity. Throughout the novel, he often travels to the desert to find peace. El Paso functions as a metaphorical panopticon, as explained by Michel Foucault in *Discipline and Punish* (1975), where all of Ari's actions seem to be observed and judged. On the contrary, an isolated and quiet space like the desert allows him to feel free; it is here Ari confesses his feelings to Dante and where they kiss for the first time.

After the kiss Ari understands the reason for his constant anger and violent outbursts:

> This was what was wrong with me. All this time I had been trying to figure out the secrets of the universe, the secrets of my own body, of my own heart. All of the answers had been so close and yet I had always fought them without even knowing it. From the minute I'd met Dante, I had fallen in love with him. I just didn't let myself know it, think it, feel it. (359)

This is the first time that Ari recognizes his feelings for Dante. For almost the entirety of the novel, the protagonist tries to put aside any feelings that may suggest sexual attraction and feelings towards Ari. In this sense, throughout the narrative, the reader infers his queerness not by what Ari relates as a narrator, but by what he does not say and prefers to hide.

The end of *Aristotle and Dante* can be considered utopian, since the parents of Ari and Dante end up being friends and the coming-out process does not present itself in a conflictive way as would generally occur in other novels written or developed in the eighties. This rarity is precisely one of the most significant successes of the novel. That is, it is important not only that these queer stories are told, but also that they are narrated in a positive way and avoid falling into the past tropes where the queer characters rarely managed to empower themselves from their subjectivity.

Visibility and Validation: the Implications of Positive Representation

Carla Trujillo and Benjamín Alire Sáenz question the binaries of sexuality and gender that were disseminated as normative within the foundational genre of Chicanx literature. Both texts analyzed in this chapter use violence as the element that triggers a series of events that will lead the protagonists to understand and accept their sexual identity. The inclusion of friendships and desire in both novels also shows how even in the most policed spaces of a heteropatriarchal society, young Chicanxs manage to experience and validate their queerness.

As Anzaldúa states in the epigraph of this essay, Trujillo and Sáenz "rewrite the stories others have miswritten about me, [and] about you" (161). *What Night Brings* and *Aristotle and Dante Discover the Secrets of the Universe* validate a group of people that has often been relegated to its own community. As they do this, they provide young Chicanx queers the opportunity to see themselves portrayed in a positive way, which contrasts other cultural representations where their identities usually condemn them ultimately to a life of distress.

Considering the violence surrounding queer youth—bullying in school, family rejection, and suicide—positive representation in literature is not just entertainment; it is a vital source of support and empowerment.

Notes

1. Quote from *This Bridge Called My Back*, page 161.

2. Most of these characters continue to be gays, lesbians, and very few bisexuals. The transgender, asexual, aromantic, and pansexual communities continue to have scarce or null representation.

3. According to Dino-Ray Ramos, although the number of LGBTQ characters on television is rising, the vast majority are still white and male, and in the last two years (August 4, 2017), "62 gay and bi women characters were killed off on TV shows" (Ramos).

4. The novel was removed from a school district in Kansas City until a judge ruled that the removal of the book from the school district's libraries was unconstitutional (Scales 22–32). Garden also stated that the book was burned "on the steps of the building housing the Kansas City School Board" (261).

5. This does not mean that Latinx youth have not experienced discrimination and homophobia in the past. However, the constant statements of President Trump and Vice President Pence regarding Mexicans and homosexuals, respectively, have been public and severe, which in turn has legitimized a sector of the US population that supports and shares these positions.

6. *What Night Brings* is generally not considered a YA novel. Nonetheless, the book is narrated by the protagonist's child voice as she tries to develop her identity. Trujillo also includes topics usually covered in YA novels such as first love, friendships, family, and identity

issues. Regardless of its classification, the analysis presented in this chapter is centered on the novel's coming-of-age characteristics as well as the coming out of the closet component.

7. Two of the foundational Chicanx novels were written as coming-of-age books, . . . *y no se lo tragó la tierra* (1971) by Tomás Rivera and *Bless Me, Ultima* (1972) by Rudolfo Anaya.

8. Esquibel discusses lesbian-erotic interactions in fictional girlhood friendships that other critics have ignored or disregarded. The novels that she studies in this chapter are Sandra Cisneros' *The House on Mango Street* (1984), Denise Chávez's *The Last of the Menu Girls* (1997), Terri de la Peña's *Margins* (1992), and Emma Pérez's *Gulf Dreams* (1996).

9. A woman is responsible for ultimately freeing Marci and her sister from the abusive situation in which they live: Grandma Flor. The characterization of this woman differs completely from that of her daughter Delia. She is a character with agency in both the private and the public spaces, as evidenced by different situations that Marci narrates. She owns a bar, confronts her husband, and she is the only adult who defies Eddie. Flor empowers Marci with her words and actions, including giving her a knife to defend herself from her father.

10. This is a characteristic that can be observed in other protagonists of the canonic Chicano coming-of-age stories such as the unnamed boy from . . . *y no se lo tragó la tierra* and Antonio Marez in *Bless Me, Ultima*.

11. In the essay "The Virgin of Guadalupe and Her Reconstruction in Chicana Lesbian Desire," Carla Trujillo gives a brief account of the myth of the Virgen de Guadalupe and her importance within Chicanx culture, even in individuals who do not practice Catholicism. Trujillo includes a sarcastic note at the end of her text where she considers what she would do if the Virgen decided to be her lover. In this situation, Trujillo assures her an equal treatment to the male figures of Catholicism. "Lupe" would not have to live subjugated to a patriarchal hierarchy within a world of lesbians, enjoying completely her sexuality and without being forced to procreate. Anzaldúa and other Chicana feminists and queer academics have also pointed out the relevance of the Virgen de Guadalupe in Chicanx culture.

12. Trujillo personifies some of the women of the story, and especially Delia as gatekeepers of heteronormativity. The author is critiquing the role of some Chicana mothers in promoting and perpetuating heterosexual and patriarchal relationships. In *Chicana Lesbians* she states the following: "Though our fathers had much to do with imposing sexual conformity, it was usually our mothers who actually whispered the warnings, raised the eyebrows, or covertly transmitted to us the 'taboo nature' of same sex relationships" (x). Hence the subtitle of her book: *The Girls Our Mothers Warned Us About*.

Works Cited

Almaguer, Tomás. "Chicano Men: A Cartography of Homosexual Identity and Behavior." *The Lesbian and Gay Studies Reader*, 1993, pp. 355–73.

Anzaldúa, Gloria *Borderlands / La Frontera: The New Mestiza*. Spinsters/Aunt Lute, 2007.

Cacho, Lisa Marie. "'If I Turn into a Boy, I Don't Think I Want Huevos': Reassessing Racial Masculinities in *What Night Brings*." *GLQ: A Journal of Lesbian and Gay Studies*, vol. 18, no. 1, 2012, pp. 71–85.

"Carla Trujillo: January Portrait of the Month." *The Robert Giard Foundation*, 7 Jan. 2015, robertgiardfoundation.org/news/detail/carla-trujillo-january-portrait-of-the-month.

Clark, Caroline T., and Mollie V Blackburn. "Scenes of Violence and Sex in Recent Award-Winning LGBT-Themed Young Adult Novels and the Ideologies They Offer Their

Readers." *Discourse: Studies in the Cultural Politics of Education*, vol. 37, no. 6, 2016, pp. 867–86.

Danielson, Marivel T. *Homecoming Queers: Desire and Difference in Chicana Latina Cultural Production*. Rutgers University Press, 2009.

Esquibel Catrióna Rueda. *With Her Machete in Her Hand: Reading Chicana Lesbians*. University of Texas Press, 2006.

Foucault, Michel. *Discipline and Punish: The Birth of the Prison*. Vintage Books, 1995.

Garden, Nancy. *Annie on My Mind*. Farrar Straus Giroux, 2007.

Herrera, Cristina. "'The Girls Our Mothers Warned Us About': Rejection, Redemption, and the Lesbian Daughter in Carla Trujillo's *What Night Brings*." *Women's Studies*, vol. 39, no. 1, Jan/Feb2010, pp. 18–36.

Leitich Smith, Cynthia. "Interview: Children's-YA Author Nancy Garden." *Cynthia Leitich Smith*. cynthialeitichsmith.com. Accessed 3 March 2018.

Moraga, Cherríe, and Gloria Anzaldúa *This Bridge Called My Back: Writings by Radical Women of Color*. Kitchen Table, Women of Color Press, 1983.

Ramos, Dino-Ray. "GLAAD Seeks More LGBTQ People of Color, Less 'Bury Your Gays' Trope on TV-TCA." *Deadline*. http://deadline.com/2017/08/glaad-diversity-inclusion-lena-wiathe-stephanie-beatriz-wilson-cruz-pete-nowalk-megan-townsend-1202142831/. Accessed 1 March 2018.

Pérez, Emma. "Queering the Borderlands: The Challenges of Excavating the Invisible and Unheard." *Frontiers: A Journal of Women Studies*, vol. 24, no. 2/3, 2003, pp. 122–31.

Sáenz, Benjamin Alire. *Aristotle and Dante Discover the Secrets of the Universe*. Simon & Schuster, 2012.

Scales, Pat R. *Protecting Intellectual Freedom in Your School Library: Scenarios from the Front Lines*. American Library Association, 2009. Web.

Trujillo, Carla M. *Chicana Lesbians: The Girls Our Mothers Warned Us About*. Third Woman Press, 1991.

Trujillo, Carla M. "La Virgen de Guadalupe and her Reconstruction in Chicana Lesbian Desire." *Living Chicana Theory*, Third Woman Press, 1998, pp. 214–31.

Trujillo, Carla M. *What Night Brings: A Novel*. Curbstone Press, 2003.

"Welcome to the Pura Belpré Award home page!" American Library Association. www.ala.org/alsc/awardsgrants/bookmedia/belpremedal. Accessed 3 March 2018.

Contributors

Carolina Alonso is an assistant professor of borders and languages and of gender and sexuality studies at Fort Lewis College, in Durango, Colorado. She holds a PhD from the University of Houston and an MA and BA from the University of Texas Rio Grande Valley. Dr. Alonso's research interests include US Latinx literature, Latin American literature, gender and sexuality studies, and queer theory. Her recent publications include "Abriendo caminos con las huellas del pasado: El Proyecto de Recuperación de la Herencia Literaria Hispana de los Estados Unidos" and a forthcoming book chapter titled "Teaching Queer Chicana Writers through Historical Research, Online Blogs and Podcasts" (2020). Currently she is working on a book manuscript about queer Latinx literature and exiles. Dr. Alonso has translated two children's books published by Arte Público Press. She is the founder of Bibliotierra, a mobile library that takes Latinx children and YA books to parks and community centers around her community. She is a border native from Reynosa, Tamaulipas, Mexico, and the Rio Grande Valley region in Texas.

Elena Avilés investigates contemporary US Latinx and Chicanx expression and production. Her specializations include Chicanx/Latinx studies, the literary and visual arts, and US Spanish studies. She teaches courses in the humanities as praxis to engage students in transnational/global exchanges inclusive of the Chicanx/Latinx diaspora. She is currently elaborating on artistic and literary work by Chicanas drawing from feminism, ethnography, and critical heritage studies to theorize on identities in public spaces. Her publications appear in *U.S. Latinx Literature in Spanish: Straddling Identities, Voices of Resistance: Essays on Chican@ Children's Literature, Bilingual Review/Revista Bilingüe*, and *Label Me Latina/o: Journal of Twentieth and Twenty-First Centuries Latino Literary Production*. She earned a BA in Spanish and Chicana/o studies from UCLA, an MS in Counseling from CSU Los Angeles, and a PhD in Hispanic languages and literature from the University of New Mexico. She is an assistant professor of Chicano/Latino studies at Portland State University.

Trevor Boffone is a Houston-based scholar, educator, writer, dramaturg, and producer. He is a member of the National Steering Committee for the Latinx Theatre Commons and the founder of the 50 Playwrights Project. Trevor has a PhD in Latinx theatre and literature from the Department of Hispanic Studies at the University of Houston, where he holds a Graduate Certificate in Women's, Gender, & Sexuality Studies. His first book project, *Eastside Latinidad: Josefina López, Community, and Social Change in Boyle Heights*, is a study of theatre and performance in East Los Angeles, focusing primarily on Josefina López's role as a playwright, mentor, and community leader in Boyle Heights. He is the co-editor of *Encuentro: Latinx Performance for the New American Theater* (Northwestern, 2019) and *Teatro Latino: Nuevas obras de los Estados Unidos* (La Casita Grande, 2019). His writing on contemporary Latinx theatre has appeared in *Theatre Journal, Aztlán: Journal of Chicana and Chicano Studies, American Theatre Magazine, Latin American Theatre Review, GESTOS, Label Me Latina/o, Theatre, Gender Forum, The Rocky Mountain Review, El Mundo Zurdo 4, Voces del Caribe, Upstage*, Café Onda, HowlRound, *Houston Press*, and *Arts + Culture TX*.

Christi Cook is an assistant professor of language and literature at Southwestern Oklahoma State University, where she teaches literature, women's studies, and composition. Author of *Sacred Sex: Integrating Our Bodies and Our Spirituality* (2010), Dr. Cook's research concerns comparative studies of gender and sexuality in recent Chicanx and Anglo young adult literature. She is currently co-writing a book on Beyoncé, feminism, and popular culture with the University Press of Mississippi. In 2013, she earned her PhD in English at the University of Texas at Arlington. Dr. Cook also enjoys competing in triathlons and marathons as a somatic complement to her academic life.

Ella Maria Diaz is an associate professor in English and Latina/o studies at Cornell University. She was a lecturer for six years at the San Francisco Art Institute (2006–2012). Diaz's book *Flying under the Radar with the Royal Chicano Air Force: Mapping a Chicano/a Art History* (2017) explores the art, poetry, performance, and political activism of a vanguard Chicano/a art collective founded in Sacramento, California, in the 1970s and in the context of the US civil rights movement. Diaz has published in several anthologies as well as articles with *Aztlán: A Journal of Chicano Studies, Chicana-Latina Studies Journal*, and *ASAP/Journal*.

Amanda Ellis is an assistant professor in the Department of English at the University of Houston. She specializes in twentieth- and twenty-first-century Mexican American literary and cultural criticism, ethnic studies, health humanities, and Chicana feminist theory. She earned her MA and PhD in English from Rice University in Houston. She also holds an MA in ethnic studies from San Francisco State University in addition to a BS in psychology. An interdisciplinary scholar who understands the value of emerging forms of literary and cultural inquiry, her essays have appeared in *Chicana/Latina Studies: The Journal of Mujeres Activas en Letras y Cambio Social and Aztlán: A Journal of Chicano Studies*. Ellis is currently finalizing her manuscript tentatively titled: *Letras y Limpias: Decolonial Medicine and Holistic Healing in Mexican American Literature*.

Guadalupe García McCall is the author of *Under the Mesquite* (Lee & Low Books), a novel in verse. *Under the Mesquite* received the prestigious Pura Belpré Author Award, was a William C. Morris finalist, received the Lee Bennett Hopkins/International Literacy Promising Poet Award, the Tomas Rivera Children's Book Award, and was included in Kirkus Review's Best Teen Books of 2011, among many other accolades. Her second novel, *Summer of the Mariposas* (Tu Books, an imprint of Lee & Low Books), won a Westchester Young Adult Fiction award, was a finalist for the Andre Norton Award for Young Adult Science Fiction and Fantasy, was included in the 2013 Amelia Bloomer Project List, the Texas Lone Star Reading List, and the 2012 School Library Journal's Best Books of the Year. She has published two YA historical fiction novels, *Shame the Stars* (Tu Books, 2016) and *All the Stars Denied* (Tu Books, 2018). Ms. Garcia McCall was born in Piedras Negras, Coahuila, Mexico. She immigrated with her family to the United States when she was six years old and grew up in Eagle Pass, Texas (the setting of both her novels and most of her poems). She is currently an assistant professor of English at George Fox University.

Cristina Herrera earned her PhD in English from Claremont Graduate University and is Professor and Chair of Chicano and Latin American Studies at California State University, Fresno. She is the author of the 2014 study *Contemporary Chicana Literature: (Re)Writing the Maternal Script* and has co-edited multiple books on Latinx literature, including the first book-length volume on Chicanx children's literature, *Voices of Resistance: Interdisciplinary Approaches to Chican@ Children's Literature* (with Laura Alamillo and Larissa Mercado-López, 2017). Cristina has published articles in *Chicana/Latina Studies, Women's Studies: An Interdisciplinary Journal, Critique: Studies in*

Contemporary Fiction, Children's Literature, The Lion and the Unicorn, and other journals. She is currently working on a number of projects related to Chicana and Latina young adult literature, including a book manuscript entitled *Brown and Nerdy: The ChicaNerd in Chicana Young Adult Literature.*

Domino Renee Perez is an associate professor in the Department of English and the Center for Mexican American Studies at the University of Texas at Austin. She regularly teaches courses in literature, film, popular culture, and cultural studies. Her book *There Was a Woman: La Llorona from Folklore to Popular Culture* examines one of the most famous figures in US-Mexican folklore, plotting her movement from post-conquest oral narratives into contemporary cultural productions. Perez has published numerous book chapters and articles on topics ranging from film and indigeneity in Mexican American studies to young adult fiction and folklore.

Adrianna M. Santos earned a BA in English from University of Texas at Austin and an MA and PhD in Chicana/o studies with an emphasis in feminist studies from UC Santa Barbara. She teaches classes on Chicanx/Latinx literature as an assistant professor of English at Texas A&M University–San Antonio, where she acts as faculty advisor for the Mexican American Student Association and co-coordinator of the Mexican American, Latinx, and Borderlands Studies minor. She was a member of the National Women's Studies Association's Women of Color Leadership Project and has volunteered at the Santa Barbara Rape Crisis Center, Martinez St. Women's Center, and Child Advocates of San Antonio. She has published and spoken on anti-violence advocacy and writing as resistance in *El Mundo Zurdo, Aztlán, Chicana/Latina Studies,* and the conferences of NACCS, MALCS, MLA, and ALA, and she is working on a book manuscript called *Beyond Survival: Trauma Studies and Chicanx Poetics in the Literary Borderlands.*

Roxanne Schroeder-Arce is Director of Fine Arts Education in the College of Fine Arts and associate professor in the Department of Theatre and Dance at the University of Texas at Austin. She is also a faculty affiliate in the Center for Mexican American Studies, the Teresa Lozano Long Institute of Latin American Studies, and the Center for Women's and Gender Studies. In addition to teaching, Professor Schroeder-Arce is a scholar, director, and playwright. She has published articles in journals such as *Youth Theatre Journal, International Journal for Education & the Arts,* and *Theatre Topics,* as well as chapters in books such as *Latinos and American Popular Culture.* Schroeder-Arce's plays are published by Dramatic Publishing. Schroeder-Arce is a proud graduate of

Emerson College and the University of Texas at Austin. She is also an alumna of the Keene State College Upward Bound Program. She grew up in Springfield, Vermont. Her website can be found at www.roxannearce.com.

Lettycia Terrones is pursuing her PhD in information science at the University of Illinois. She employs interdisciplinary methods, particularly Chicana feminist theory and performance studies, to interrogate strategies for minoritarian resistance deployed in the picture-book art form. She holds a BA in English from UC Berkeley and a master of library science degree from UCLA. Lettycia has served as a member of the Pura Belpré Award and Ezra Jack Keats Book Award. She is from Boyle Heights, East Los Angeles.

Tim Wadham earned a PhD in comparative literature from the University of Texas at Arlington, with an emphasis in children's literature. As a fluent speaker, reader, and writer of Spanish, much of his professional work has centered around Spanish-language and bilingual literature for young readers. He published *Programming with Latino Children's Materials: A How-To-Do-It Manual for Librarians* and *Libros Esenciales/Essential Books: Building, Marketing, and Programming a Core Collection of Spanish Language Children's Materials* with Neal-Schuman. He has also published a picture book, *The Queen of France*, with Candlewick Press. Wadham currently works as an online adjunct instructor for Brigham Young University–Idaho, teaching advanced research and literary analysis. Additionally, he has taught information literacy for Dixie State University and face-to-face and virtual graduate courses in children's literature for the University of Arizona (Tucson). There he developed a course for them in the evaluation of children's books. He organized and presented a mini-conference on the work of Ursula K. Le Guin at Arizona State University in conjunction with her Arbuthnot lecture there. He has also presented at the Southwest Popular Culture Association and has published articles in *The Horn Book* magazine and *Children and Libraries*.

Index

Made in the USA
Las Vegas, NV
09 October 2021